The English Dream Vision

The English Dream Vision

ANATOMY OF A FORM

J. Stephen Russell

Ohio State University Press • Columbus

Copyright © 1988 by the Ohio State University Press.

Quotations from the works of Chaucer are taken from *The Complete Works of Geoffrey Chaucer*, ed. Fred Norris Robinson, 2nd ed. (Boston: Houghton Mifflin, 1961).

The discussion of *Pearl* is a revision of "*Pearl*'s 'cortaysye': A critique of Eschatology" *Renascence* 35, 3 (Spring 1983): 183–95. The present revision is included with the permission of the editors of *Renascence*.

Library of Congress Cataloging-in-Publication Data

Russell, J. Stephen.
  The English dream vision : anatomy of a form / J. Stephen Russell.
    p.   cm.
  Bibliography: p.
  Includes index.
  ISBN 0-8142-0451-1
  1. English poetry—Middle English, 1100–1500—History and
criticism.   2. Dreams in literature.   3. Visions in literature.
4. Literary form.   5. Chaucer, Geoffrey, d. 1400—Criticism and
interpretation.   I. Title.
PR317.D7R87   1987
821'.1'09—dc 19   87–16594
                                                                       CIP

to my parents

Contents

ACKNOWLEDGMENTS

I would like first to express my gratitude to the late Donald R. Howard, to Stanley E. Fish, and Lee W. Patterson, who first stirred my interest in Chaucer and the dream vision in 1977 and 1978. In the dissertation that profited so much from their advice, "The Grammar of the Dream Vision," lie the beginnings of this book, especially its nontraditional treatment of medieval dream authorities and its approach to the *Hous of Fame*.

Among several colleagues who read and commented on the manuscript at various stages of its development, I single out for thanks R. A. Shoaf of the University of Florida, who read the manuscript carefully and aggressively. This is a stronger book for his queries and suggestions.

An earlier version of "*Pearl* and the Discourse of Eschatology" appeared in *Renascence*; I am indebted to the editors for permission to reprint it here.

My children, Mary, Elizabeth, and Catherine, aided and abetted this project more than they know. They missed out on many an evening and many a Saturday because this quote was incorrect, that argument needed tightening, and so on. They also disposed of tons of scrap paper.

My wife suffered with me all of the valleys that inevitably precede the peak of any publishing venture. She read drafts and checked quotations, proofread and collated, and, most important of all, kept the faith. Thanks, Helen.

INTRODUCTION

The following is a study of the late medieval English dream vision and, like any study of a poetic kind or form, certain presuppositions lie behind it. The purpose of this introduction is to make these presuppositions explicit and to argue, at least provisionally, that they are valid ones. The basic assumptions, then, are these:

> that the term "dream vision" refers to a definable and recognizable set of literary works, and that medieval dream vision writers were aware that they were making this certain kind of poem (and not simply using a set of unrelated conventions);
>
> that an understanding of the dynamics of the dream vision will tell us something worth knowing about the poems.[1]

The first assumption—an obligatory one for genre studies—requires a sort of double vision. On the one hand, a genre is a set of tactics or details or motifs, conventions which, in the right combination, cause a poem to be of a certain kind. When enough of the required motifs or images are present, in, for example, *The Divine Comedy*, then the poem looks like a dream vision to the modern reader. Does the presence of enough such motifs, however, make *The Divine Comedy* a dream vision? Does the presence of some of the motifs, as J. V. Cunningham has discovered in the General Prologue of the *Canterbury Tales*,[2] make this poem somewhat of a dream vision?

On the other hand, a poet's choice of a genre is a self-conscious one, and the resulting poem is, at least in that poet's mind, a romance, a pastoral, an elegy, or a dream vision. When such a poet, as Deguileville, for example, excludes (or botches) some of the motifs which seem crucial—the dreamer in *La Pelerinage de la Vie Humaine* makes up parts of the dream report which he has forgotten—does this affect the genre of the poem? To cite another example, Long Will wakes up at the end of Passus Six of *Piers Plowman* and then falls asleep again and dreams the remaining passus; does this matter? Finally, Boethius, Martianus Capella, Alanus de Insulis, and Dante do not report falling asleep at all and make no references to dream lore in the prologues of their poems; are these poems dream visions?

There are no simple answers to these questions, but there are safe answers, answers suggested in my first assumption: to be a dream vision (or to be a poem of any predefined kind), a poem must *both* contain certain motifs *and* be the product of a poet's intention to follow a tradition or imitate a generic model.

This complex and rigorous set of requirements is necessary in this case beause the dream vision in late medieval English literature is more than a conventional frame or an obsolescent authenticating device. In the hands of Chaucer and Langland and the *Pearl* poet, the dream vision genre with its accompanying rhetorical effects is essential to the themes and contents of the poems and not simply a convenient fiction. In adopting the special, problematic discourse created by Cicero and explicated by Macrobius, the discourse bounded and defined by Boethius and Dante, Guillaume de Lorris, Chaucer, and the others wrote poems *ipso facto* about reference, authority, the limitations of the human intellect, and the contingency of earthly knowledge, contents, and concerns enhanced and actually enabled by the dream vision form.

This interdependence of form and content is the reason for my second assumption—that looking at these poems as dream visions will tell us something important about them. The dream vision had its origin in the gaps, the interstices of two parallel taxonomies in medieval thought, taxonomies of real and literary dreams. An understanding of the way the poems invaded and deconstructed these two taxonomies will help us look again at the ostensible subjects of the poems and to see these subjects in powerful new, though thoroughly medieval ways.

No medieval writer ever used the term "dream vision" or discussed this kind of poem, but this fact should neither surprise nor daunt us when we remember how generally casual medieval writers were about kinds of poems. Chaucer, the medieval English poet who talks more about literary kinds than any other, uses a notoriously eclectic set of terms. He sees *Troilus and Criseyde* as a tragedy (III, 1786) and promises a few lines later to work next on "som comedye," presumably a reference to the *Canterbury Tales*.[3] On his other works, sadly, Chaucer is less specific: in the Retraction to the *Canterbury Tales*, he refers to his dream visions—*Book of the Duchess, Hous of Fame, Parlement of Foules*, and *The Legend of Good Women*—simply as "books," a term he seems to be using to differentiate these works from "songs and lecherous lays" (13-19). In the Prologue to *The Legend of Good Women*, he refers to his dream visions once more, but this passage sheds only limited light on the problem of how he saw the dream vision:

> He made the book that hight the Hous of Fame,
> And eke the Deeth of Blaunche the Duchesse,
> And the Parlement of Foules, as I gesse,
> And al the love of Palamon and Arcite
> Of Thebes, thogh the storye ys knowen lyte;
> And many an ympne for your halydayes,
> That highten balades, roundels, virelayes;
> And, for to speke of other holynesse,
> He hath in prose translated Boece,
> And maad the lyf also of Seynt Cecile.
> He made also, goon ys a gret while,
> Origenes upon the Maudeleyne.
>
> (F, 417–28)

Elsewhere, Chaucer refers to his dream visions either as "books" or "things." All that can be learned from this is that Chaucer did not have a single term which he used exclusively to denote his dream-frame poems: they are "books," a category that includes not only the dream visions but also integated works like the *Troilus* (Retraction) but *not* the *Canterbury Tales*, to which he never refers except in the plural (both in the Retraction and also, implicitly, in his references to the Knight's and Second Nun's Tales in the Prologue to the *Legend of Good Women*).

Chaucer refers to two other dream visions in his poetry. In the Prologue to the *Legend of Good Women*, he is accused of translating the *Romaunt of the Rose*, a work so despicable to the God of Love that it requires no generic label. In the Retraction, Chaucer claims to have translated "the book of the Leoun," presumed to be a (lost) redaction of Machaut's *Dit du Lyon*, a dream vision. Thus, Chaucer seems consistently to use the term "book" to refer to major works, including dream visions, which have a definable structure and an obvious integrity: the category includes the *Troilus* and his translations of other people's dream visions. He does *not* use the designation "book" to refer to his translations of Pope Innocent's *De misera humanae conditionis* or of Boethius' *Consolation of Philosophy*, even though this second work is clearly a forerunner of the dream vision.

Chaucer, then, seemed to know what he meant by "dream vision": it was a "book," an artistic integrity like the tragedy of Troilus; it was a poetic artifact with the standard Chaucerian persona and not a prose treatise like those of Innocent and Boethius; it was a form more complex (though less concretely defined) than those of the balade, roundel, or virelay; and the "book" was always identified by a representative or metonymic item such as the house of Fame, the "deeth" of Blanche, or the lion. The evidence is tantalizing but incomplete; even late in life and during the tense reign of Richard II, he would refer to these early *books* in the Retraction, a list which included a memorial to the wife of John of Gaunt, no royal favorite. To be sure, they were "enditynges of worldly vanitees," he says, but he "revokes" these juvenalia with a pride and satisfaction which shows he still thought highly of them.

Even if, perhaps, there was no medieval word for this kind of "book," an empirical look at the structure or shape of the dream vision reveals the form to be a conscious design and not merely a collection of motifs. At the simplest level, a dream vision is the first person account of a dream; the dream report is usually preceded by a prologue introducing the dreamer as a character and often followed by an epilogue describing the dreamer's reawakening and recording the dream report in verse. The *prologue*, though typically short and allusive, is by far the most conventionalized and formulaic part of the dream vision. Along with establishing the frame narrative, the purpose of the prologue seems to be to introduce the character of the dreamer-poet. It is here that the reader often learns that the dreamer was distressed or concerned about some unnamed problem or worry, such that he found it hard to get to sleep on that fateful night. Though readers are encouraged and emboldened to guess the natures of these distresses—Chaucer's love languor at the opening of the *Book of the Duchess* is patently obvious—it appears to be obligatory that the poet-dreamer not tell. The dreamer (or soon-to-be-dreamer) sometimes represents himself as a poet in the prologue and sometimes mentions that he tried to divert his mind by reading or meditation to get to sleep. Chaucer, for example, meditates on the daisy (the *Legend of Good Women*) or reads the story of Ceys and Alcione (the *Book of the Duchess*).

Following this introductory frame narrative, the *dream report* begins. The dream is usually a record of a *debat* or less formal conversation with one or more characters, sometimes real, sometimes allegorical. Usually there are several interlocutors and various topics of conversation: *Pearl*, with its singular figure of authority and tightly focused dialogue, seems the exception rather than the rule in its imitation of Boethius. There seems to be no particular narrative shape to this, the heart of the dream vision: motifs described by others such as the *hortus conclusus*, preternatural light, talking animals, or a personified figure of authority are common but not obligatory.[4] Chaucer's dream visions, for example, sometimes have earthly settings (the *Book of the Duchess*, the *Parlement of Foules*; also *Piers Plowman*); sometimes unearthly (the *Hous of Fame*, the *Legend of Good Women*). They sometimes feature preternatural animals like the talking birds of the *Hous of Fame* and the *Parlement of Foules*, while elsewhere the animals are either realistic details, emblematic or allegorical, like the whelp and the hart in the *Book of the Duchess*.[5] The dream reports can be self-consciously allegorical (Piers Plowman, Skelton's *Bouge of Court*, or the *Roman de la Rose*), superficially naturalistic (the *Book of the Duchess*), or set in the "real" other world of Christian eschatology like *Pearl* and other visions related to the apocalypse (such as the *Hous of Fame*). In all of this, the only constant seems to be the complex central figure of the dreamer-narrator-character: unlike most absent, omniscient, impersonal medieval narrators, the dreamer is *always* a character in his dream narrative.[6]

This dream report makes up the bulk of the poem and, at its conclusion, there is often a brief framing *epilogue* describing the reawakening of the dreamer and occasionally offering interpretive comments on the dream report. This conclusion often reminds the reader of the identity of the poet and the dreamer: sometimes the identification is symbolic, as when a dream event turns into a waking one (the tolling bell of the *Book of the Duchess* or the river crossing of *Pearl*); sometimes it is explicit, as with the dreamer's intention to produce a verse redaction of his experience (the *Book of the Duchess* again and Deguileville's *Pelerinage de la Vie Humaine*). In any case, the concluding frame gives the poems a technical (or "formal") closure that the dream reports themselves frequently lack. The dream report of *Pearl*, for example, seems enigmatic and violently interrupted by the jueler's attempt to cross the river, but the epilogue makes it clear that, though the *dream* was cut off, the *poem* is finished and esthetically complete. Like the couplet of a sonnet, the concluding frame asserts the architectural finish of the artifact and challenges the reader to perceive its artistic closure.

This description is the last and best proof that the dream vision was a "kind of poem" in the minds of medieval artists. If dream poems were nothing more than collections of unrelated and optional motifs, then we should expect to find these motifs throughout the poems. In fact, the typical motifs are clustered at the beginning of the poem: the introduction to the dreamer, the dreamer's allusive distress, his insomnia and diversions, and his appearance as the central character in the dream report all suggest that the motifs work together to help determine the structure of the poem.

The first dream vision in Western literature is the *Somnium Scipionis* of Cicero, and unlike other first instances, this mysterious work exerted a profound, though accidental, influence on the development of the form through the later Middle Ages. This dream, recounted by Scipio Africanus the Younger at the conclusion of Cicero's *Republic*, seems to be a conscious imitation of "Vision of Er," the death ecstasis at the end of Plato's *Republic*. Following his Greek model, Cicero ends his examination of the ideal state with the vision of a universe which embodies cosmological versions of the very ethical and political principles just prescribed for the perfect state. In doing this, Cicero replaces the magic of Er's extracorporeal journey to the spheres with a more quotidian dream; the frame he uses to introduce the dream, however, damages the dream's credibility as a revelation or ecstasis. On landing in Africa, Scipio recalls, he spends an evening with King Masinissa of Numidia, an old friend of his late grandfather, Scipio the Elder:

> Post autem apparatu regio accepti, sermonem in multam noctem produximus, cum senex nihil nisi de Africano loqueretur, omniaque eius non facta solum sed etiam dicta meminisset. deinde ut cubitum discessimus, me et de via fessum, et qui ad multam noctem vigilassem, artior quam solebat somnus complexus est. hic mihi—credo equidem ex hoc quod eramus locuti; fit enim fere ut cogitationes sermonesque nostri pariant aliquid in somno tale, quale de Homero scribit Ennius, de quo videlicet saepissime vigilans solebat cogitare et loqui—Africanus se ostendit ea forma quae mihi ex imagine eius quam ex ipso erat notior; quem ubi agnovi, equidem cohorrui; sed ille: 'ades' inquit 'animo et omitte timorem Scipio, et quae dicam trade memoriae.

> And later, after we had dined amidst regal state we prolonged our talk until far into the night. The old man would talk about nothing except of Africanus and remembered not only all that he had done but all as well that he had said. Then, when we had parted to take our rest a sleep much deeper than was usual fell upon me, for I was very weary from my journey and had stayed awake until very late. And then—(I suppose it was a

result of what we had been talking about; for it happens often that the things that we have been thinking and speaking of bring about something in our sleep. So Ennius relates in his dream about Homer, of whom in hours of wakefulness he used so often to think and speak)—Africanus stood there before me, in figure familiar to me from his bust rather than from life. I shuddered with dread as I recognized him but he said, "Be calm, Scipio, and have no fear, but fail not to remember the things that I shall tell.[7]

Effectively, what is introduced here is the day-residue dream of a great man, Scipio Africanus the Younger. The introduction implies that the details of the dream (if not the entire experience) are the products of the exhausted mind of an impressionable young man who has spent the night hearing stories of his adoptive grandfather. Scipio himself says as much in comparing his experience to that of the poet Ennius; the comparison firmly suggests that neither dream, inspired by waking thought and surrounded by coincidences, ought to be taken seriously as a revelation.[8] Indeed, Scipio takes care to mention that his namesake appeared to him in resemblance to a statue the younger man remembered; this is a telling little detail, for Scipio the Younger, who was two when his grandfather died, would not have *remembered* him in life. Even Macrobius, whose *Commentary* on the *Somnium* preserved the text for the modern world, sees the frame as self-consciously fictional and not supernaturally revelatory.[9]

What follows this introduction is a spectacular but fairly predictable vision of the great world in the Platonic affective tradition, a vision designed to legitimize Cicero's conservative republican virtues of *pietas* and civic obligation. The elder Scipio, the dreamer's guide in the ecstasis, concludes by drawing a crisp moral lesson from the rapturous vision of the spheres:

cum pateat igitur aeternum id esse quod se ipsum moveat, quis est qui hanc naturam animis esse tributam neget? inanimum est enim omne quod pulsu agitatur externo; quod autem est animal, id motu cietur interiore et suo; nam haec est propria natura animi atque vis; quae si est una ex omnibus quae se ipsa moveat, neque nata certe est et aeterna est. hanc tu exerce in optimis rebus! sunt autem optimae curae de salute patriae, quibus agitatus et exercitatus animus velocius in hanc sedem et domum suam pervolabit, idque ocius faciet, si iam tum cum erit inclusus in corpore, eminebit foras, et ea quae extra erunt contemplans quam maxime se a corpore abstrahet.

Since then that which is self-moving is everlasting, who would dare deny that this is the essential nature given to living spirits? For everything that is set in motion by an outside force is without a spirit within it, but that which is animated by spirit is moved by its own power within, for this is the essential property and power of spirit,—which, since it is the only thing among all things which moves itself, cannot have had a beginning nor can it ever have an end. Devote this, then to the highest tasks! Of these surely the noblest are those on behalf of one's fatherland: a spirit dedicated and devoted to these will swiftly wing its way to this, its own abode and home. And more swiftly will it speed here if, while still prisoned in the body, it soars above it and fixing its gaze on things beyond, it rids itself as much as is in its power from the body.[10]

The work thus continues to draw moral lessons from the vision, seemingly unimpeded by the problematic nature of the dream; despite the introductory section which casts the dream into doubt, the moral lessons drawn from the visions of history and of the Platonic cosmos are responsible and salutary. In part, this is because it is a responsible man who dreams the vision; by this point in the *Republic*, Scipio the Younger has been established by Cicero as a stoic Republic saint, moral touchstone of a fast-fading golden age. The dream of such a person, even if it is nothing more than the product of his mind freed in sleep from the constraints of rationality and day-to-day existence, is a precious possession: dreamer valorizes dream. At the same time, though, the evident piety and moral probity of the vision is a credit to the mind that produced (received?) it: dream valorizes dreamer. So the reader is left with a vision of the other world that need not be taken literally to be appreciated or treasured (as this work certainly was). Even if the *Somnium Scipionis* is nothing more than a day-residue dream, it is nonetheless valuable both for the truth it obviously tells and because it is a great man's dream.[11]

It is unlikely that Cicero analyzed the rhetoric of the *Somnium Scipionis* in this way, or even that he was fully conscious of the formal issues which his choice of a dream frame raised: Macrobius' suspicion that he chose the dream frame to avoid the intrusive incredibility of Er's out-of-body experience seems entirely reasonable. More important than his motives for his choice, though, was its effect: in changing the frame from apotheosis to dream, Cicero complicated and psychologized the visionary experience. Surely dreams are more commonplace than visions, even in the ancient world;[12] more surely, though, dream intelligence is less credible, less dramatic, more dangerous than messages in waking visions. In fact, after Cicero (and after the Macrobean *Commentary* to which the *Somnium Scipionis* was always appended), a remarkably strict distinction in visionary literature is established between the somatic experience and the waking vision. As I will illustrate in detail later, the poet's choice of a waking vision suggests that the didactic message of the vision is the poet's priority; the choice of the dream as frame is based on psychological, affective, and rhetorical motives antithetical to the visionary's purpose in writing.

Surely it is such considerations that lay behind Boethius' choice of a frame narrative for *The Consolation of Philosophy*. A century after Macrobius, Boethius begins his treatise by approximating the drama of the *Somnium Scipionis* but, conscious of the ambiguity of the dream, he soon departs from his Ciceronian model:

> Carmina qui quondam studio florente peregi,
>   Flebilis heu maestos cogor inire modos.
> Ecce mihi lacerae dictant scribenda camenae
>   Et veris elegi fletibus ora rigant.
> Has saltem nullus potiut pervincere terror,
>   Ne nostrum comites prosequerentur iter.
> Gloria felicis olim viridisque iuventae
>   Solantur maesti nunc mea fata senis.
> Venit enim properata malis inopina senectus
>   Et dolor aetatem iussit inesse suam.
> Intempestivi funduntur vertice cani
>   Et tremit effeto corpore laxa cutis.
> Mors hominum felix quae se nec dulcibus annis
>   Inserit et maestis saepe vocata venit.
> Eheu quam surda miseros avertitur aure
>   Et flentes oculos claudere saeva negat.

Dum levibus male fida bonis fortuna faveret,
Paene caput tristis merserat hora meum.
Nunc quia fallacem mutavit nubila vultum,
Protrahit ingratas impia vita moras.
Quid me felicem totiens iactastis amici?
Qui cecidit, stabili non erat ille gradu.

I who once wrote songs of keen delight am now by sorrow driven to
take up melancholy measures. Wounded Muses tell me what I must
write, and elegiac verses bathe my face with real tears. Not even terror
could drive from me these faithful companions of my long journey. Poetry, which was once the glory of my happy and flourishing youth, is still
my comfort in this misery of my old age.

Old age has come too soon with its evils, and sorrow has commanded
me to enter the age which is hers. My hair is prematurely gray, and slack
skin shakes on my exhausted body. Death, happy to men when she does
not intrude in the sweet years, but comes when often called in sorrow,
turns a deaf ear to the wretched and cruelly refuses to close weeping eyes.

The sad hour that has nearly drowned me came just at the time that
faithless Fortune favored me with her worthless gifts. Now that she has
clouded her deceitful face, my accursed life seems to go on endlessly. My
friends, why did you so often think me happy? Any man who has fallen
never stood securely.[13]

This prologue shows that Boethius had a clear understanding of the
visionary tradition. Like Cicero, he shows quite clearly that his
dreamer was distressed and preoccupied prior to his visionary experience. The poignant lyricism of this first metrum, in fact, far better
captures the distressed state of the visionary than Scipio's pale
prose. For precisely these reasons, Boethius departs radically from
the dream conventions in the first prosa:

Haec dum mecum tacitus ipse reputarem querimoniamque lacrimabi-
lem stili officio signarem, adstitisse mihi supra verticem visa est mulier
reverendi admodum vultus, oculis ardentibus et ultra communem hominum valentiam perspicacibus . . .

While I silently pondered these things, and decided to write down my
wretched complaint, there appeared standing above me a woman of ma-
jestic countenance whose flashing eyes seemed wise beyond the ordinary
wisdom of men.[14]

11

Unlike Cicero, Boethius specifically chooses to keep his visionary awake, and his reasons for doing are serious and telling. Unlike the *Somnium Scipionis*, the *Consolation of Philosophy* is to be a treatise with a first-person narrator, and this structural change so weakens the didactic impact of the dream vision that Macrobius must suppress the dream frame to give his text any semblance of seriousness. To explain, in the *Somnium Scipionis*, we noted the mutual valorization of dream and dreamer; this happens only because Cicero and his audience already reverenced both Scipio and the doctrines he espouses. In Boethius, however, the change to the first person, the highly emotional state of the visionary, and the searching investigative program of the poem, taken together, preclude immediate valorization of either the vision or the visionary. Thus, were Boethius to begin his poem and say *in his own voice* that he is in complete despair *and then* to report his inspired consolatory experience, the delicate balance would shift too far in the direction of the subjective. The dream vision, quite the opposite of Boethius' form here, explodes the delicate balance of credibility: however precious a dream vision might be, it must perforce always be indeterminate, always remain suspended between the two poles, neither assuredly somatic nor assuredly divine.

In general, the implicit distinction visible in the opening of the *Consolation of Philosophy* is carefully maintained by visionary poets ever since. From Martianus Capella through the Chartrean naturalists and Dante to the allegorical visionary poets of the sixteenth century, the balance between objective (didactic) and subjective (somatic) is a careful one. In the next chapter, we will see that the two poles of this opposition—the dream as an event in third person narratives and the waking vision—developed and conserved well-defined ontological statuses throughout the Middle Ages.

In this very restricted sense of the dream vision, the form does not reappear until the eighth century in Anglo-Saxon England. Dreams, apocalypses, visions, and other somatic and marvelous reports were very common in French and Neolatin literature, but it is not until the Old English "Dream of the Rood" that the full complexity and ambivalence of the form reappears. The "Dream of the Rood" is a striking dream dialogue between the dreamer-narrator and the Rood and an imaginative exploration of its crucial but inglorious part in God's plan of redemption. But it is finally even more: in the last analysis, it is a profoundly psychological poem, an exploration of faith and despair which purposely calls the status of the dream into question. Phrases early in the dream-report (there is no introductory frame) suggest that the dreamer-narrator feels despair and shame over his sinfulness, a state that makes him a poignant analogue to the unwilling, shame-ridden instrument of the Savior's death:

Beheoldon þær engeldryhta feala
faegere þurh forδgesceaft;　　ne wæs þær huru fracodes gealga,
ac hine þær beheoldon　　halige gastas,
men ofer moldan,　　and eall þeos maere gesceaft.
　　Syllic wæs se sigebeam,　　and ic synnum fah,
forwundod mid wommum.

　　　　I beheld there a host of the angels of the Lord
fair from their creation;　　this was no felon's gallows
but beholding it there were　　holy spirits,
men of the earth　　and all this splendid creation.
　　Wondrous was the victory-tree　　and I stained with sin
wounded with defilement.[15]

The poem goes on to suggest a typological relationship between the narrator and the Rood; both are shameful but the same redemption that transformed the Rood can glorify the sinful dreamer:

On me bearn Godes
þrowode hwile;　　for þan ic þrymfæst nu
hlifige under heofenum,　　and ic haelen mæg
aeghwylcne anra　　þara þe him biδ egesa to me.
Iu ic wæs geworden　　wita heardost,
leodum laδost,　　aer þan ic him lifes weg
rihte gerymde,　　reordberendum.

On me the Son of God
suffered for a time;　　therefore, now in glory
I tower under Heaven,　　and I can save
any one　　who is in awe of me.

13

> Long ago I was made to be   the cruelest of torments,
> hateful to men,   but that was when I opened up
> the true way of life   for men.[16]

Like the *Somnium Scipionis*, this poem evades the question of the authenticity of the dream; there are hints that the dream may be a projection of the dreamer's guilty conscience, but these hints do not obtrude on the traditional theological *sentence* of the vision. Dreamer and dream are mutually valorized here: the humble dreamer comes to terms with his sin in the dream, while the inherent worth of the dream credits the consciousness that conceived it.

Despite this native facility with the dream vision form in the Old English period, the dream vision masterpieces of the fourteenth century owe virtually nothing to rich, primitive works such as "The Dream of the Rood," Cynewulf's "Elene," or to the story of Caedmon's dream in Bede. The later works, the poems of Chaucer and of the alliterative revival in the second half of the fourteenth century, are the direct descendants of the remarkably original invention of Guillaume de Lorris, *Le Roman de la Rose*. While *Roman* source studies ably demonstrate Guillaume's wide reading (to say nothing of Jean de Meun's encyclopedic vision), the originality of the *idea* of the *Roman* remains completely intact: even comparisons with the poems of Machaut, Froissart, Houdenc, and other early French writers of vision-poems cannot account for the grand blasphemy, the extraordinary deadpan, and finally the profound beauty of this poem. More to our present purpose, no poet before Guillaume de Lorris understands and exploits the rich ambiguity of the dream frame, the mutual valorization of dream and dreamer, and the strange energy of the self-conscious dream report:

> Aucunes genz dient qu'en songes
> n'a se fables non et mençonges;
> mes l'en puet tex songes songier
> qui ne sont mie mençongier,
> ainz sont aprés bien aparant,
> si en puis bien traire a garant
> un auctor qui ot non Macrobes,
> qui ne tint pas songes a lobes,

14

ançois escrit l'avision
qui avint au roi Scypion.
Qui c'onques cuit ne qui que die
qu'il est folor et musardie
de croire que songes aviegne,
qui se voudra, por fol m'en tiegne,
quar endroit moi ai ge fiance
que songes est senefiance
des biens as genz et des anuiz,
que li plusor songent de nuiz
maintes choses covertement
que l'en voit puis apertement.

(1-20)

Many men sayn that in sweveninges
Ther nys but fables and lesynges;
But men may some swevenes sen
Whiche hardely that false ne ben,
But afterward ben apparaunt.
This may I drawe to warraunt
An authour that hight Macrobes,
That halt nat dremes false ne lees,
But undoth us the avysioun
That whilom mette kyng Cipioun.
And whoso saith or weneth it be
A jape, or elles nycete,
To wene that dremes after falle,
Let whoso lyste a fol me calle.
For this trowe I, and say for me,
That dremes signifiaunce be
Of good and harm to many wightes,
That dremen in her slep a-nyghtes
Ful many thynges covertly,
That fallen after al openly.[17]

The key to the passage is Guillaume's mention of Macrobius and the *Commentary on the Somnium Scipionis*. As we shall see in chapter 3, Macrobius does assert the existence of divine, revelatory, or premonitory dreams, but Macrobius would hardly have considered this dream a revelatory one, given its context and circumstances. If any-

15

thing, the mention of Macrobius puts this present dream into even more question, for Macrobius' prime example of the anxiety- or day residue-dream—the lover's dream of possessing his beloved—is the very dream to which Guillaume here calls Macrobius to witness. The use of the *Commentary* as intertext or context thus puts Guillaume's opening strategies into sharp relief; invoking the authority of Macrobius makes the choice Guillaume offers his readers—"Let whoso lyst a fol me calle"—a legitimate one.[18]

So, as in the other cases, there is good reason here to doubt the revelatory nature of the dream, but at the same time the content of the dream valorizes the dreamer as a worshipper of the God of Love, just as the dream of the rood valorized the dreamer in that poem. The same situation, in which neither the dream nor the dreamer is trustworthy in isolation but each justifies the other when taken together, inheres in the artificial courtly ambience of the *Roman de la Rose*. For the follower of courtly love, a true lover's dream is *ipso facto* an object of value, while the stately, masque-like decorum of the dream is a credit to its dreamer.

The *Roman de la Rose* is the single most important work in the history of the dream vision in the later Middle Ages. By grafting a moribund doctrinal form onto the mischief and vigor of courtly love, the *Roman* brought new life to the poetic form and turned it, once more, inward, focusing its energies not on messages from beyond but on tensions within. Guillaume de Lorris could give his readers lush religious ecstasy one moment, light and disreputable burlesque the next, and could enclose all within a frame that blithely defers all questions of source, credibility, and authority.

Thanks to Guillaume, the dream vision form with all its subtleties became the undisputed poetic fashion in France and later in England during the thirteenth and fourteenth centuries. Scores of greater and lesser poets adopted the form, and related literary kinds such as the Neoplatonic ecstasis experienced a rebirth throughout Europe. *De Planctu Naturae*, the *Anticlaudianus*, and the *Divina Commedia* each share, to some degree, the ancestry of the love visions of Froissart and Machaut, but these works move away from the intensity of the dream vision toward other identities and for other poetic effects. The famous opening lines of the *Divina Commedia*, for example, suggest the initial situation of the dream vision but do so only obliquely:

> Nel mezzo del cammin di nostra vita
> mi ritrovai per una selva oscura,
> che la diritta via era smarrita.
> Ahi quanto a dir qual era è cosa dura
> esta selva selvaggia e aspra e forte
> che nel pensier rinova la paura!
> Tant' è amara che poco è più morte;
> ma per trattar del ben ch'i' vi trovai,
> dirò de l'altre cose ch'i' v'ho scorte.
> Io non so ben ridir com'i' v'intrai,
> tant' era pien di sonno . . .

Midway in the journey of our life I found myself in a dark wood, for the straight way was lost. Ah, how hard it is to tell what that wood was, wild, rugged, harsh; the very thought of it renews the fear! It is so bitter that death is hardly more so. But, to treat of the good that I found in it, I will tell of the other things I saw there.

I cannot rightly say how I entered it, I was so full of sleep at the moment I left the true way; but when I had reached the foot of a hill, . . .[19]

Clearly, from these first lines, Dante does not have the dream vision in mind. The verb "ritrovai" is nicely ambiguous and seems to suggest a sleep, but the reader soon learns that the sleep, like all else in this dream landscape, is figurative. Only a figurative or allegorical life's journey could have a "mezzo" and only after a metaphorical sleep could the Wayfarer find himself in this backdrop. Dante is not interested in his frame, as Scipio, Guillaume de Lorris, and other dream vision writers are; in a real sense, the *Divina Commedia* does not have a frame, preferring instead the less comforting and forgiving wrench of the reader's perspective from the earthbound to the polysemous.[20] This dislocation, the tracklessness of the dark forest, stands in contrast to the (actually overdetermined) conventional prologue of the dream vision, just as the mysterious Wayfarer contrasts with the conventionalized and languishing dreamer. Dante certainly wants us to mistrust his simulacrum, but he wants this mistrust to be on a moral, not a narrative level (and he wants the mistrust to develop slowly through the early cantos of *Inferno*). The dreamer's debility, so critical an element in the dream vision, here calls the Wayfarer's moral probity into question, not his credibility.[21]

While poems like the *Commedia* and the allegories of the Chartrean Naturalists spring in part from the same creative ferment that inspired Guillaume de Lorris, his true heirs were the great English dream vision poets of the fourteenth century. Chaucer, the most prolific English writer of dream visions, wrote complex poems which drew deeply on the wide French love vision tradition of which Guillaume was the flower. The *Book of the Duchess*, usually thought to be Chaucer's first major poem, is the most French of Chaucer's dream poems and alludes to Froissart's *Paradys d'Amours*, Machaut's two *Jugement* poems and the *Dit du Lyon*, and of course to the *Roman*. The *Parlement of Foules* also traces its ancestry to the *Roman* but also owes much in theme and technique to Jean de Meun and to the Chartrean Naturalists. While the *Hous of Fame* clearly echoes Dante and Classical models, it too is finally a work after the *Roman de la Rose*, in which the unreliability of the narrator becomes the crucial counter in a web of disreputed and disreputable authorities. Only the anthology of lives of the Saints of Cupid, called the *Legend of Good Women*, a work often thought to have been commissioned by the court and one in which Chaucer's interest seems to have failed, employs the frame but fails to develop it as a psychological motif.

Outside London, the dream frame narrative experienced an equally remarkable renaissance in the alliterative revival of the fourteenth century. Poems such as *Pearl* and *Piers Plowman* use the imagery of courtly love, personification allegory, estates satire, and eschatology within the flexible poetic form. Later writers in the Chaucerian tradition such as Lydgate, Dunbar, James I, and Skelton continued to use the frame into the fifteenth century for amorous and satiric purposes but, with the new vogue of Italianate lyric models in the late fifteenth century, the form essentially disappears in the antiquarian voice of Edmund Spenser, to subsist marginally in the Renaissance and beyond as the bankrupt vehicle of ecstatics, mystics, and political satirists. We can only speculate about the reasons for the dream vision's demise, but poetry's new devotion to human emotion and Protestantism's new suspicions about dreams must surely have made the form seem plodding and mechanical. In a literary environment where life is a dream, where Prosperos and Redcrosses live in poems, the line between this world and the mind's own habitat need not be drawn before art can begin.

CHAPTER ONE

DREAM AND APOCALYPSE

*T*he dream vision is often placed under the general heading of revelation literature or is considered as merely an unsurprising development of the general fascination with dreams in Classical or Biblical narratives, but this classification is too general and actually blunts the special dynamics of the form as Guillaume de Lorris, Chaucer, and the rest understood it.[1] Though the form borrows much from revelation literature and from the many narratives of antiquity which feature dreams as events, its origins lie elsewhere, in the psychology, philosophy, and literary theory of the late Middle Ages. Nonetheless, to understand the impact of the late medieval dream vision we must perceive its special relationship to the apocalypse and to the dream-as-narrative-event, because these two "real" categories define the ontological space which the dream vision occupies.

For the dream vision is a self-conscious anomaly, an unaccountable and "impossible" experience, unlike the apocalypse and the somatic dream. It exists, we shall see, in the space between the literary categories of apocalypse and narrative dream. As an analogy, consider Todorov's definition of the fantastic:

> In a world which is indeed our world, the one we know, a world without devils, sylphides, or vampires, there occurs an event which cannot be explained by the laws of this same familiar world. The person who experiences the event must opt for one of two possible solutions: either he is a victim of an illusion of the senses, of a product of the imagination—and

the laws of the world then remain what they are; or else the event has indeed taken place, it is an integral part of reality—but then this reality is controlled by laws unknown to us. Either the devil is an illusion, an imaginary being; or else he really exists, precisely like other living beings—with this reservation, that we encounter him infrequently.

The fantastic occupies the duration of this uncertainty. Once we choose one answer or the other, we leave the fantastic for a neighboring genre, the uncanny or the marvelous. The fantastic is that hesitation experienced by a person who knows only the laws of nature, confronting an apparently supernatural event.[2]

In Todorov's definition, the "neighboring genres" of the uncanny and the marvelous are both directly apprehensible: the first is finally seen to acquiesce in the laws of nature while the second does not. The fantastic, in Todorov's definition, neither affirms nor violates those laws of nature: it is somehow neither *A* nor *not A*. And its power as a literary mode directly derives from its impossible, anomalous hesitation or suspension between comprehensible ontological statuses.

It is a similar notion of hesitation, of suspense, that characterizes the dream vision, and a similar assault on law, on category, on taxonomy that characterizes its effect.[3] The purpose of this chapter and the next is to present and analyze the two twin medieval taxonomies within which or above which the dream vision is suspended. Here I will examine the literary context of the dream vision, the two apprehensible poles of dream-as-narrative-event and apocalypse between which the dream vision existed. In the next chapter I will describe the development and maturity of a *parallel* psychological or scientific taxonomy of dreams and visionary experiences derived from Macrobius and Patristic sources and will show that the literary form consciously and deliberately beggars both of these systems of classification to achieve its unique poetic effect.

Both this chapter and the next will include texts and examples familiar to medieval writers like Chaucer, but they will also include examples utterly *un*familiar to them. The reason for discussing such texts as the *Oneirocriticon* of Artemidorus of Daldis or *Gilgamesh* or the *Oresteia* is to show that the literary and oneiric classifications of dreams and visions which the dream vision deconstructs are not only ancient and ubiquitous but also essential for the rational ordering of experience in any culture.

The Dream-as-Narrative-Event

As a motif in narrative literature, the dream is as old as literature itself. In fact, the earliest extant work of literature, the epic of Gilgamesh, King of Uruk, is a surprisingly appropriate place to begin a characterization of the dream as an event in third person narratives. A representative use of the dream as a message from the gods (a "theogonic" dream) is this passage at the beginning of the narrative, following the report of Gilgamesh's dream foretelling the coming of the wildman Enkidu:

> Now Gilgamesh got up to tell his dream to his mother, Ninsun, one of the wise gods. 'Mother, last night I had a dream. I was full of joy, the young heroes were round me and I walked through the night under the stars of the firmament, and one, a meteor of the stuff of Anu, fell down from Heaven. I tried to lift it but it proved too heavy. All the people of Uruk came round to see it, the common people jostled and the nobles thronged to kiss its feet; and to me its attraction was like the love of woman. They helped me, I braced my forehead and raised it with thongs and brought it to you, and you yourself pronounced it my brother.'[4]

The situation seems simple—the goddess Ninsun sends her son a dream telling him to expect Enkidu, a monstrous alter ego with whom Gilgamesh must do battle before the two "brothers" become friends and set out on their adventures together. This interpretation is obvious to the reader, who has reached this point in the narration after reading of the gods' displeasure with the hero, his wildness, his recklessness, and his need for an equal "like him as his own reflection, his second self, stormy heart for stormy heart."[5] Further, in the passage immediately preceding the dream report above, the magic lover of Enkidu tells him that Gilgamesh will be informed of his coming in a dream.

The difficulty of course is that the dream fails to do this, fails to communicate its intended message to Gilgamesh, who must turn to the source of the dream to ask what it (she) meant. Thus, given the fact that the dream is so enigmatic that it fails to impart its message and serves only as the occasion for Gilgamesh to ask Ninsun to interpret it, why then include it at all? Why not simply have Ninsun tell her son to expect Enkidu?

The answer to this question is crucial to our understanding of the dream as a narrative event, for this "unnecessary" and ineffective dream produces many of the same psychological and esthetic effects as does the *Book of the Duchess* or *Pearl.* First and most important, the dream is here, however paradoxically, a device of literary realism: in *Gilgamesh,* the gods speak, at least initially, not in clouds or apparitions but through a medium that each of us has experienced. Considered in this way, dream-events bridge the gap between the highly favored hero and us lesser folk and thus allow the pleasure of vicarious adventure to be found in primitive narratives such as *Gilgamesh.* In this perspective, the fact that Gilgamesh cannot unravel his dream is not at all remarkable—we cannot usually unravel our dream-messages from the gods either. This tiny fact allows readers the momentary thrill of wild imaginings; if they could but remember and interpret their dreams as Gilgamesh can, then perhaps the riddles of their lives could be solved and they too could hear the *arcana verba,* a privilege allowed to none on earth.

The second psychological effect of the dream is almost as important as the first, and one which builds on the matters of interpretability and enigma just introduced. We have seen that the text of *Gilgamesh* is constructed so as to make the dream immediately apprehensible to readers but not to the dreamer himself, who must rely on the interpretive powers of his goddess-mother. The obvious effect of this structure is to enhance the readers' pleasure by predetermining their intellectual superiority to the hero: not only can readers imagine themselves in Gilgamesh's situation; they can imagine themselves handling it better. This sense of superiority will become a conventional element in the dream vision throughout its history—Amant, Geffrey, Margery's father, Long Will, and Skelton's Drede all share an absolute inability to see what is right there in front of them. The ultimate use of this motif, that of the naive-obtuse-unfit narrator in the dream vision, is far more sophisticated

24

than it is here, but the early interpretive superiority of readers to dreamer in the dream vision plays a crucial role in suspending the poem between forms.

These two qualities, the realistic depiction of communication with the gods and the element of enigma (if only for the dreamer), are common to most uses of the dream in primitive or Classical narrative literatures. Their combination for dramatic purposes is nicely illustrated in the report of Clytaemnestra's snake dream in *Choephori*. At the grave of Agamemnon, Orestes asks the chorus why Clytaemnestra has ordered funeral offerings for the man she murdered:

Chorus:
I know, child, I was there. It was a dream she had. The godless woman had been shaken in the night by floating terrors, when she sent these offerings.

Orestes:
Do you know the dream too? Can you tell it to me right?

Chorus:
She told me herself. She dreamed she gave birth to a snake.

Orestes:
What is the end of the story then? What is the point?

Chorus:
She laid it swathed for sleep as if it were a child.

Orestes:
A little monster. Did it want some food?

Chorus:
She herself, in the dream, gave it her breast to suck.

Orestes:
How was her nipple not torn by such a beastly thing?

Chorus:
It was. The creature drew in blood along with the milk.

Orestes:
No void dream this. It is the vision of a man.

Chorus:
She woke screaming, out of her sleep, shaky with fear, as torches kindled

all about the house, out of the blind dark that had been on them, to comfort the queen. Now she sends these mourning offerings to be poured and hopes they are medicinal for her disease.[6]

The principal curiosity of this passage from Aeschylus is that Clytaemnestra evidently did not understand the meaning of her dream, which is so clear to both Orestes and to readers. The simplest explanation for this lack of insight on her part is that, like her victim Cassandra, Clytaemnestra is cursed with prophetic powers from which she cannot benefit, powers manifest in haunting, fatalistic realizations apprehended by all but the seer. This dream, like that of Pilate's wife in the Gospels (see page 32), is not a revelation or a warning from on high but a vaguely decorative taunt, almost a divine tease. The gods clearly approve of Orestes' plan of revenge and, in effect, participate in it by supplying psychological torment for Clytaemnestra. At the very least, the gods use the dream to underscore the ineluctability of the events to come. The effect of this dream is, then, like that of Gilgamesh's: to make visible to readers the immanent divine order controlling the narrative. The dreamer, even if he is a hero, is regularly denied this intelligence by divinities who keep the evidence of their intervention hidden from *actors* and reveal it only to seers, on whom wise heroes rely for information and advice.

Clytaemnestra's dream illustrates yet another use to which the dream was regularly put in ancient (and medieval) narratives: dream events serve as substitutes for depictions of the inner life of characters. Literature has always been faced with the problem of describing the inner turmoil of characters in narratives; actions need motives and characters, if they are to be realistic, must somehow be provided with reasons for doing the things they do. The literatures of various periods have developed various conventional mechanisms to meet this need, such as psychomachia, the dramatic aside or soliloquy, and the modern convention of the omniscient narrator. The dream-event was often used as another such mechanism, a device especially useful in accounting for unexpected or remarkable decisions or transformations in characters (and a mechanism, by the way, neither more nor less artificial than any other). Clytaemnestra's offering at Agamemnon's grave and Ebeneezer Scrooge's Yuletide metamorphosis are both explained or "covered" by dramatic dream events. Especially for cultures that lacked popular terminology for (or interest in) the inner life, ones which lacked words like "tension," "emotion," and "motive" borrowed from physics and metaphors like being "torn between" two courses of action, dreams were a useful device for imposing (if not achieving) psychological realism. There may have been others available, such as the portent ("In hoc signo vinces") or the apparition, but the dream is far more interesting and dramatically rich because its origins are so ambiguous: Scrooge's disclaimer to Marley about undigested beef and Clytaemnestra's "I accept nothing from a brain that is dulled with sleep"[7] both testify with Pertelote's dissertation that dreams can have mundane causes. On one level, these mundane causes allow dreamers to discount their dreams while readers do not; more importantly, though, the ambiguity of the dream allows authors to portray powerful, even obsessive motivation in characters without needing explicitly to resort to supernatural agency or to the hyperbolic language that so often invades poetry during and after the Renaissance.

The most extended treatment of the dream as a narrative event in Greek literature must be the crucial series of dreams in Book Seven of Herodotus' *History*. A long and painful session with his advisors had finally convinced Xerxes that it was unwise to lead an army into Greece:

> When he had thus made up his mind anew, he fell asleep. And now he saw in the night, as the Persians declare, a vision of this nature—he thought a tall and beautiful man stood over him and said, "Hast thou then changed thy mind, Persian, and wilt thou not lead forth thy host against the Greeks, after commanding the Persians to gather together their levies? Be sure thou doest not well to change; nor is there a man here who will approve thy conduct. The course that thou didst determine on during the day [i.e., to attack, a decision Xerxes reached before the Council], let that be followed."[8]

The dream troubles Xerxes, but on its authority alone he does not

27

change his mind about the invasion; thus, the next morning, on the advice of his uncle Artabanus, he announces once more that he will not lead the Persian host against Greece.

The next night, Xerxes receives another dream visitation, and this time the interlocutor is perturbed that his earlier advice was ignored by the king:

> Son of Darius, it seems thou hast openly before all the Persians renounced the expedition, making light of my words, as though thou hadst not heard them spoken. Know therefore and be well assured, that unless thou go forth to the war, this thing shall happen unto thee—as thou art grown mighty and puissant in a short space, so likewise shalt thou within a little time be brought low indeed.[9]

This second visitation rattles Xerxes, who sends for Artabanus and recounts to him the oracular experiences he has had now for two nights. Artabanus is highly sceptical but finally accedes to a rather harebrained test of the dreams' value: he agrees to wear Xerxes' robe and crown and to sleep on the king's couch to see if he too might receive the dream. Artabanus sensibly objects that a prescient god might conceivably recognize that the sleeper isn't Xerxes but, in the end, falls asleep on his nephew's couch and, sure enough, dreams a dream himself:

> Thou art the man, then, who, feigning to be the tender of Xerxes, seekest to dissuade him from leading his army against the Greeks! But thou shalt not escape scathless, either now or in time to come, because thou hast sought to prevent that which is fated to happen. As for Xerxes, it has been plainly told to himself what will befall him, if he refuses to perform my bidding.[10]

The awakened Artabanus, not surprisingly, now argues passionately *for* the invasion, convinced that the three dreams proceeded from the gate of horn, the gate of true revelation.

And of course the dreams did reveal that the Persian invasion of Greece was fated, though it was no less fated that the invasion should fail. Thus, the Greek historian records what we must take to be a case of monstrous divine duplicity, the gods sending a tantalizing invitation to the haughty enemy of the Greeks, an invitation which, when followed, humbled him before his divinely favored enemies.

A look at the dream-event in Scripture reveals both similarities to the Greek examples and profound differences as well. The dream in the Old Testament is still a device of literary realism, but it is one from which most of the ambiguity, enigma, and hence danger, have been removed. The dream in the Bible is typically symbolic like the examples just considered, but the Biblical dreams are normally interpreted both by their dreamers and by others without difficulty, a change owing (in part, no doubt) to the revolutionary Hebrew conception of a benevolent god, a deity lacking the capriciousness and perversity of the Olympians and other primitive gods. Jacob's dream at Bethel is a representative example:

> Viditque in somnis scalam stantem super terram, et cacumen illius tangens caelum: angelos quoque Dei ascendentes et descendentes per eam, et Dominum innixum scalae dicentem sibi: Ego sum Dominus Deus Abraham patris tui, et Deus Issac: Terram, in qua dormis, tibi dabo et semini tuo.
>
> (Genesis 28: 12–14)
>
> And he saw in a dream a ladder standing upon the earth with its top touching Heaven. Angels of God ascended and descended it, and, resting against the ladder, the Lord said to him: "I am the Lord God of Abraham your father and the God of Isaac. The land on which you sleep I give to you and to your progeny."[11]

Jacob's comment on awakening, "Vere Dominus est in loco isto, et ego nesciebam" ("Truly the Lord is in this place, but I did not realize it"), identifies the dream as a true vision of God and not as a meaningless everyday dream.

The dream of Jacob's ladder is fairly representative of the use of the dream as a narrative event in Scripture. It is at once believable and special because, while all of us have dreams, few of us have dreams which are so strikingly communicative. It is true that this dream is a sign of Jacob's special favor with God; it is, however, also true that, like the dreams of Gilgamesh or Clytaemnestra, this dream functions as a source of motivation in literature that had no vocabulary for describing the powerful impulses that move characters in religious narratives. It would not have done to say simply that Jacob got the feeling that Bethel was an especially holy place; the Scripture writer needs (for various reasons) to exteriorize this intuition by giving it a divine origin. Like the voice of God speaking through the mouths of the prophets, the dream motif is a technique for normalizing and exteriorizing—for "realizing" in the original sense of that word—the sure and special presence of God.

In its enigma too, this dream resembles the Sumerian and Greek examples. As a symbolic artifact, this dream is not appreciably clearer than Gilgamesh's or Clytaemnestra's dreams: all are figurative with specific personal applications which must be grasped by their dreamers. Their principal difference lies in the mere fact of their interpretability—Jacob understands his dream because God sees to it that he does. This is not, I stress, owing to the transparency of Jacob's dream or to the opacity of the others but is *a fact of the narrative*. Perhaps the Jews are smarter than the Greeks or Sumerians, and perhaps God inspires them—it is never explained; in whichever case, whenever a Jew or another person in favor with God has a dream in the Old Testament, the favored dreamer can regularly figure out what it means. When an enemy has a dream, that is frequently another matter.

The implications of this difference—interpretability—are important ones for the dream vision. In Western Judeo-Christian religious narratives, the dream is not regularly enigmatic or elusive: the God of the Jews and Christians did not regularly play games with humans as the Olympians did. Thus, to claim that the late medieval dream vision draws on the enigmatic excitement of the Scriptural dream is somewhat misleading. The enigma of dreams in the Middle Ages (as in the Bible) generally lay not in what God was saying but in whether or not it was God that was talking; that is, in whether the dream had earthly or divine origins. Old Testament writers regularly condemned dream interpretation as a form of magic and paganism because (we may infer) Yahweh does not treat His people so contemptuously as to speak to them in riddles. When the God of Abraham your father and Isaac decided to speak to one of His creatures, He did so openly and explicitly.

In Greek literature and in the Old Testament, then, we may generalize that dreams were used to show the dreamer's favor with God and to move stories along in a way that would not strain credibility. Everyone dreams, yet few of us can remember our dreams in great detail and fewer still of us can rehearse our dreams so that their relevance to our life and its decisions becomes clear. In the nonscriptural examples, the dreamer needs another party to explain the meaning of the dream, a fact which permits folk like Elektra or Chryses or Ninsun to interpret them or remain silent for their own gain or to the ruin of wrongdoers. The God of the Old Testament, consistently more personal and paternal, communicates with people in the same way, although His enigmatic dreams are almost always interpretable to those who receive them.

The Gospels also contain many premonitory and prophetic dreams and, as a rule, these dreams are even less ambiguous and mysterious than the Old Testament examples (and considerably less arresting as narrative events). An angel appears to Joseph in Nazareth, for example, to lay to rest any doubts he had about his pregnant fiancée; this dream, with deft comic touches added, became a favorite feature of medieval plays of the Annunciation. The two best examples of this sort of dream event, though, are those granted to Joseph and to the Magi, dreams warning them of the danger to the Christ Child:

> Et responso accepto in somnis ne redirent ad Herodam, per aliam viam reversi sunt in regionem suam. (Matthew 2: 12)

> And, following the advice which came to them [the Magi] in a dream, that they not return to Herod, they returned to their own land by another route.

> Domini apparuit in somnis Ioseph, dicens: Surge, et accipe puerum, et matrem eius, et fuge in Aegyptum, et esto ibi usque dum dicam tibi. Futurum est enim ut Herodes quaerat puerum ad perdendum eum. (Matthew 2: 13)

> The Lord appeared to Jospeh in a dream, saying: Arise and take the boy and his mother from here until I tell you to return, for Herod is going to seek out the boy to kill him.

These are not ordinary dreams, either to us or to medievals, and the very terminology used to describe them seems to underscore this.

31

Specifically, the warnings were not the dreams: the preposition "*in*" in both cases tells us that the extraordinary communications occurred "in" (i.e., during) sleep or dreams, taking advantage of the spiritual or psychic openness which, it was commonly believed, was a property of sleep.[12]

If these dreams seem somewhat shrouded in mystery, in special phrasing that seems to set them apart from our own everyday dreams, the dream of Pilate's wife seems more commonplace, more fully realizing the ambiguity of the Greek examples. As he sits in judgment on Jesus, Pilate receives a message from his wife:

> Sedente autem illo pro tribunali, misit ad eum uxor eius, dicens: Nihil tibi, et iusto illi: multa enim passa sunt hodie per visum propter eum.
> (Matthew 27: 19)

> Even as he sat in judgment on Jesus, his wife sent a message to him: Have nothing to do with this just man, for I have learned much about him in a dream today.

This dream is an important contrast to the wonderful dreams of the beginning of the New Testament, the passages "in somnis" just considered, for this dream is a true quotidian premonition, a mysterious, in some ways egregious, piece of divine intelligence. Pilate's wife appears in no other place in the Gospels, and the mention of her dream at this point in the Passion serves no narrative purpose other than to heighten the drama and pathos of a scene that needs more of neither. Indeed, the dream is, in its narrative, actually more than egregious: if Pilate had heeded his wife's warning and had not turned Jesus over to the Jews, then the Redemptive act, the center of human history, would have been thwarted. This fact alone should call the origin of the dream into question.

In some ways, this dream is like Clytaemnestra's dream of the snake, little more than a gratuitous reminder that the readers are witnessing important events fraught with theological significance, tensions that express themselves in premonitions. The phrase, "per visum," itself suggests this nonauthoritative origin, or at least it would have to medieval readers. *Visum* was a technical term in medieval oneiromancy which never referred to a divinely inspired dream; a *visum* was normally characterized as a hallucination or daydream or (in its more sinister sense) the incubi or bogeymen experienced in the moments between waking and sleep.[13] This would mean, at least to a medieval reader of the Bible and of dream visions, that the dream of Pilate's wife was not one of those special and rare communications from God but was something more mysterious and exciting, perhaps Satan's last attempt to frustrate Salvation History by preventing the sacrifice of the Son of God.

The complexity and suggestivity of the dream motif in narrative is best illustrated in Roman literature. In ways that the writers of Scripture could not, the Latin poets used the dream as an effective dramatic device—taunting, premonitory, yet always ambiguous. One of the best examples of the dream as a narrative event in Latin literature can be found in Book Four of the *Aeneid*: Aeneas' dream on the night before he leaves Carthage illustrates fully both the power and the enigma of the motif. Earlier in the book, in a waking vision, Aeneas receives a scolding from Mercury:

> tu nunc Karthaginis altae
> fundamenta locas pulchramque uxorius urbem
> exstruis? heu, regni rerumque oblite tuarum!
> ipse deum tibi me claro demittit Olympo
> regnator, caelum et terras qui numine torquet,
> ipse haec ferre iubet celeris mandata per auras:
> quid struis? aut qua spe Libycis teris otia terris?
> si te nulla mouet tantarum gloria rerum
> [nec super ipse tua moliris laude laborem,]
> Ascanium surgentem et spec heredis Iuli
> respice, cui regnum Italiae Romanaque tellus
> debetur.

> Are you
> now laying the foundation of high Carthage,
> as a servant to a woman, building her
> a splendid city here? Are you forgetful
> of what is your own kingdom, your own fate?
> The very god of gods, whose powers sway
> both earth and heaven, sends me down to you

> from bright Olympus. He himself has asked me
> to carry these commands through the swift air:
> What are you pondering or hoping for
> while squandering your ease in Libyan lands?
> For if the brightness of such deeds is not
> enough to kindle you—if you cannot
> attempt the task for your own fame—remember
> Ascanius growing up, the hopes you hold
> for Iulus, your own heir, to whom you are owed
> the realm of Italy and the land of Rome.[14]

Such an experience has very little to do with the medieval dream vision; it is closer, oddly enough, to the divine visitations of the New Testament than to the *Hous of Fame*. Mercury does not speak to Aeneas in a dream; the passage is represented as an apparition, which always marked a privileged communication from a divine protector. Further, the message of the vision is not truly premonitory but rather speaks of Aeneas' fated future with casual assurance. Aeneas is represented as dragging his feet in the divinely ordered plan for the founding of Rome: he is an insider, a full and fully informed participant who needs to be reminded of his special role.

Later in the same book, Aeneas has a dream. On the evening before he is to leave Carthage, he sleeps on the stern of his ship and sees Mercury again:

> Aeneas celsa in puppi iam certus eundi
> carpebat somnos rebus iam rite paratis.
> huic se forma dei uultu redeuntis eodem
> obtulit in somnis rursusque ita uisa monere est,
> omnia Mercurio similis, uocemque coloremque
> et crinis flauos et membra decora iuuenta:
> 'nate dea, potes hoc sub casu ducere somnos,
> nec quae te circum stent deinde pericula cernis,
> demens, nec Zephyros audis spirare secundos?
> illa dolos dirumque nefas in pectore uersat
> certa mori, uariosque irarum concitat aestus.
> non fugis hinc praeceps, dum praecipitare potestas?
> iam mare turbari trabibus saeuasque uidebis,

conlucere faces, iam feruere litora flammis,
si te his attigerit terris Aurora morantem.
heia age, rumpe moras. uarium et mutabile semper
femina.' sic fatus nocti se immiscuit atrae.

Aeneas on the high stern now was set
to leave; he tasted sleep; all things were ready.
And in his sleep a vision of the god
returned to him with that same countenance—
resembling Mercury in everything:
his voice and coloring and yellow hair
and all his handsome body, a young man's—
and seemed to bring a warning once again:
"You, goddess-born, how can you lie asleep
at such a crisis? Madman, can't you see
the threats around you, can't you hear the breath
of kind west winds? She conjures injuries
and awful crimes, she means to die, she stirs
the shifting surge of restless anger. Why
not flee this land headlong, while there is time?
You soon will see the waters churned by wreckage,
ferocious torches blaze, and beaches flame,
if morning finds you lingering on this coast.
Be on your way. Enough delays. An ever
uncertain and inconsistent thing is woman."
This said, he was at one with the black night.[15]

This passage stands in subtle but important contrast to the earlier vision. While the earlier waking experience was a warning, it alerted Aeneas not to any impending danger but rather chastised him for his forgetful and irresponsible behavior in staying at Carthage. The vision expressed the gods' displeasure with a hero who had put aside his fated duty in favor of Dido, Carthage, and the saner life of a mere man. In fact, the waking visitation of Mercury is the precise opposite of a warning of impending danger in that the remainder of the *Aeneid* is a record of the tribulations which lie in the direction in which Mercury nudges the hero in this vision.

The dream, however, is premonitory in the short fall, a warning of immediate danger. While it certainly looks forward to Aeneas' future misson in Italy—he could not fulfill his destiny if he is cut down in Carthage—this dream-warning is considerably less far-sighted than the vision, more rooted in the here and now. Beyond this, a medieval dream interpreter would have noticed crucial differ-ences in Aeneas' state of mind just before the two experiences, dif-ferences which serve to distinguish the literary vision or fictional apocalypse from the dream event.[16] Before the first (which Vergil clearly intends for us to understand as a real visitation from Mer-cury), Aeneas is blithely going about Dido's business without the brooding restlessness of the inactive hero. The vision is actually aimed at this very state of mind—rather than warning Aeneas against external dangers, it seeks to amend his own mind, a grave *internal* threat to his destiny. A medieval dream interpreter would have seen this fact as evidence that the vision was a true apparition, because it is obviously not the product of the hero's troubled conscience.

The dream, however, is far more ambiguous, far more successful as a dramatic device. Unlike the earlier vision, the dream happens at a time of worry and foreboding—unable to sleep, Aeneas sits on the stern of his ship—and is preceded in the narrative by Dido's painful speech searching for a response to Aeneas' decision to leave. Thus, both Aeneas and the readers have reason to fear the worst and thus to suspect that this second visit of Mercury is an anxiety-dream. Further, Mercury is not explicitly identified in the dream (as he was in the vision); in the later passage the reference is to "similis dei . . . redeuntis" ("the god's image returned"), which implies, if only weakly, that this present image, so remarkable for its fidelity to the first, may in fact have the first as its origin. The verb phrase "uisa monere est" similarly weakens the credibility of the dream: although the phrase is not as ambivalent in Latin as its translation, "seemed to bring a warning," might suggest, the phrase nonetheless grounds the dream in the sleeping metaphorical sight of the hero. As with the other examples, then, the use of the dream in the *Ae-neid* is at least potentially ambiguous, perhaps suggesting divine communication, perhaps serving as a window into the emotional life of the character, and surely advancing the narrative by providing character motivation.

As a final example of the dream as a narrative event, we may cite the following passage in the *Confessions* of St. Augustine, a writer not otherwise known for credulity in such matters. Late in Book Three, Augustine relates the dream of his mother Monica and, more important, his unsuccessful attempt to deflect its meaning away from himself:

> Vidit enim stantem se in quadam regula lignea, et advenientem ad te juvenem splendidum, hilarem atque arridentem sibi, cum illa esset moerens et moerore confecta: qui cum causas quaesisset ab ea moestitiae suae quotidianarumque lacrymarum, docendi, ut assolet, non discendi gratia, atque illa respondisset perditionem meam se plangere; jussisse illum quo secura esset, atque admonuisse ut attenderet et videret, ubi esset illa, ibi esset me. Quod illa ubi attendit, vidit me juxta se in eadem regula stantem.

> She saw herself standing upon a certain wooden rule, and coming towards her a young man, splendid, joyful, and smiling upon her, although she was grieved and crushed with grief. When he asked her the reasons for her sorrow and her daily tears—he asked, as is the custom, not for the sake of learning but of teaching—she replied that she lamented for my perdition. Then he bade her rest secure, and instructed her that she should attend and see that where she was, there was I also. And when she looked there she saw me standing on the same rule.[17]

Augustine the author has absolutely no doubt about the divine authority for this dream, though elsewhere in the same book of the *Confessions*—and the proximity is not accidental—he reserves his most caustic rhetoric for the superstitious beliefs of the Manichees, beliefs too absurd even for his unregenerate self (see chapter 3 below for a quotation).

Augustine's memory of his pathetic, defensive response to his mother's dream forms the coda of the story:

> Unde illud etiam, quod cum mihi narrasset ipsum visum, et ego ad id trahere conarer, ut illa se potius non despararet futuram esse quod eram; continuo sine aliqua haesitatione, *Non*, inquite, *non enim mihi dictum*

est, Ubi ille, ibi ettu; sed, Ubi tu ibi, et ille. Confiteor tibi, Domine, recordationem meam quantum recolo, quod saepe non tacui, amplius me isto per matrem vigilantem responso tuo, quod tam vicina interpretationis falsitate turbata non est, et tam cito vidi quod videndum fuit, quod ego certe, antequam dixisset, non videram; etiam tum commotum fuisse, quam ipso somnio, quo feminae piae gaudium tanto post futurum, ad consolationem tunc praesentis sollicitudinis, tanto ante praedictum est.

Whence too was this, that when she had narrated the vision to me and I attempted to distort it to mean rather that she should not despair of becoming what I already was, she immediately replied without any hesitation: "No!" she said, "It was not said to me, 'Where he is, there also are you,' but 'Where you are, there also is he.' " I confess to you, Lord, that my memory of this, as best I can recall it, and I often spoke of it, is that I was more disturbed by your answer to me through my mother—for she was not disturbed by the likely-seeming falsity of my interpretation and quickly saw what was to be seen, which I certainly did not see before she spoke—than by the dream itself. By this dream the joy of that holy woman, to be fulfilled so long afterwards, was predicted much beforehand so as to bring consolation in her present solicitude.[18]

While Augustine is certain of the special nature of the dream, it is for him subsumed into the universal, immanent hand of the Father leading him ineluctably on the path he is fated to take. Always the logician and rhetorician, Augustine is more unnerved at being bested in disputation by his mother (coached from on high, to be sure) than by her eerie, premonitory dream. In short, for Augustine, Monica's dream is of a piece with the death of Alypius, the encounter with Faustus, and even with *Tolle, lege*: it is no less and no more than another of God's ubiquitous incursions into his errant life.

These dreams as narrative events are an important literary context for the medieval dream vision, one of the two categories between which the poetic form asserted itself. These dream events in third person narratives constitute proof that everyday dreams are sometimes significant, sometimes, remarkably, vehicles for enigmatic messages from beyond. More importantly, however, these dream-events serve as powerful narrative catalysts: they suggest, inspire, and usually result in decisive, often heroic action, and therefore can be seen as a conventional method of depicting a character's motivation in the largely externalized literatures of the ancient world. These dreams are thus the literary forebears of works such as *Psychomachia*, the *Consolation of Philosophy*, and *Le Roman de la Rose*, in which the action that the allegory represents is wholly an intellectual one, one depicted in an external psychological grammar that is, in all fairness, the forerunner of Freud's superego, ego, and id. We shall see that the dream vision used this fundamentally psychological thrust of the narrative dream, still and always tantalized by the possibility that its origins may be more than psychological.

The Apocalypse

The second of the two literary contexts of the late medieval dream vision is apocalyptic writing, the traditional literary form which begins (in the Christian era) with the Book of Revelation and comes soon to include a remarkable body of early Christian reports of visions, ecstasies, divine or angelic visitations, and deathbed ravishments into Heaven.[19] At first glance, these works might not seem separable from the dreams-as-narrative-events just discussed (and even less separable from the dream vision), but their differences from these other forms would have been obvious and crucial to medieval readers. The most important difference, as I suggested earlier, is the context of the vision, its circumstances. Aeneas' dream of Mercury, for example, comes at a high dramatic moment in Book Four of the *Aeneid*: on the evening before his departure from Carthage, Aeneas himself senses this tension, is at first unable to sleep, and then finally falls into an uncomfortable slumber on the stern of his ship. He dreams a classic anxiety dream, resurrecting the mental image of Mercury from his earlier vision and exteriorizing his fears about Dido's response to his departure. A medieval expert would have given this dream as much credence—and the same sort of credence—as a modern psychologist would: the dovetailing of day residue in an unquiet mind thoroughly impugns the dream as a divinely originating premonition.

The apocalypse, however, has a completely different context. If an apocalypse occurs in a larger work at all, this larger work is typically "factual," a history or chronicle or spiritual biography. The visionary is never depicted as distressed or anxious; in fact, he is always represented as worthy, pure, and totally free from worldly cares. The psychic emptiness of the visionary is conventionally emphasized in mystical tracts such as *The Cloud of Unknowing*, and its history as a requirement for mystical experience is long and distinguished: only a vessel empty of earthly concerns can accept the indwelling of the Divine Presence.[20] And the emptiness must be a conscious emptiness, a simplicity of heart and an abstinence of mind: visionaries may occasionally be tranced or even on the point of death, but never asleep.

The other difference between the dream-event and the apocalypse is in content. The dream events in larger narratives are generally without striking or memorable content: their purpose is to advance their narratives and not to move the readers with their messages. Even Clytaemnestra's dream, however striking its imagery may be, shares this merely *personal* relevance, for the image of the snake is, within Aeschylus' fiction, Clytaemnestra's and not ours, and the dream report is a projection of her guilt and dramatic situation, not the readers'. The apocalypse, however, succeeds only insofar as its content is compelling and universal: the Apocalypse, for example, is comprehensible *as a revelation* merely by the application of Semitic and Christian iconography without any need to resort to the personality or circumstances of St. John. The Apocalypse is a framed narrative, of course, but it is one whose frame has no dramatic or formal relationship to the visionary report which it introduces: the frame of an apocalypse serves only to authenticate the vision and to normalize the visionary, that is, to assure the readers that the vision did take place and that the visionary was sane, sober, and unencumbered by emotional or physical distress. The frame thus readily dispensed with, the vision takes over completely, with all its symbols, colors, and eschatological meanings supporting a universal ethical or theological truth. To put it simply, Clytaemnestra's dream is finally about her guilt and Joseph's dream is about the imminent danger to the child Jesus, while John's vision has no personal context at all: it is from first to last an artifact transmitted by God to be experienced by all as universally applicable.

The distinction can be seen by briefly examining two later works in the apocalypse tradition, the *Visio Sancti Pauli* and the *Visio Wettini* of Walahfrid Strabo. The *Visio Sancti Pauli* is one of the earliest and most important of the large body of apochryphal visions. It was probably written in the second century and was alleged by its author to be the lost narrative of the experience to which St. Paul refers in 2 Corinthians:

Si gloriari oportet (non expedite quidem) veniam autem ad visiones et revelationes Domini. Scio hominem in Christo ante annos quatuordecim, sive in corpore nescio, sive extra corpus nescio, Deus scit, raptum huiusmodi usque ad tertium caelum. Et scio huiusmodi hominem sive in corpore, sive extra corpus nescio, Deus scit: quoniam raptus est in paradisum: et audivit arcana verba, quae non licet homini loqui. Pro huiusmodi gloriabor; pro me autem nihil gloriabor nisi in infirmitatibus meis.
(2 Corinthians, 12:1-5)

I must continue boasting—it serves no purpose—and turn now to visions and revelations of the Lord. I know a man in Christ who, some fourteen years ago—whether in the body or outside of the body I do not know; God knows—was rapt into the third heaven. And I know that this man—either in his body or outside of it (I do not know; God knows)—was taken up into Paradise itself and there heard secret words which men are not permitted to speak. About this I boast; about myself I boast of nothing save my infirmities.

The document which purports to be the account of this vision, the *Visio Sancti Pauli,* generates from this scant Scriptural allusion a rich, dramatic first-person account of the Apostle's rapture. The frame prologue to the vision report, a masterful little story in itself, places Paul's *visionary* experience in sharp contrast to the everyday dreams of lesser men:

Consule Theodosio Augusto minore et Cynegio, tunc habitante quodam honorato Tharso, in domum que fuerat sancti Pauli, angelus per noctem apparens reuelauit ei dicens ut fundamenta domus dissolueret et quod inuenisset palam faceret; *haec autem fantasmata esse putauit.*

In the consulship of Theodosius Augustus the Younger and of Cynegius, a certain nobleman living in Tarsus, in the house which was that of Saint Paul, an angel at night appeared to him, saying that he should open the foundations of the house and should publish what he found, *but he thought that these things were dreams.*[21] (my emphasis)

As the frame narrative continues, we learn that the homeowner refused to follow the instructions of the angel until the heavenly visitor had come a second, and then a third time: his feeling after three such messages was that these might be more than "fantasmata." Set beside Paul's meticulous insistence on having been rapt into Heaven, this sympathetic depiction of the homeowner's scepticism about dreams *in somnio* amounts to a convenient index to the different perceptions of dream and vision in the early Christian era. The dream was suspect and unreliable: no one could expect the poor homeowner to tear his house down on the authority of a mere dream. Only after three such messages—recall the cumulative effect of the repeated dreams in Herodotus—does the homeowner, still with misgivings, dig up his foundation.

The apocalyptic vision is different, special. Paul does not report that he was asleep when he had it, and his Apostolic authority and reputation for no-nonsense bluntness make the *Visio* instantly authoritative and precious (or at least this was the intention of the author). The reference to dreams in the frame prologue is thus a rhetorical strategy designed to place the subsequent vision in a context which will remind readers of the received distinctions between the worthless dream and the divine revelation.

This formula for revelation-writing, based ultimately on the *Book of Revelation* itself and locally on the *Visio Sancti Pauli* and its contemporaries, became the ironclad convention for a millennium of Christian ecstasis writers. Literally scores of visions, ecstatic accounts, and at least one "visionary novel" (*The Pastor of Hermes*) were written in the first centuries of the Christian era, and all of these emphasize the implicit ground rules of the *Visio Sancti Pauli*: that visions are not dreams and that the context, introduction, and "environment" of a vision must identify it as a qualitatively different experience from that of the dream. Time after time in these apochryphal writings, the authors use the Pauline formulas "raptus in caelum" and even "sive in corpore, sive extra corpus." Along with this conscious adherence to the tradition, these writings, such as the visions of Sedrach, Our Lady, St. John, and many others, explicitly insist that they are records of waking visions and not of dreams, an

emphasis that continued throughout the long history of the apocalypse genre. In the ninth century, for example, Walahfrid Strabo
elaborately assures us that the visionary Brother Wetti is awake:

> Tum frater: "Non mensa placet, non pabula prosunt.
> Cedo locum, compellor enim feritate doloris
> Strata videre mea. Haec aliam portate sub umbram."
> Tolluntur stramenta aliamque feruntur in aedem
> Continguam cellae quam cenatum ante petivit.
>   Ergo ubi membra suo componit languida lecto,
> Conclusis oculis penitus dormire nequiebat.
> Spiritus ecce doli foribus processit apertis
> Clericus in specie, frontis latuere fenestrae,
> Ut nec signa quidem parvi videantur ocelli.

Then brother Wetti said: "It upsets me to be at table; the food does me
no good. I give up my place; a severe pain forces me to look to my bed;
please carry this bed to another room." His bed was lifted up and taken to
another room next to the cell to which he had come to take his meal.

He had laid down his limbs on his couch, closed his eyes, but had not
yet been able to fall into a deep sleep, when suddenly the spirit of guile
came through the open doorway. He was dressed as a priest; the aper-
tures of his brow were shouded in darkness so that not so much as the
gleam of an eye could be seen.[22]

The quotation is significant because it represents a late but still "serious" survival of the tradition, the conventions of which have been
solidified into final guarantors of verity. Strabo, Hincmar, Bede, and
the rest, out of touch with the original Christian impulse to apocalypse, imitated the form conscious of dangers not appreciated or
realized in the first centuries of the Christian era: what if this is just
a silly dream, a phantasm? Of what value is it then? To protect the
truth claims of these narratives, the writers typically included elaborate disclaimers (such as Strabo's above), shrilly assuring readers
that the visionary is not asleep—at the point of death, in ecstasy,
semiconscious, even delirious from starvation, *but not asleep.*

Another crucial convention in these writings is their absolute insistence on third person narration. Even in 2 Corinthians, St. Paul
adopts the form to describe his own experience: "Scio hominem in
Christo" ("I know man in Christ"). In his introduction to the *Visio*

Wettini, David Traill theorizes that this third person narration became conventional for a variety of reasons: to avoid the credibility problems in relying on the visionary as reporter as well, and to provide a voice external to the experience to assure readers that the visionary was a normative and trustworthy individual, one, for example, who hadn't eaten that night and would thus have no pollutants in his stomach. In short, the narrator was a moderator who could take pains to investigate and guarantee the validity of the vision (at least circumstantially), pains avoided with a vengeance by dream vision writers.[23]

The later history of the apocalypse is outside the scope of this study, but it is relevant to show just how it diverged rhetorically and thematically from the medieval dream vision. In the eleventh century, we find the *Visio Episcopus Goliardis,* which uses the conventional motifs for playful, parodic purposes:

> A tauro torrida lampade Cynthii
> Fundente iacula ferventis radii,
> Umbrosas nemoris latebras adii,
> Explorans gratiam lenis Favonii.
> Aestivae medio diei tempore,
> Frondosa recubans Iovis sub arbore,
> Astantis video formam Pythagorae;
> Deus scit, nescio, utrum in corpore.
> Ipsam Pythagorae formam aspicio,
> Inscriptam artium schemate vario.
> An extra corpus sit haec revelatio,
> Ultrum in corpore, Deus scit, nescio.

> In May, when fall Apollo's rays
> Like bright hot spears in showers,
> I wander, sweetened by Zephyrus
> In secret woodland bowers.
> At noon, upon this summer's day
> In Jove's oak's shade, as I resting lay,
> I see Pythagorus' form stand there:
> God knows if in body—I cannot say.
> I see Pythagorus himself,
> Who wrote, of all the arts, the scheme,

44

> But if this vision be out of body
> Or in, God knows, but I can't deem.[24]

In this vision, the standard Pauline formula is put into a comic, even satiric context. This does not mean, of course, that the revelation form was bankrupt in the eleventh century; it does mean, when one notices how its conventions have become merged with the terminology of classical antiquity, that if the form was not obsolescent by this time, it was at least dryly and predictably conventional.[25]

A semisecular tradition of vision writing also exists in the later Middle Ages, a tradition dating back to the "Vision of Er." Though works in this lineage often swing close to the overtly religious apocalypse (and less often to the dream vision), their development is fairly independent. The major works in this Platonic visionary tradition are Prudentius' *Psychomachia*, Martianus Capella's *De Nuptiis Mercuriae et Philologiae*, and, of course, *The Consolation of Philosophy*. For a variety of reasons, these important poems lie outside the provenance of this book; though their influence on Guillaume de Lorris and Chaucer is unarguable, these allegorical visions do not have a direct *formal* relationship to the dream vision.

First and most important, the manner of these poems is unilaterally and uncompromisingly discursive and their mode is either naively allegorical or dialogic, unlike religious apocalypses which often included typological or historical figures as figurative elements. Consequentially, the Platonic visions seem to care little about literal credibility: it hardly matters that readers do not believe the literal truth of the "Vision of Er" or *The Consolation of Philosophy*, for the fruit of these texts is their doctrine and not the literal truth of their fabulous imagery. While it is appropriate that Boethius have such a vision at this low point in his life, the Boethian doctrine dramatically realized by Lady Philosophy is easily detachable from the fictional frame. In contrast, the literal truth of the religious apocalypse was crucially important to its medieval readers, as evidenced by the ecclesiastical scrutiny given to visionaries whose writings were innocuous or even completely orthodox. The Platonic vision frame was a disposable convention, while that of the Christian apocalypse was not.

The later history of the Platonic revelation only serves to illustrate the conventionality of the form and its use for naive didactic allegory. The form experienced a major resurgence in the twelfth century in the luxuriant allegories of such as Alain de l'Isle and Bernard Silvestris. *Anticlaudianus, De Planctu Naturae,* and the *Cosmographia* were roughly contemporary with the *Visio Episcopus Goliardis* just quoted, but these poems, despite their power and beauty, exploit the apocalypse frame for only the barest conventional purposes. Thus, we must not confuse the profound doctrinal or philosophical influence of these works—for example, that of the *Pleynt of Kynde* on the *Parlement of Foules* or on the *Roman de la Rose*—with *literary* influence: Guillaume de Lorris, Chaucer, and Jean de Meun were greatly indebted to the Chartrean Naturalists and to other Neo-Platonists for ideas about love, nature, and even about allegory, but the form they chose to express these ideas had, we shall see, very different origins.

These two forms—the dream as narrative event and the apocalypse—are the two *literary* poles between which the dream vision found its existence. Their carefully contrived essences and conventions, which seem to be as old as literature itself, create a taxonomy, a structure that includes two and only two kinds of experience: one a dream in a story, a dream fraught with ambiguity and ambivalence like our own, the other a singular communication from God sent to humanity through the agency of a privileged individual. From the very beginning, the distinction between these two sorts of experience was carefully maintained by the perpetuation of formal conventions which clearly identified a given work as either a dream or a revelation. Dreams (like Clytaemnestra's or Monica's or those in the Bible) were either ordinary, albeit curious, or somebody else's; apocalypses (like St. John's or Wetti's) were, irrelevantly, somebody else's too, but their message was universal, hence impersonal, hence everybody's and nobody's.

In the beginning and within purely literary circles, this taxonomy

—it is either somebody else's dream or everybody's revelation—developed accidentally and innocently: we shall see in the next chapter that a remarkably similar, even parallel, scientific structure of exclusion, based on classical and medieval oneiromancy, developed alongside its literary analogue. This second taxonomy, one dividing dreams into revelatory dreams and your dreams, was far from accidental: it was the serendipitous discovery of the conservative fathers of the Church, which they set in stone to protect the institutional Church from dangerous visionaries and their chaotic dreams. The ultimate effect of the twin taxonomies or classifications, one literary, the other scientific, was exclusion, the exclusion of the everyday somatic dream of the ordinary person which somehow spoke to universal concerns—in short, the relevant dream.

By virtue of pressures more within the province of the psychiatrist than that of the literary historian, the dream vision was born in the space between the dream event and the apocalypse, a space between wholly dramatic and wholly didactic purposes. At one extreme, the dramatic, is the dream event. Its energy is completely focused on the story of which it is a part. In the case of the Magi or Aeneas, the dream is a source of character motivation, an internal event which advances the external events of the narrative (the return by another route, the departure from Carthage). As such, the dreams are quite pointless outside their contexts and have no didactic value: we are not moved by them to flee to Egypt or to anticipate an armed attack (or even to muse on how inconstant a thing is woman). Their point and purpose are wholly psychological: they are evidence of their dreamers' reasons (inspired or otherwise) for doing what they did. No one could live in St. Paul's house in Tarsus and not fancy that it might contain some relic, and the writer of the *Visio Sancti Pauli* understands this well; the homeowner's dream must play three times before he thinks anything of it and takes pick and shovel. Dreams as narrative events move texts.

The revelation, however, *is* a text. The apocalypse is generally narrated by an objective third party whose function is to add credibility to the report, and the visionary is invariably depicted as straightlaced, holy (and rather boring)—a person who doesn't have

47

nightmares, doesn't eat the wrong foods, and doesn't talk to imaginary playmates. This person, often a saint, and one commonly on the point of a holy, peaceful death, is so trustworthy, so far above suspicion, that he generally disappears from his own text: after all, the vision has nothing special to do with him—there is ideally no "him" for the vision to have to do with—but a special communication to the world from God that merely uses this person as a medium. Having thus neutralized the dramatic potential in the text and having established a special claim of divine communication, the vision writer is free to represent God's revealed truth without obstruction or impediment.

The dream vision draws much from these two forms. From the dream event it takes drama and an abiding interest in the personality of the dreamer as the esthetic center of the work. Like the dreams of Clytaemnestra or of Pilate's wife, the dreams of Chaucer or of the "jueler" of *Pearl* are uniquely psychological events inextricably tied to the personalities of their dreamers. From the apocalypse the dream vision takes a fascinated, unblinking report of a remarkable inner occasion. The form of the dream vision, a lengthy dream report framed by a brief prologue and epilogue, invites a sort of forgetfulness on the part of its readers, invites them to treat the dream report as an important, even supernal message only accidentally enclosed within an "insignificant" dream. While the dream vision does not owe a direct debt to the Apocalypse and its tradition, it is impossible to imagine a medieval reader of *Pearl* or of *Piers Plowman* or even of the *Hous of Fame* failing to think of St. John and his glimpse of Heaven and allowing himself to consider this unlikely revelation as a vicarious affirmation of the revelatory powers of one's own dreams.

But the dream vision did not simply establish itself between these two forms: it transcended them. Neither the narrative dream event nor the revelation can lay any special claim to irresistible *rhetorical* power. The dream event has little specifically rhetorical value at all, for it is simply one of a series of events in a story subject only to the limitations of realism and to the grammar of narrative causation. The revelation, while powerful, is hardly *rhetorically* so: ecstasis writers generally make little attempt to enlist the readers' support or agreement beyond providing the explicit assurance that the text's import is revelatory. To do more than this would cheapen the divine message, freely given and embraceable in faith by those of faith. The dream vision, however, does have a strategy, a typical rhetorical thrust. This strategy is the subject of chapter 4, but we may note here that the strategy inheres in the simple description of the form: the story of a man (dream event) *and* his dream (apocalypse). The form takes the didactic integrity and brilliance of the apocalypse and puts it in the head and in the "story" of a suspect, individual dreamer and, ultimately, draws its energy from its position or space between the two forms, a space within which readers can never be sure whether the words they read are God's or those of one who has dreams.

CHAPTER TWO

MEDIEVAL DREAM
AUTHORITIES

As every reader of medieval literature well knows, the Age of Freud was not the only great period of dream analysis in Western science. Another period of intense interest in dream lore or oneiromancy came in the late Middle Ages, an age that was heir to a tremendous body of classical oneiromancy beginning with Plato and Aristotle and including such figures as Artemidorus, Cicero, and Macrobius. The challenge for the Catholic Middle Ages was to make sense of this corpus of authoritative opinion passed on to them by the ancients; to consider, codify, and reconcile the categories of the classical psychologists and encyclopedists with the New Dispensation. Augustine, Aquinas, and scores of other Church fathers in fact succeeded in this hermeneutic task; they reconciled the overwhelmingly sceptical teachings of the Greek and Roman philosophers with the unavoidable evidence of Sacred Scripture, evidence that made absolute scepticism untenable. As we shall see, the seams between classical and patristic approaches to dreams are tidy, if not completely invisible, and the consensus of these writers is remarkably rational, sensible, and close to prevailing modern views on the subject of dreams. In fact, while modern dream writers can be neatly divided into two irreconcilable camps—the pathological and the revelatory—medieval authorities are much more open-minded. As evidence, perhaps, of the perceptual openness that Carolly Erickson describes in *The Medieval Vision*, medieval dream authorities were able to combine a healthy scepticism about dreams as somatic experiences with a blithe acquiescence to the existence of dream experiences which were quite other than merely somatic.[1] It was not by accident that medieval Christian oneiromancers and patristic authorities treated the question of the interpretability of dreams with such care, for the matter of dream interpretation was a volatile one on practical levels for the Middle Ages. The early Christian era, the post-Apostolic centuries, inspired, as we have seen, an enormous number of devotional and eschatological ecstasis writers, and one might imagine that the trade in apochryphal visions, ecstases, raptures, and apocalypses was brisk in this age. We shall see that these writers of ersatz revelations had circumstantial Scriptural authority for their experiences—after all, God had spoken to others in dreams, so why not to them as well? Soon, however, the Church grew larger and more strictly institutionalized and, as evidence as early as the Epistles of Saint Paul testifies, the central authority of the Church was constantly plagued with strange divergences or dangerous positions held by far-flung outposts of the new religion and spawned, often, by somebody's vision, extracorporeal experience, or dreams. The evidence in the *Patrologia Latina* for the development of this conservative position on dreams and visions is spotty at best, but what we do have suggests that warnings to the credulous are virtually as old as the Church itself.[2] At any rate, by the fourth century, Augustine can announce without bitterness (in *De Genesi ad Litteram*) that the age of miracles is past and that we are never on safe ground believing that our dreams are inspired. The necessity of this position at the managerial level is obvious and unremarkable; what is important about the Church's ultimate conservatism on the dream question is that it allowed the Middle Ages to draw on, legitimize, and therefore perpetuate a strikingly uniform classical scepticism about dreams, a classical-patristic detente that codified dreams into a scientific taxonomy in the interstices of which the poetic form developed.

Classical Scepticism

As it seems everything else does, dream science begins with Plato.[3] Plato was extremely cautious about dreams, recognizing both the danger inherent in the vivid, effective dream and the predictable rational objections to uncritical credulousness.[4] He often alludes to Socrates' dreams, the most famous of which is his dream that his own execution would be delayed until the return of the ceremonial ship from Delos (*Crito*, section 43). Even this dream, however, like several others in the dialogues, receives little serious comment from either Plato or Socrates and seems principally intended as dramatic and sympathetic, the literary device of a literate philosopher. A more pointed discussion of dreams can be found in the *Timaeus*, a mystic psychological assertion that would prove the foundation for the Neo-Platonic apocalpyses of the twelfth century:

> No man, when in his wits, attains prophetic truth and inspiration; but when he receives the inspired word, either his intelligence is enthralled in sleep or he is demented by some distemper or possession. And he who would understand what he remembers to have been said, whether in a dream or when he was awake, by the prophetic and inspired nature, or would determine by reason the meaning of the apparitions which he has seen, and what indications they afford to this man or to that, of past, present or future good or evil, must first recover his wits. But, while he continues demented, he cannot judge of the visions which he sees or the words which he utters; the ancient saying is very true—that "only a man who has his wits can act or judge about himself and his own affairs," and for this reason it is customary to appoint interpreters to be judges of the true inspiration.[5]

Even this statement, however, must be viewed with a certain circumspection. Plato is acknowledging the existence of a category and offering an explanation of its existence, but he carefully surrounds the acknowledgment of the revelatory dream with insistent reminders about the necessity of rational control and with cautions about the uncertainty of the visionary state. His persistent references to dementia, the cautions implicit in the beginning of the quotation, and the final suggestions concerning professional oneiromancers radically delimit the possibilities opened by the statement, so much so that Socrates, in another mood, might say the same things only to conclude that, given the dangers and uncertainties, revelation through dreams is not worth the effort.

Plato considers dreams again in the *Republic*, but this time the thrust is thoroughly sceptical. Near the end of the treatise, Socrates describes the appetites of the Despotic Man, appetites which

> . . . bestir themselves in dreams, when the gentler part of the soul slumbers and the control of reason is withdrawn; then the wild beast in us, full-fed with meat or drink, becomes rampant and shakes off sleep to go in quest of what will gratify its own instincts.[6]

The passage continues, describing the outrages the Despotic Man commits "in phantasy," but comes to acknowledge, in fairness, that

> It is otherwise with a man sound in body and mind, who, before he goes to sleep, awakens the reason within him to feed on high thoughts and questionings in collected meditation.[7]

The paragraph concludes, however, with an unmistakable warning to even such pure men, a warning which, in fact, apologizes for the preceding digression on the rare revelatory dream:

> However, we have been carried away from our point, which is that in every one of us, even those who seem most respectable, there exist desires, terrible in their untamed lawlessness, which reveal themselves in dreams.[8]

This final position is remarkably close to the standard Christian teaching in the high Middle Ages: the revelatory dream is a real category, representing a phenomenon that exists in fact, but such dreams are exceedingly rare and the everyday dreams of mere mortals ought never to be assumed to be communications from the gods. They are indices of a man's nature (and may therefore be precious or admirable if that nature is so), but only the very purest natures might hope to attain some transcendent truth through them.

It is difficult to find another classical authority as open-minded about dreams as Plato. Aristotle, in two short tracts in the *Parva Naturalia*, is considerably less sanguine about even the possibility of the revelatory or miraculous dream and treats dreams as thoroughly physiological phenomena. The longer and more important of these two tracts, *Peri enypnion (On Dreams)*, acknowledges with Plato that the dream operates in the absence of the senses and rational faculties but offers an uncompromising psychological explanation for its origin:

[In *On the Soul*] Imagination was agreed to be a movement produced by perception in a state of activity, and the dream seems to be some sort of mental picture (for we call a mental picture appearing in sleep a dream, either simply so or, at any rate, in some sense); it is clear that dreaming belongs to the sensitive faculty and is related to it in the same way as imagination.[9]

With typical Aristotelean closure, the discussion concludes "from all this that a dream is one form of mental image, which occurs in sleep,"[10] a position which Aristotle amplifies in *On Prophecy in Sleep*, a short and summary dismissal of its topic:

Generally speaking, seeing that some of the lower animals also dream, dreams cannot be sent by God, nor is this the cause of their appearance, but they are miraculous, for human nature is miraculous, though it is not divine.[11]

While this extreme position was not entirely acceptable to later classical authorities (and certainly not to Christian ones), the eminence of Aristotle and the rational, clinical approach he took to the dream question exerted a profound conservative influence on later opinions. His emphasis on the physiological causes for dreams, taken with similar assertions in Plato's *Republic*, established a solid sceptical position which was passed on to Latin authorities such as Lucretius and Cicero.

De Rerum Natura contains an extended discussion of sleep, treating the subject in a clinical manner reminiscent of Aristotle and taking the conventional position that it is a state of partial withdrawal of the senses and the intellect:

principio somnus fit ubi est distracta per artus
vis animae partimque foras eiecta recessit
et partim contrusa magis concessit in altum.
dissoluuntur enim tum demum membra fluuntque.
nam dubium non est, animai quin opera sit
sensus hic in nobis, quem cum sopor impedit esse,
tum nobis animam perturbatam esse putandumst
eiectamque foras; non omnem; namque iaceret
aeterno corpus perfusum frigore leti.

First of all, sleep comes to pass when the strength of the soul is scattered about among the limbs, and in part has been cast out abroad and gone its way, and in part has been pushed back and passed inward deeper within the body. For then indeed the limbs are loosened and droop. For there is no doubt that it is thanks to the soul that this sense exists in us; and when sleep hinders it from being, then we must suppose that the soul is disturbed and cast out abroad; yet not all of it; for then the body would lie bathed in the eternal chill of death.[12]

This notion of sleep as a demi-death, of which this is an early testimony, is an important one for the apocalypse tradition as well as for that of the dream vision, but Lucretius makes in this passage no explicit case for revelation in sleep while strongly suggesting that the resting spirit is typically affected by external waking circumstances; for example,

> deinde cibum sequitur somnus, quia, quae facit aer,
> haec eadem cibus, in venas dum diditur omnis,
> efficit. et multo sopor ille gravissimus exstat
> quem satur aut lassus capias, quia plurima tum se
> corpora conturbant magno contusa labore.
> fit ratione eadem coniectus partim animai
> altior atque forus eiectus largior eius,
> et divisior inter se ac distractior intust.

Again, when sleep follows after food, because food brings about just what air does, while it is being spread into all the veins, and the slumber which you take when full or weary, is much heavier because then more bodies than ever are disordered, bruised with the great effort. In the same manner the soul comes to be in part thrust deeper within; it is also more abundantly driven out abroad, and is more divided and torn asunder in itself within.[13]

Lucretius takes up dreams in the next lines, a change of subject that suggests, even before he presents his thesis, that Lucretius views dreams as manifestations of a troubled spirit:

> Et quo quisque fere studio devinctus adhaeret
> aut quibus in rebus multum sumus ante morati
> atque in ea ratione fuit contenta magis mens,
> in somnis eadem plerumque videmur obire;
> causidici causas agere et componere leges,
> induperatores pugnare ac proelia obire,
> nautae contractum cum ventis degere duellum,
> nos agere hoc autem et naturam quaerere rerum
> semper et inventam patriis exponere chartis.

And for the most part to whatever pursuit each man clings and cleaves, or on whatever things we have before spent much time, so that the mind was more strained in the task than is its wont, in our sleep we seem mostly to traffic in the same things; lawyers think that they plead their cases and compose contracts, generals that they fight and engage in battles, sailors that they pass a life of conflict waged with the winds, and we that we pursue our task and seek for the nature of things at all times, and set it forth, when it is found, in writings in our country's tongue.[14]

To emphasize this physiological explanation for dreams, Lucretius turns, in the final lines of the discussion, to the dreams of animals (as Aristotle did)—to sweating horses and panting dogs—and finally to the wet dream. The only allusion in *De Rerum Natura* to even the possibility of dream-visitations or of revelations in dreams occurs in a semidigression early in the same book (Book Four), as Lucretius introduces the notion of the mental image:

Atque animi quoniam docui natura quid esset
et quibus e rebus cum corpore compta vigeret
quove modo distracta redirect in ordia prima,
nunc agere incipiam tibi, quod vementer ad has res
attinet, esse ea quae rerum simulacra vocamus;
quae, quasi membranae summo de corpore rerum
dereptae, volitant, ultroque citroque per auras,
atque eadem nobis vigilantibus obvia mentis
terrificant atque in somnis, cum saepe figuras
contuimur miras simulacraque luce carentum,
quae nos horrifice languentis saepe sopore
excierunt, no forte animas Acherunte reamur
effugere aut umbras inter vivos volitare
neve aliquid nostri post mortem posse relinqui,
cum corpus simul atque animi natura perempta
in sua discessum dederint primordia quaeque.

And since I have taught what was the nature of the mind, and whereof composed it grew in union with the body, and in what way rent asunder it passed back into its first-beginnings: now I will begin to tell you what exceedingly nearly concerns this theme, that there are what we call idols of things; which, like films stripped from the outermost body of things, fly forward and backward through the air; and they too when they meet us in waking hours afright our minds, yea, and in sleep too, when we

56

often gaze on wondrous shapes, and the idols of those who have lost the light of day, which in awful wise have often roused us, as we lay languid in sleep; lest by chance we should think that souls escape from Acheron, or that shades fly abroad among the living, or that something of us can be left after death, when body alike and the nature of mind have perished and parted asunder into their several first-beginnings.[15]

Such a position forecloses the possibility of the dream from Heaven and places the dream phenomenon clearly in the realm of mental, imaginative activities with physical, mundane causes or stimuli. The crucial link between the seminal Greek authorities and the Middle Ages is Cicero, considered among medievals—recall Dante—to be the universal genius: philosopher, moralist, rhetorician. On the subject of dreams, their causes and their worth, Cicero is as clear-headed and emphatic as Lucretius: despite his having been elected augur in 53 B. C., Cicero wrote (in *De Divinatione*) a blistering attack on the notion of revelation in dreams, lumping oneiro-mancers together with magicians and other charlatans. The following passage from *De Divinatione* recalls the pointed rejection of Aristotle:

Hi cum sustinetur membris et corpore et sensibus, omni certiori cernunt, cogitant, sentiunt. Cum autem haec subtracta sunt desertusque animis languore corporis, tum agitatur ipse per sese. Itaque in eo etformae versantur et actiones, et multa audiri, multa dici vindentur. Haec scillicet in imbecillo remissaque animo multa omnibus modus confusa et variata versantur, maximeque 'reliquiae' rerum earum moventur de quibus vigilantes aut cogitavimus aut egimus;

When the soul is supported by the bodily members and by the five senses its powers of perception, thought, and apprehension are more trustworthy. But when these physical aids are removed and the body is inert in sleep, the soul then moves of itself. And so, in that state, visions flit about it, actions occur and it seems to hear and see many things. When the soul itself is weakened and relaxes many such sights and sounds, you may be sure, are seen and heard in all manner of confusion and diversity. Then especially do the 'remnants' of our waking thoughts and deeds move and stir within our soul.[16]

Like all of the others, with the single exception of Aristotle, Cicero takes care elsewhere to allow that the gods do occasionally speak to us in dreams, but by now the inclusion of this disclaimer seems little more than ceremonial. Indeed, there is remarkable unity among the great dream authorities of antiquity on this important question: the lore shows us undeniably that revelatory dreams do occur, but we are ill-advised to fancy that our own dreams might be such.

It should be added that there is an equally insistent literature in support of the revelatory nature of dreams in Greek and Roman antiquity, but such oneiric speculation was by and large out of the mainstream of classical thought, at least as this was passed down to and understood by the Middle Ages. Divination and incubation were important elements in Greek and Roman religions, but a dispassionate survey of the major intellectual figures of Greece and Rome (emphasizing those widely read in the Middle Ages) shows a deep-seated scepticism about oneiromancy. Thus, authors such as Morton Kelsey are correct in claiming that there was great interest in dream interpretation in Greece and Rome, just as I would be correct in claiming that twentieth century Americans are fascinated with, say, flying saucers (and I could support my claim with a huge bibliography of our tabloid "chronicles"). In neither case, though, is the fascination "official," authoritative, or even representative of the leading minds of the periods. We are, thus, both more accurate and more responsible in concentrating on the classical authors, revered and trusted by medieval thinkers, however unrepresentative of *their* age and civilization they may be.

The Encyclopedists

Nearly contemporary with Cicero, another tradition in Western oneiromancy begins to surface. The *Oneirocriticon* of Artemidorus of Daldis (or, sometimes, of Ephesus; second century A. D.) is an important Greek dream manual, possibly showing some familiarity with Cicero but probably deriving from Posidonius and other Eastern sources. A final determination of Artemidorus' sources, such as that conducted by Claes Blum, is unnecessary for our purposes, since his work seems to mark the introduction of this body to the West, and since the seminal discussion of dream analysis in Macrobius' *Commentary on the Somnium Scipionis* (fourth century) is traceable with certainty no further back than to Artemidorus and to the mainstream Greek and Latin authorities just examined.

At first glance, the *Oneirocriticon* seems a striking departure from the brief and summary discussions of dreams in Lucretius and Cicero; it is a complex, carefully organized, five-volume manual for the interpretation of dreams as portents of future events.[17] Nonetheless, the difference between Artemidorus and, say, Cicero, is one of degree and emphasis: while Artemidorus' principal interest is in the revelatory dream, he divides dreams, just as Cicero did, into categories and assigns values and levels of importance to each category.

Accordingly, the first division of the *Oneirocriticon* is one between significant and insignificant dreams, called *oneiros* and *enhypnion* respectively. The precise distinction Artemidorus makes here is important: *oneiri* are significant in the waking world of the dreamer (that is, to present or future conditions) while *enhypnioni* lose their significance when the dreamer awakens (hence *"enhypnion"* or "in sleep"). *Oneiri* are next subdivided into two classes: the "theorematic" *oneiros*, in which the communication or portent is direct, requiring no interpretation, and the "allegorical" *oneiros*, the true significance of which is veiled or coded. The bulk of the *Oneirocriticon* is, naturally enough, devoted to rules and examples of interpretation of this last allegorical variety.

Artemidorus' classification of dreams was his most important contribution to medieval dream lore. Though unaware of its source, nearly every medieval dream writer used Artemidorus' categories and even his terminology: following Macrobius, the standard term in medieval oneiromancy for a meaningless day residue dream is *"insomnium"* (translating Artemidorus' *"enhypnion"*), and Macrobius even repeats Artemidorus' quaint etymology for the term. Moreover, the division of significant dreams into theorematic and allegorical—or representational and figurative—neatly corresponds to the Macrobean distinction between the *somnium* and the *visio* (respectively), a formal or "generic" distinction which will prove crucial in the eventual "occupation" of this scientific taxonomy by the medieval dream vision.

Above all, however, like the others before him, Artemidorus counsels caution and scepticism in assessing the worth of specific dreams. Even in a treatise as enthusiastic as the *Oneirocriticon* on the subject of dream portents, Artemidorus offers careful and dispassionate advice to would-be oneiromancers, suggesting, for example, that dream analysts consider such factors as the dreamer's homeland and personal habits (Books Four and Five). Thus, if we search for a credulous dream interpreter in the waning years of the classical era, we will not find him in Artemidorus, who was, with Cicero, the most important source of the seminal document for dream interpretation in the later Middle Ages, the *Commentary on the Somnium Scipionis* of Ambrosius Theodosius Macrobius.

Macrobius' commentary on the "Dream of Scipio" is far and away the most influential theoretical treatment of dreams and dream interpretation that the Middle Ages knew and, considering the work as a whole, this is a curious legacy. Macrobius never intended to write a treatise on dream interpretation, a subject which takes up only a few pages in the *Commentary* (and these by way of introduction), and yet it is for these pages that Macrobius is most revered.

In fact, the *Commentary on the Somnium Scipionis* is an encyclopedic gloss on the Ciceronian text, a compendium of all knowledge loosely structured as a running commentary on the ecstatic conclusion of Cicero's *Republic*. Operating on the first principle that "there is nothing more complete than this work [the *Somnium*], which embraces the entire body of philosophy," Macrobius uses the topics of Scipio's dream as occasions for lengthy discussions of numerology, mathematics, physical science, astronomy and, naturally enough, dream lore. Thus, early in the *Commentary*, Macrobius comes to terms with the form of the revelation and (essentially glossing the passage quoted earlier), offers his own rather eclectic taxonomy of dreams. According to Macrobius,

omnium quae videre sibi dormientes videntur quinque sunt principales et diversitates et nomina. aut enim est ὄνειρος secundum Graecos quod Latini somnium vocant, aut est ὅραμα quod visio recte appellatur, aut est χρηματισμός quod oraculum nuncupatur, aut est ἐνύπνιον quod insomnium dicitur, aut est φάντασμα quod Cicero, quotiens opus hoc nomine fuit, visum vocavit.

All dreams may be classified under five main types: there is the enigmatic dream, in Greek *oneiros*, in Latin *somnium*; second, there is the
prophetic vision, in Greek *horama*, in Latin *visio*; third, there is the
oracular dream, in Greek *chrematismos*, in Latin *oraculum*; fourth, there
is the nightmare, in Greek *enhypnion*, in Latin *insomnium*; and last, the
apparition, in Greek, *phantasma*, which Cicero, when he has occasion to
use the word, calls "visum."[18]

Macrobius next goes into some detail on each of the varieties, beginning with the insignificant types:

est enim ἐνύπνιον quotiens cura oppressi animi corporisve sive fortunae, qualis vigilantem fatigaverat, talem se ingerit dormienti: animi, si
amator deliciis suis aut fruentem se videat aut carentem, si metuens quis
imminentem sibi vel insidiis vel potestate personam aut incurrisse hanc
ex imagine cogitationum suarum aut effugisse videatur: corporis, si
temeto ingurgitatus aut distentus cibo vel abundantia praefocari se aes-
timet vel gravantibus exonerari, aut contra si esuriens cibum aut potum
sitiens desiderare, quaerere, vel etiam invenisse videatur, fortunae cum
se quis aestimat vel potentia vel magistratu aut augeri pro desiderio aut
exui pro timore.

Nightmares may be caused by physical or mental distress, or anxiety
about the future; the patient experiences in dreams vexations similar to
those that disturb him during the day. As examples of the mental variety,
we might mention the dream of the lover who dreams of possessing his
sweetheart or of losing her, or the man who fears the plots or might of
an enemy and is confronted with him in his dream or seems to be fleeing
him. The physical variety might be illustrated by one who has overin-
dulged in eating or drinking and dreams that he is either choking with
food or unburdening himself, or by one who has been suffering from
hunger or thirst and dreams that he is craving and searching for food or
drink or has found it. Anxiety about the future would cause a man to
dream that he is gaining a prominent position or that he is being de-
prived of it as he feared.[19]

After making a similar disclaimer on the subject of the *phantasma*
or *visum*, Macrobius concludes:

his duobus modis ad nullam noscendi futuri opem receptis, tribus ceteris
in ingenium divinationis instruimur.

The two types just described are of no assistance in foretelling the future;
but by means of the other three we are gifted with the powers of
divination.[20]

Macrobius next turns to descriptions of these "tribus ceteris," the three significant varieties:

> et est oraculum quidem cum in somnis parens vel alia sancta gravisve persona seu sacerdos vel etiam deus aperte eventurum quid aut non eventurum, faciendum vitandumve denuntiat. visio est autem cum id quis videt quod eodem modo quo apparuerat eveniet. amicum peregre commorantem quem non cogitabat visus sibi est reversum videre, et procedenti obvius quem viderat venit in amplexus. depositum in quiete suscepit et matutinus ei precator occurit mandans pecuniae tutelam et fidae custodiae celanda committens. somnium proprie vocatur quod tegit figuris et velat ambagibus non nisi interpretatione intellegendam significationem rei quae demonstratur, quod quale sit non a nobis expondendum est, cum hoc unus quisque ex usu quid sit agnoscat.

> We call a dream oracular (*oraculum*) in which a parent, or a pious or revered man, or a priest, or even a god clearly reveals what will or will not transpire, and what action to take or to avoid. We call a dream a prophetic vision (*visio*) if it actually comes true. For example, a man dreams of the return of a friend who has been staying in a foreign land *thoughts of whom never enter his mind*. He goes out and presently meets this friend and embraces him. Or in his dream he agrees to accept a deposit, and early the next day a man runs anxiously to him, charging him with the safekeeping of his money and committing secrets to his trust. By an enigmatic dream (*somnium*) we mean one that conceals with strange shapes and veils with ambiguity the true meaning of the information being offered, and requires an interpretation for its understanding. We need not explain further the nature of this dream since everyone knows from experience what it is.[21] [emphasis mine]

Macrobius concludes this passage by referring to the five varieties of *somnia* outlined by Artemidorus—personal, alien, social, public, and universal—and offers brief commentaries on each.

Such was the authoritative classification for dreams for over a millennium. Later writers might alter the Macrobean categories slightly, but except for such minor alterations and shifts in emphasis, the taxonomy stays intact through Freud and even Edgar Cayce. Macrobius clearly recognizes that the dream is often the fulfillment of a wish, the product of transmuted thoughts, experiences, and desires, yet he simultaneously maintains that, at special times to special people, the same dreams are vehicles for divine communication.

The taxonomy, while seemingly very neat, raises more questions than it answers: how, for example, are we to tell if a dream that fits the formal description of a *visio* (or *oraculum* or *somnium*), yet is possibly traceable to day residue (and hence is an insignificant *insomnium*), is worthy of interpretation? How, for example, should I interpret last night's dream that a distinguished colleague had praised this book? Formally, the dream is a *visio* since it seems to reveal the future directly and clearly ("apertly," Chaucer would say); at the same time, though, the dream is also manifestly the fulfillment of its dreamer's wish and thus an *insomnium*. What are we to do with such commonplace dream experiences (and the even more common one of the *somnium-insomnium*, the enigmatic dream interpreted to portend the fulfillment of a wish)?

Macrobius does not answer this sort of question explicitly, but his implied answer, gleaned from the quotations just presented, would seem to be that the possibility that a dream might have originated in the waking concerns of the dreamer is, in and of itself, sufficient to raise questions about its authenticity. This at least would seem to be the medieval interpretation, not only because it is a point heavily emphasized by medieval dream writers, but also, paradoxically, because it helps account for the separate existence of the "apocalypse tradition" with formal constraints very different from those of the dream vision. The insistence on the waking state of the visionary, on his serenity, and especially on minutiae such as his fasting prior to the experience, when viewed in light of Macrobius' taxonomy, suggests that the apocalypse conventions developed as means of protecting holy experience from "disqualification by causes" when judged according to standards such as Macrobius'

Thus, Macrobius' categories are (or at least were interpreted by medievals to be) extremely conservative, all but precluding the possibility of a dream-revelation except under extraordinarily "sterile" and controlled circumstances. Otherwise, it would seem that, according to Macrobius, we ought never to consider our dreams revelatory.

Select Medieval Authorities

With all of its inconsistencies and contradictions, the dream taxonomy which reached fruition in the *Commentary on the Somnium*

Scipionis suited the purposes of medieval dream writers perfectly, for it contained all of the elements required by their ancient theology and their contemporary philosophical scepticism. In the *Liber de Spiritu et Anima*, for example, St. Augustine repeats Macrobius' fivefold classification almost verbatim:

> Omnium quae sibi videre videntur dormientes, quinque sunt genera; videlicet, oraculum, visio, somnium, insomnium, et phantasma. Oraculum est, cum in somnis parens vel aliqua sancta gravisque persona, seu sacerdos, vel etiam Deus eventurum aliquid aperte vel non eventurum, faciendum vel devitandum denuntiat. Visio est, cum id quis videt quod eodem modo quo apparuerat, eveniet. Somnium est figuris tectum, et sine interpretatione intelligi non potest. Insomnium est, quando id quod fatigaverat vigilantem, ingerit se dormienti; sicut est cibi cura vel potus, vel aliqua studia, vel artes, vel infirmitates. Secundum namque studia quae quisque exercuit, somniat; et solitarum artium simulacra in praesentia mentis impressa apparent in somnis. Juxta etiam infirmitatum diversitates diversa accidunt somnia. Etaim secundum morum et humorum varietates variantur somnia. Alia namque vident sanguinei, alia cholerici, alia phlegmatici, alia melancholici. Illi vident rubea et varia; isti, nigra et alba. Phantasma est, quando qui vix dormire coepit, et adhuc se vigilare aestimat, aspicere videtur irruentes in se, vel passim vagantes formas discrepantes et varias, laetas vel turbulentas.

Of those experiences which sleepers seem to have, there are five varieties: *oraculum, visio, somnium, insomnium,* and *phantasma.* It is an *oraculum* when in sleep a parent or a holy and respectable person, a priest or even God Himself announces what shall or shall not come to pass, or what one should or should not do. It is a *visio* when that which is revealed happens in the very way it appeared in the dream. A *somnium* is made of images and cannot be understood without interpretation. It is an *insomnium* when that which oppressed the person awake returns to afflict him when asleep; for example, some disturbance from food or drink, or certain avocations or arts, or certain infirmities. It follows of an avocation when that in which one labors is what one dreams of; and images of those very arts impressed on the waking mind appear in sleep. Likewise, certain dreams result from various infirmities, and are also affected by various habits or bodily humors. Some dreams are sanguine, some choleric, some phlegmatic, some melancholic. Some see red and other colors, others only black and white. It is a *phantasma* when, barely asleep, one thinks himself still awake and seems to see fleet images or various flitting shapes, sometimes joyful, sometimes troubled.[22]

I quote the passage at length both to show Augustine's great unacknowledged debt to Macrobius and to his system and also to illustrate his conscious decision to emphasize the somatic dream (the *insomnium*) in this expanded version of his original.

Leaving out Macrobius' charming case of the dream of the return of the long missed friend "quem non cogitabant" and his other examples of prophetic or premonitory dreams, Augustine chooses to expand on the *insomnium*, stressing the range of everyday preoccupations (*studia et artes*) which can bring on such dreams. Similar remarks can be found in the *Confessions*, only five chapters away from Augustine's recollections of his mother's dream of the young man on the rule (discussed earlier, in chapter 1):

> Cibus in somnis simillimus est cibus vigilantium, quo tamen dormientes non aluntur; dormiunt enim: atilla nec similia erant nullo modo tibi, sicut nunc mihi locuta es; quia illa erant corporalia phantasmata, falsa corpora, quibus certiora sunt vera corpora ista quae videmus visu carneo, sive coelestia sive terrestria: cum pecudibus et volatilibus videmus haec; et certiora sunt, quam cum imaginamur ea. Et rursus certius imaginamur ea, quam ex eis suspicamur alia grandiora, et infinita quae omnio nulla sunt, qualibus ego tunc pascebar inanibus; et non pascebar.

> Food in dreams is very much like the food of waking men, but sleepers are not fed by it: they merely sleep. But those fantasies [i.e., the teachings of the Manichees] were in nowise similar to you, as you have now told me, because they were corporeal fantasies, false bodies, and real bodies, whether in the heavens or on earth, are more certain than they. These things we behold in common with beasts of the field and birds of the air, and they are more certain than those which we conjure up in imagination. Again, there is more certainty when we fashion mental images of these real things than when by means of them we picture vaster or unlimited bodies that do not exist at all. On such empty phantoms I was fed—and yet I was not fed.[23]

Elsewhere in his writings, Augustine is equally careful to maintain what was rapidly becoming the orthodox viewpoint, acknowledging the miraculous nature of the dreams recorded in Scripture while lambasting at every turn credulous beliefs in one's own dreams. In *De Cura pro Mortibus*, for example, Augustine discounts dream visitations from the dead, explaining that the images of loved ones produced in the dreamer's mind are purely phantasmal.[24]

Thus, while Augustine can credit a divine source to Monica's dream, he is careful in more analytical contexts to maintain a thoroughgoing scepticism about dreams. Even in his exegesis of the Pauline ecstasis in Book 12 of *De Genesi ad Litteram*, Augustine carefully prefaces his remarks on the three levels of vision with a brief discussion of dreams and their relationship to the mind of the dreamer:

> Quis enim cum a somno evigilaverit, non continuo sentiat imaginaria fuisse quae videbat, quamvis cum ea videret dormiens, a vigilantium corporalibus visis discernere non valebat? Quanquam mihi accidisse scio, et ob hob etiam aliis accidere potuisse vel posse non dubito, ut in somnis videns, in somnis me videre sentirem; illasque imagines, quae ipsam nostram consensionem ludificare consueverunt, non esse vera corpora, sed in somnis eas praesentari firmissime, etiam dormiens, tenerem atque sentirem.

> Does not everyone, when awake, still feel that the images he saw while asleep were real? Who is really able to distinguish between what he has seen asleep and waking, corporeal sights? I know these things have happened to me and I have no doubt that they have happened to others (and will continue to happen): when I dream certain sights, I also dream that I see them in fact. These images, with whose games we are all familiar, are not corporeal, but when I am asleep, they surely seem so to me, such that I can hold and feel them.[25]

Even the word "somnium" occurs only rarely after this point in the *De Genesi ad Litteram*, as Augustine analyzes Paul's rapture into the third Heaven: the word consistently used for the experience, not surprisingly, is "visio," a term sanctified by the *Visio Sancti Pauli* and one which short-circuits Macrobius' categories. Even so, Augustine interrupts himself again in the exegesis to detail the several varieties of revelatory experience in terms which subtly recall Macrobius:

> Ego visa ista omnia visis comparo somniantium. Sicut enim aliquando et haec falsa, aliquando autem vera sunt, aliquando perturbata, aliquando tranquilla; ipsa autem vera, aliquando futuris omnino similia, vel aperte dicta, aliquando obscuris significationibus et quasi figuratis locutionibus praenuntiata: sic etiam illa omnia.

> I might compare these visions to those experienced in dreams. Some are false, some true; some unsettled, some serene. Some offer images of the

future, sometimes plainly announced, while at other times the prophecies are given through enigmatic meanings or figurative pronouncements.[26]

Though here the decided emphasis is on revelatory or significant experiences (the *visio* suggested by "aperte," the *somnium* by "obscuris," and the *oraculum* by "figuratis locutionibus"), Augustine still begins with the ubiquitous disclaimer, "aliquando . . . haec falsa."

Writing not long after Augustine, Gregory the Great is considerably less open-minded than even Augustine was, reflecting the growing official conservatism on the dream question, which Morton Kelsey calls "The Coming of Darkness." From the point of view of dream enthusiasts, the term is apt, for there seems to develop at this stage of patristic writings a concerted attempt on the part of the Church establishment to minimize (though not, of course, to eliminate thoroughly) the possibility of the significant, revelatory dream:

> Aliquando namque somnia ventris plenitudine, vel inanitate, aliquando vero illusione, aliquando cogitatione simul et illusione, aliquando revelatione, aliquando autem cogitatione simul et revelatione generantur.

> Dreams are generated either by a full stomach or by an empty one, or by illusions, or by our thoughts combined with illusions, or by revelations, or by our thoughts combined with revelations.[27]

This statement seems intentionally confused, featuring the sort of manic randomness we associate with the Prologue to Book One of the *Hous of Fame*: Gregory carefully includes "revelationes" among the possible causes for dreams, but he does so in a singularly unpromising way, refusing even to give this worthy cause single status in his list. Still, however sceptical this statement may seem, it is only so by degree and, considering the insistence of Augustine on mundane causes for dreams, a small degree at that. Given this attitude—acknowledgment of revelation in dreams but contrived pessimism about identifying such agency—it is not surprising that Gregory next repeats advice as old as Aristotle, Cicero, and Cato:

> Somnia etenim nisi plerumque ab occulto hoste per illusionem fierent, nequaquam hoc vir sapiens indicaret dicens: *Multos errare fecerunt*

somnia, et illusiones vanae (Eccli. 34: 7). Vel certe: *Non augurabimini, nec observabitis somnia* (Levit. 19: 26). Quibus profecto verbis, cujus sint detestationis ostenditur quae auguriis conjunguntur.

If dreams did not frequently come from illusions of the Devil, the wise man surely would not have said, "For dreams have led many astray, and vain illusions as well" (Ecclesiasticus 34: 7), or "You shall not divine or observe dreams" (Leviticus 19: 26), words which anathemize those who dabble in auguries.[28]

This attitude toward dreams became the standard one among the Church Fathers in the succeeding centuries of the Middle Ages, of whom I shall include only two examples before turning to Thomas Aquinas' mature Scholastic view. Writing in the ninth century *Commentary on Ecclesiastes*, Rhabanus Maurus includes a dismissal of dream credulity as memorable and shrill as can be found in the period:

> Vana spes, et mendacium viro insensato; et somnia extollunt imprudentes. Quasi qui apprehendit umbram, et persequitur ventum: sic et qui attendit as visa mendacia. Hoc secundum hoc visio somniorum; ante faciem hominis, similitudo alterius hominis. Ab immundo quis mundabitur? et a mendace quid verum dicitur?

> A vain hope and a lie to insensate men; dreams only coddle fools. Like those who attend to shadows and those who follow the very wind—such as these pay heed to lying visions. What can be learned from such visions in sleep?—before the face of man, but the image of man himself. And who can be cleansed by filth? And who can learn the truth from a liar?[29]

Addressing his sister in the *Liber de Modo Bene Vivendi*, Bernard of Clairvaux uses some of the same imagery as Rhabanus did, equating dream credulity with folly, though doing so more positively and gently:

> Qui in somniis vel augurliis spem suam ponit, non confidit in Deo: et talis est qualis ille qui ventum sequitur, aut umbram apprehendere nititur. Auguria mendacia, et somnia deceptoria, ultraque vana sunt. Non debemus credere somniis, ne forte decipiamur in illis. Spes nostra in Deo semper sit firma, et de somniis nulla nobis sit cura.

> He who puts his faith in dreams or divinations has none in God; he is

like one who follows the wind or who tries to grab at shadows. Lying divinations and deceptive dreams are equally vain. Let us not believe in dreams lest we be ensnared by them. Let our faith rest ever firm in God, and let us care nothing for dreams.[30]

Thomas Aquinas and the *Summa Theologicae* might well serve as the watershed for this discussion, since the later Middle Ages saw the return of a substantial part of Aristotle's work largely through Thomas' Christianizing mirror, and since Thomas has no trouble discovering the total scepticism of "The Philosopher" on dreams. There is no extended discussion of dreams and oneiromancy themselves in the *Summa* (a fact I take to be significant in itself), but Thomas' fugitive statements on dreams and dream interpretation may be collected to give a clear picture of his (very negative) thinking. The best known passage in the *Summa*, Ia. III; 3, *responsio*, explains how "angeli revelant aliqua in somnis":

Unde Aristoteles, assignans causam apparitionis somniorum, dicit quod, *cum animal dormit, descendente plurimo sanguine ad principium sensitivum, simul descendunt motus*, idest impressiones relictae ex sensibilium motionibus, quae in spiritibus sensualibus conservatur, et *movent principium sensitivum*, ita quod fit quaedam apparitio, ac si tunc principium sensitivum a rebus ipsis exterioribus mutaretur. Et tanta potest esse commotio spirituum et humorum, quod hujusmodi apparitiones etiam vigilantibus fiunt: sicut patet in phreneticis, et in aliis hujusmodi. Sicut igitur hoc fit per naturalem commotionem humorum; et quandoque etiam per voluntatem hominis, qui voluntarie imaginatur quod prius senserat; ita etiam hoc potest fieri virtute angeli boni vel mali, quandoque quidem cum alienatione a corporeis sensibus, quandoque autem absque tali alienatione.

Hence Aristotle says, in analysing the cause of dream images, that *when an animal is sleeping most of the blood descends to its seat and sense movements accompany this*. In other words, the impressions left from the objects of the senses are retained in the animal spirits and *induce change in the seat of the senses*. And thus a kind of image is produced as though the seat of the senses were at that moment being caused to change by external objects themselves. In fact, the disturbance of the spirits and humors may be so great that hallucinations of this sort may occur even in those who are awake as, for example, in the insane and the like. Therefore, just as this happens through a natural disturbance of the humors, and sometimes through the will (as when a man deliberately imagines what he had previously experienced), so also this can occur through the power of good and bad angels, both at times when we are disconnected from our bodily senses and at other times when we are connected with them.[31]

This is a crucial passage because it effectively collapses Macrobius' "distinction by causes" by sensibly claiming that God can use anything, even human physiology, for His purposes; it does not, however, engender hopes that such divine intervention can be recognized for what it is.

Elsewhere (at 2a. 2ae; 95, 6), Thomas discourses briefly on the causes of dreams: internal (physiological or emotional imbalance) or external (evil spirits, good spirits, God), with only divine causation valorizing the dream. Thus, on the subject of prophecy, Thomas is technically open-minded but rhetorically stern:

> Sic ergo dicendum quod si quis utatur somniis ad praecognoscenda futura secundum quod somnia procedunt ex revelatione divina, vel ex causa naturali, intrinseca sive extrinseca, quantum se potest virtus talis causae extendere, non erit illicita divinatio. Si autem hujusmodi divinatio causetur ex revelatione daemonum cum quibus pacta habentur expressa, quia ad hoc invocantur, vel tacita, quia hujusmodi divinatio extenditur ad quod se non potest extendere, erit divinatio illicita et superstitiosa.

> To conclude, if anyone uses dreams to foretell the future when he knows that they come from a divine revelation, or, observing its limits, from some natural cause, internal or external, then this is not unlawful divination. But if the foretelling comes from the disclosure by demons with whom a pact has been made, whether express, by invoking them, or tacit, by seeking knowledge out of human reach, then this is superstitious and unlawful divination.[32]

The subject of dreams comes up twice more in purely ethical contexts in the *Summa*, specifically on the degree of guilt incurred in wet dreams (at 2a. 2ae; 154-55 and again at 3a. 80; 7); in the second discussion, Thomas' psychological explanation for the wet dream allows monks so afflicted to take the Eucharist the next morning, provided their dreams were wholly the products of their unconscious minds.

I conclude this survey of medieval scepticism on the dream question with three later authorities whose popularity and importance to medieval thought are hardly questionable: John of Salisbury, Boccaccio, and Bartholomeus Angelicus. It cannot be ascertained, of course, that Chaucer or the *Pearl*-poet or Langland knew their thinking on dreams, but nonetheless the *Polycraticus*, the *De Casibus Virorum Illustrorum*, and the *De Proprietatibus Rerum* were, in their respective fields, widely admired and revered books thoroughly in the mainstream of philosophical, historical, and medical learning.

John of Salisbury takes up the dream question in Book Two of the *Polycraticus*, as an example of "Quia Deus signis suam praemunire dignatur creaturam" or of how God by signs deigns to forewarn His creatures, a proof of "divinae miserationis" ("divine pity"):

> Signa etenim interdum vera, interdum falsa sunt. Quis nescit somniorum uarias esse significationes quas et usus approbat et maiorum confirmat auctoritas? In eis utique quoniam sompnis est, animales virtutes, scillicet sensus, qui dicuntur corporis et sunt animale quiescunt, sed naturales intenduntur.

> At times signs are true; at times false. Who is ignorant of the various meanings of dreams which experience approves and the authority of our forefathers confirms? In dreams especially, since it is the sleeping state, the animal properties (that is to say the senses which are called corporeal but are in reality spiritual) are quiescent, but the natural properties are intensified.[33]

The snippet of traditional psychology which concludes this passage, along with John's admission that certain dreams do have meaning, seems to promise a clear, practical discussion of the method of differentiating and interpreting dreams. The rhetorical question, "Who is ignorant . . . " reminds us that John is aware of the existence of true revelations, and the rest of the passage seems a calm prelude to a final, clinical solution to the dream question. The passage seems to promise that psychology and theology, human nature and Biblical tradition can be brought together to solve this vexing problem.

The promise is not fulfilled.[34] What follows this chapter in the *Polycraticus* is nothing more than Macrobius' distinction between *somnia* and *insomnia* (which asserts that the two sorts of dream are distinct but not practically differentiable; chapter 15) and a tentative analysis of interpretive principles which somewhat anticipates Freud's notions of transference and condensation (chapter 16). Finally in chapter 17, John's own voice intrudes on the growing but contradictory evidence to introduce a sunny, reasonable conclusion that completely dismantles the edifice of lore:

Sed dum has coniectorum traditiones exequimur, uereor ne merita non tam coniectoriam exequi, quas aut nulla aut inanis ars est, dormitare videamur. Quisquis enim somniorum sequitur uanitatem, paruum in lege Dei uigilans est, et dum fidei facit dispendium, perniciosissime dormit. Ueritas siquidem ab eo longe facta est, nec eam facilius potest apprehendere quam urionem expungere vel puncto curare carcineam qui caligantibus in meridei palpat.

In describing the methods of the interpreters of dreams, I fear it may seem that I am not describing the art but am myself nodding, for it is no art at all or at best a meaningless one. For whoever involves himself in the deception of dreams is not sufficiently awake to the law of God, suffers a loss of faith, and drowses to his own ruin. Truth is indeed far removed from him, nor can he grasp it any more effectually than he who with blinded eyes gropes his way in broad daylight can lance a boil or treat a cancer.[35]

Boccaccio's approach to dreams is like that of John of Salisbury, though his "solution" to the question is finally not as crashing as that of the *Polycraticus*. In Book Two of the *De Casibus Virorum Illustrorum*, Boccaccio introduces dreams in relation to his notions of the soul and of allegory:

Etenim maximus quiddam diuinitatis occultam infixum mortalium animis est. Eoque agente curis sol ti ceu minus corporea depressi inde plura sopito corpore aut visione certissima aut tenui sub velamine audimus vidimusque.

. . . there is a certain divine something implanted in the souls of men; when the body is asleep, this something is released by our thoughts and is less imprisoned by the solidity of the body. It is then that we hear and see the things that will take place either in actual visions or under the veil of allegory.[36]

Like the first passage quoted from the *Polycraticus*, this introduction seems to augur well for an open, less totally sceptical consideration of dreams, and, in the paragraphs that follow this one, Boccaccio carefully reminds us of the well-attested dreams of figures such as Simonides, Calpurnia, Atterius, and Pharaoh. All comes, however, to an abrupt, rather open-ended conclusion:

> Nolim tamen ab hoc arbitretur quisquam etsi se de corpus sompno detineatur immobile animam semper sua divinitate frui. Quum diuni muneris illud sit quando contingit. Variis quippe et plurimus agentibus causis per ambages frequenter deducitur. Et ideo si quandoque visis fides integra adhibenda sit: nam tamen eisdem semper credendem est. Sicut in ceteris inter spernandum credendumque discretione preuia discernendum est. Ut non negligamus quod ad salutem ostenditur: et conuerso innocuis non turbemur.

Of course, no one must believe that every time he dreams there is a divine communication, or that each dream is a present from God. For many reasons a man's spirit is frequently led into confusing obscurities. Therefore, even if one puts complete faith in dreams, they cannot always be believed. As in everything, above all one should carefully weigh between rejecting a dream or believing in it. In that way we will not neglect anything that is for our benefit, nor, on the other hand, will we be disturbed by something harmless.[37]

This is certainly good and sound advice, the chief difficulty of which, we have seen, inheres in that very process, "discernere."

Bartholomeus Anglicus, a central figure in the history of medicine in the Middle Ages who wrote about a hundred years after John of Salisbury, will conclude this brief anthology of medieval dream authorities. Bartholomeus is predictably specific about the causes of dreams, citing Aristotle and Augustine's *De Genesi ad Litteram* (Book 12; see pages 65–66 above) in his eclectic, derivative discussion. His formal pronouncements on dreams (in John of Trevisa's translation) have the same peremptory ring that sounded earlier in John of Salisbury, as well as his subterranean perplexity:

> Also somtyme sweuenes beþ trewe and somtyme fals, somtyme clere and playne and somtyme troubly. Sweuenes þat beþ trewe buþ somtyme opun and playne and somtyme iwrappid in figuratif, mistik, and dim and derke tokenynges and bodinges, as it ferde in Pharaoes sweuene.[38]

However,

> Somtyme Satanas his aungel desgisiþ hym as þey3 he were an angel of li3t and makeþ siche images to begile and deceyue man to his purpos, whanne me trowiþ him in doinges þat beþ opunlich goode . . . .

> Also diuers sweuenes comeþ of diuers causes, somtyme of complex-
> ioun, as he þat is *sanguineus* haþ glad and likinge sweuenes, *malancolius*
> metiþ of sorwe, *colericus* of fire and of firy þinges, and *flewmaticus* of
> reyne and snowe, and of watres and of watery þinges and of oþire such.
> And so eueriche man metiþ sweuenes acordinge to his complexioun,
> witt, and age. So seiþ Constantius. And somtyme sweuenes comeþ of
> appetite, affeccioun, and desire, as he þat is anhongred metiþ of mete,
> and a dronken man þat is aþurst metiþ of drinke, . . .[39]

Thus, like Macrobius, Augustine, and all the others before him, Bartholomeus admits that there may be some dreams, under rare circumstances, that come from God and may contain wisdom, but by
now this gesture is no more than ceremonial. The admission is
stated briefly and the theological justification—something like "divine pity"—is surely included, but the bulk of the discussion is devoted to the everyday somatic dream, the worthless, sometimes be-
guiling and troubling dream from which Alcuin prays to be spared:

> Domini Jesu Christi, miserere mei et cohibe in me omnis iniquiae concu-
> piscentiae motum; ut non me compellat corruptellarum turpitudines
> perpetrare, quae per imagines animales me usque ad carnis fluxum in
> somnis conantur seducere.

> O Lord Jesus Christ, have mercy on me and abide with me in all my
> various trials and to all my goals. Let me not be compelled to endure the
> disgraces of the corrupters who, through creatures of my mind, try to
> move me in sleep towards the dissolution of my very flesh.[40]

One wonders what Pertelote might have said to Alcuin.

Assessing the Evidence

Several facts can be deduced from the foregoing, very fragmentary
anthology of classical and medieval dream writers. The first fact is
that medieval, and especially patristic writers were caught in a curious doctrinal-philosophical tangle. The weight of the classical evidence (excluding an Arab-mystical tradition based on Artemidorus)
was decidedly sceptical, probably itself a reaction to flourishing mystery cults and popular credulity in Greece and Rome. The classical
authorities were aware of the canonical dream visitations from the
gods but were unwilling to accord these a central place in their dis-

cussions, fearing that ignorant men would be led astray by credulous beliefs that Jove or Venus might visit them too in sleep. Thus, the great medieval authority on nearly everything, Cicero, is the source of the scepticism in Macrobius, to which the encyclopedist added a "Platonic" ambivalence for what we shall see were rhetorical and not scientific reasons.

This collision of philosophical common sense and mystical tradition among classical dream writers took its toll on their descendents in the Middle Ages and is half of the reason why the medieval authorities sound so fey and discontinuous on the dream question. The discontinuity, the latent and inherent contradictions in the classical and medieval taxonomies, first becomes visible in Macrobius. Seeking to elevate the *Somnium Scipionis* in the beginning of his commentary, Macrobius sets out his five categories as we have seen only to do remarkable violence to them a page or so later:

> hoc ergo quod Scipio vidisse se rettulit et tria illa quae sola probabilia sunt genera principalitatis amplectitur, et omnes ipsius somnii species attingit, est enim oraculum quia Paulus et Africanus uterque parens, sancti gravesque ambo nec alieni a sacerdotio, quid illi eventurum esset denuntiaverunt; est visio quia loca ipsa in quibus post corpus vel qualis futurus esset aspexit; est somnium quia rerum quae illi narratae sunt altitudo tecta profunditate prudentiae non potest nobis nisi scientia interpretationis aperiri.

> The dream which Scipio reports that he saw embraces the three reliable types mentioned above, and also has to do with all five varieties of the enigmatic dream [after Artemidorus: personal, alien, and so on]. It is oracular since the two men who appeared before him and revealed his future, Aemilius Paulus and Scipio the Elder, were both his father, both pious and revered men, and were both affiliated with the priesthood. It is a prophetic dream since Scipio saw the regions of his abode after death and his future condition. It is an enigmatic dream because the truths revealed to him were couched in words that hid their profound meaning and could not be comprehended without skillful interpretation.[41]

What are we to make of this or, more to the point, what might some poor journeyman oneiromancer of twelfth century France or England make of it? Macrobius seems impressed—and expects his readers to be impressed—that the *Somnium Scipionis* embraces all "three reliable types mentioned above," but, far from adding literal dignity and credibility to the dream, this embrasure would cause a would-be dream interpreter no little unrest (as would, say, three alibis). More than this, Macrobius makes this odd proclamation on the significance(s?) of the *Somnium Scipionis* heedless of the inescapable contrary evidence in the text itself:

> hic mihi—credo equidem ex hoc quod eramus locuti; fit enim fere ut cogitationes sermonesque nostri pariant aliquid in somno tale, . . . Africanus se ostendit ea forma quae mihi ex imagine eius quam ex ipso erat notior; . . .

> And then—(I suppose it was a result of what we had been talking about; for it happens often that the things that we have been thinking and speaking of bring about something in our sleep . . .)—Africanus stood there before me, in figure familiar to me from his bust rather than from life . . . .[42]

Cicero himself seems to leave open the possibility that the *Somnium Scipionis* is really the "Insomnium Scipionis," a day residue dream. The long conversation with Masinissa before retiring, along with the telling remark that Africanus appeared not as in life but as his statue looked, strongly suggests something other than supernatural causation for Macrobius' *locus classicus*.

Macrobius is predictably silent on this difficulty, refusing to allow it to obtrude on the dream's philosophic worth. The dream *is* worthy, as I suggested earlier, because it is inherently excellent, because it contains palpable truths, and because it is a great man's dream. To claim more of it than this is dangerous.

Such a dream, in fact, beggars the categories, and violates the taxonomy by locating itself in the seam or gap in the five-part scheme: the revelatory types (*visio, oraculum,* and *somnium*), are characterized formally or "generically" according to their contents— they are either clear vision, dream conversation, or enigmatic vision—while the insignificant types (*insomnium* and *visum*) are identified externally or "symptomatically"—either as the effect of some physical or emotional imbalance or as occurring between waking and sleep. Macrobius' *decision* to judge the *Somnium Scipionis* formally rather than symptomatically (disregarding Scipio's own suggestion) and the contradictions attendant on that decision are alarming evidence that, despite their neatness, Macrobius' categories simply do not wash. Augustine's ambivalence on dreams is surprisingly like that of Macrobius. Like his pagan counterpart, Augustine knew that dreams were, for the great majority of people, the merest imaginative refuse, but, again like Macrobius, he was categorically prevented from discounting the dream altogether, for the evidence of occasional dream-visitations (in Scripture at the very least) was incontrovertible. Thus, we find the strange contradictions of Book Three of the *Confessions*, in which Augustine first derides credulous belief in dreams and then fervently recounts that of his mother. The categories of Augustine, like the fivefold taxonomy of Macrobius, are almost secondary, created by the exigencies of doctrine and common sense rather than by a direct experiential or intellectual encounter with the phenomena. The multiplicity of causes for dreams in Augustine—God, angels, demons, fumosity, and so on—hides an underlying conservative need to retain the fundamentals of doctrine without opening the door to wild, illogical, and potentially dangerous credulity in dreams. Rhabanus Maurus and Gregory the Great may be allowed their purple prose on the dream question because, like Augustine in the *De Genesi ad Litteram*, their large task in these tracts (*Moralia in Job* and *Commentary on Ecclesiastes*) was the exegesis of a Biblical text in which dreams *were* shown to be revelatory. As if to counterweight the implied approval of the hermeneutic text itself, both writers include excessive denials that other dreams, our dreams, can portend as these of the Old Testament did.

This "doublethink" on the dream question became institutionalized in the later Middle Ages, as the three final examples, from different disciplines, indicate. With the right hand, John of Salisbury and Boccaccio can blithely introduce the dream as a vehicle of divine communication and can list the significant dreams canonized by doctrine and tradition, provided they take all (or nearly all) of the others away with the left. Bartholomeus Anglicus can do the same, with that wonderfully quirky turn of phrase surely borrowed from John of Salisbury: "Also somtyme sweuenes beþ trewe and som-

77

tymes fals." Such a locution could stand as the sum of medieval knowledge of the subject of dreams. In the West at least, there was no practical, usable prescriptive taxonomy of dreams: for all the theories and categories, rules and schemes, there are two and only two firm, though facetious precepts:

I   All significant dreams are significant.
II   All pathological dreams are pathological.

Such "rules" inhered, once again, for reasons totally extrinsic to dream lore; they were the absolutely necessary precepts which allowed oneiromancy to coexist with theology and science. When a dream was excellent, such as Scipio's or Monica's, ways were found to declare it so; when dreams were subversive or revolutionary (or so enigmatic that they could be so interpreted), their believers could be shown that, because their dreams are the fulfillment of their wishes or the "reliquiae" of their daily concerns, their dreams were merely somatic experiences.

Having taken a look at the body of dream lore that was available to late medieval thinkers, we are now in a position to apply this lore to the dream vision. What my two Orwellian precepts amount to is a grand suppression—the suppression of the *relevant* dream. The argument runs like this: if dreams caused by emotional unrest or obsession are insignificant, then it follows that the dreams of persons admitting to such discomfitures are somatic, or at least one is safest in assuming so. To put it slightly more harshly, if a person's dream promises the fulfillment of a wish or the realization of fear—if the dreamer has any emotional investment in the content of the dream whatever—then the dream is meaningless.

This premise is tacitly supported by the apocalypse literature surveyed in chapter 2, where the vision-narrators took great pains to demonstrate that the visionaries were not asleep and, moreover, were level-headed holy men and women whose minds were as free from anxiety as their stomachs were free from pollutants. Strabo's elaborate introduction to the *Visio Wettini* is the *summa* for such conventions: the narrative doggedly established that Brother Wetti was holy, at peace, awake, and fasting when he had his vision. Thus, his vision is credible *qua* vision because he was a fit vessel for Divine indwelling. Dream vision narrators, on the other hand, are conventionally in turmoil. *Piers Plowman* begins with a restless soul on Malvern Hills:

> In a somer seson whan soft was the sonne
> I shope me in shroudes as I a shepe were;
> In habite as an heremite vnholy of workes
> Went wyde in þis world wondres to here.
> Ac on a May morynge on Maluerne hulles
> Me byfel a ferly, of fairy me thouȝte:
> I was wery forwandred and went me to reste
> Vnder a brode banke bi a bornes side,
> And as I lay and lened and loked in þe wateres,
> I slombred in a slepyng, it sweyued so merye.[43]

In *Pearl*, the narrator weeps and grieves, "fordolked of luf-daungere":

> Bifore þat spot my honde I spenned
> For care ful colde þat to me caȝt;
> A deuely dele in my hert denned,
> Paȝ resoun sette myseluen saȝt.
> I playned my perle þat þer waȝt spenned
> Wyth fyrce skylleȝ þat faste faȝt;
> Paȝ kynde of Kryst me comfort kenned,
> My wreched wylle in wo ay wraȝte.[44]

Chaucer's narrators also suffer anxiety, the best of example being that of the narrator of the *Book of the Duchess* (the case of the *Hous of Fame* will be discussed a bit later):

> I have gret wonder, be this lyght,
> How that I lyve, for day ne nyght
> I may nat slepe wel nygh noght;
> I have so many an ydel thoght,
> Purely for defaute of slep,

> That, by my trouthe, I take no kep
> Of nothing, how hyt cometh or gooth,
> Ne me nys nothyng leef not looth.
>
> (lines 1–8)

This strikingly consistent feature of dream vision prologues is powerful evidence that the dreams reported in poems are meant to be seen symptomatically as *insomnia* or everyday somatic dreams. Even given the careful arguments of Bloomfield, Koonce, Newman, and others—that some or all of these poems represent fictive *somnia* or *visiones* or *oracula*—it is difficult to overcome the simple fact of their dreamers' discomfiture in the light of passages like this from Macrobius:

> est enim ἐνύπνιον quotiens cura oppressi animi corporisve sive fortunae, qualis vigilantem fatigaverat, talem se ingerit dormienti: animi, si amator deliciis suis aut fruentem se videat aut carentem, . . .

> Nightmares may be caused by mental or physical distress, or anxiety about the future: the patient experiences in dreams vexations similar to those that disturb him during the day. As examples of the mental variety, we might mention the dream of the lover who dreams of possessing his sweetheart or of losing her, . . .[45]

Thus, the dream vision is, considering symptoms or external indicators, clearly an *insomnium*, a somatic dream in which "the patient experiences vexations" traceable to the sketchy but always sufficient details which we know of the dreamer's life. The content of such dreams is never described by medieval oneiromancers—what purpose would it serve?—but we may assume that Macrobean *insomnia* would be full of alien and enigmatic images or *figmenta* recognizable and comprehensible only to the dreamer.

And that is precisely the point, precisely the place where the dream vision breaks loose from the twin dream taxonomies we have been examining: the poems always record experiences that are never finally alien or incomprehensible: the *Roman de la Rose* and *Pearl* come to deal realistically with universal verities like love and the desire for life after death; *Piers Plowman* confronts the social, political, and religious corruption of fourteenth century England; the

Book of the Duchess speaks to all who mourn Blanche of Lancaster and all others who must someday mourn someone. In short, while the poems undeniably fit the external description of the insignificant *insomnium*, they fit with equal ease the internal or formal features of the *visio*, the *oraculum*, and especially the *somnium*: intrinsically and spiritually, the dream vision *is* a revelation, for, like the *Somnium Scipionis*, its content is worthy, its truth universal.

This means that the late medieval dream vision is a consciously constructed anomaly which deconstructs the literary and scientific dream taxonomies by occupying the impossible space between the pathological and the divine, the somatic and the significant. It draws its unique energy and vitality from this deconstruction for, if it were merely a fictive revelation (not somatic), it would then be simply a fictive pronouncement of truth; and if it were merely a somatic dream (not significant), then it would be self-admittedly irrelevant. Thus it is both and neither: the dream vision is the impossible record of one whose life and whose dreams are just like ours, whose dream in the course of its narration *becomes* ours, a self-conscious fiction that announces and celebrates its fictionality, thereby attaining a higher "rhetorical" truth.

The examination of these new contradictions, of truth in fiction and of the rectitude of the mind's own images, is the subject of the next chapter. We conclude this discussion and preview that next, however, by recalling Rhabanus Maurus: "Who can be cleansed by filth? And who can learn the truth from a liar?" Who indeed?

81

CHAPTER THREE

ORIGINS

𝕿 he relationship between the dream vision and its literary and scientific contexts is fairly clear: the poems filled parallel gaps in the two taxonomies with vicarious experiences the taxonomies denied to readers and dreamers. In literature, there were psychological dreams and revelatory dreams, but neither of these totally satisfied the real human need for a psychologically significant (or "realistic") experience—an everyday dream—that was also prescient. Readers could encounter tales of wondrous dream visitations to the men and women of the past, special, magical moments when, for a time, the chasm separating this world from the next narrowed a bit for the privileged individual. Such moments, which Artemidorus identified as "personal revelations," were wonderful and tantalizing, but they happened only to Joseph or to Aeneas or to the Magi. These dreams brought their dreamers crucial messages and demonstrated these persons' favor with God and special role in a divine plan. The dreams could come at any time, in fact did come when the dreamer least expected them, and *never* came when the dreamer was troubled or anxious or undecided about a course of action.

Elsewhere, readers could read apocalypses (or what Artemidorus called "universal revelations"). Unlike the personal revelations of others, these revelations were as much the readers' as the visionary's: the message belonged to all equally, and the visionary was only the medium of communication. These revelations showed readers the

Platonic World of Forms, the Christian afterlife—visions of Hell, Purgatory, and Heaven and visions of the end of the world—but they never trafficked in more mundane signs and wonders such as announcements of the return of a friend from a foreign land or hints on when to plant the crops. The medieval science of dreams offered even less comfort and satisfaction. While the dream writers seemed to provide a mechanism for determining the worth of dreams, their systems did little more in fact than to deny their readers the very dreams they most needed and wanted: the *visio, oraculum*, and *somnium* came only to those whose minds were free of perturbation, while those beset with worry and anxiety were, *ipso facto*, denied the dreams that would ease their malaise. Thus, while science denied the "relevant dream" in fact, literature teased readers by denying them even its vicarious satisfaction, telling them again and again, "Io non Enea, io non Paolo sono."

It was into this environment, and actually because of it, that the dream vision was born. On the simplest of affective levels, the poetic account of the revelant *insomnium* provided the vicarious experience missing from the two classifications; further, in filling the gaps in the taxonomies, the dream vision called the taxonomies themselves into question.

But gaps are not origins, and overworked metaphorics is not the medium of literary analysis. Someone had to perceive these gaps or inconsistencies in the literary and scientific discussions of dreams and then fill them with a carefully constructed poetic artifact, an artifact that, like modern science fiction, draws its energy from its subtle mix of the known and the unknowable, the demonstrable and the imaginable. More specifically, a rhetoric, a form, a psychology, and a metaphysics were needed to focus and loose the affective energy latent in the classifications and in the human response to their suppression. These topics—three developments that combined to make the dream vision theoretically possible—are the matter of the following pages: first, the figmental rhetoric of Augustine and Macrobius (along with its appreciation by later writers); second, the liberation of the dream frame from its doctrinal and eschatological subject matter by Guillaume de Lorris; and third, the contingent, democratic iconography inherent in the nominalism of the early fourteenth century.

A Rhetoric and a Form: Augustine and Macrobius

There is increasing evidence that hermeneutics in the Middle Ages begins with Augustine, begins in his appreciation of the subtle and sophisticated matrix of reader, text, and subject. This appreciation, gleaned from the *Confessions* and the *De Doctrina Christiana*, allows us to see Augustine anticipating the "modern" notion of a text's existence as residing in a reader's appreciation of it, a notion far from the traditional sense of medieval hermeneutics as textual alchemy. This is not the place to develop an Augustinian theory of reading: some remarks are necessary here, however, to illustrate the ways in which the semiotic theories of Augustine and Macrobius combined to form the basis for the rhetoric of the dream vision.

For Augustine, reading was not a form of communication; it was a means of verification, a celebration of the reader's possession of the truth.[1] Like every other human activity for Augustine, reading was subject to the test of *uti versus frui*, use *versus* enjoyment; much *un*like other human activities, reading radicalizes the use-enjoyment distinction in remarkable ways. In Book One of the *Confessions*, for example, Augustine seems to be making the distinction between "reading" (verb, intransitive) and "reading something" (verb, transitive), a distinction with which Hamlet would tease Polonius:

Quid autem erat causae cur graecas litteras oderam quibus puerulus imbuebar, ne nunc quidem mihi satis exploratum est. Adamaveram enim latinas, non quas primi magistri, sed quas docent qui grammatici vocantur. Nam illas primas ubi legere et scribere et numerare discitur, non minus onerosas poenalesque habebam, quam omnes graecas. Unde tamen et hoc nisi de peccato et vanitate vitae, quia caro eram, et spiritus ambulans et non revertens? (Psal. 77, 39) Nam utique meliores, quia certiores erant primae illae litterae, quibus fiebar in me, et factum est, at habeo illud ut et legam si quid scriptum invenio, et scribam ipse si quid volo, quam illae quibus tenere cogebar Aeneae nescio cujus errores, oblitus errorum meorum, et plorare Didonem mortuam, quia se occidit ob amorem, cum interea meipsum in his a te morientem, Deus vita mea, siccis oculis ferrem miserrimus.

Why I detested the Greek language when I was taught it as a little boy I have not yet fully discovered. I liked Latin very much, not the parts given by our first teachers but what the men called grammarians teach us. The first stages of our education, when we learned reading, writing, and arithmetic, I considered no less a burden and punishment than all the Greek courses. Since I was but "flesh, and a wind that goes and does not return," where could this come from except from sin and vanity of life? Better indeed, because more certain, were those first studies by which there was formed and is formed in me what I still possess, the ability to read what I find written down and to write what I want to, than the later studies wherein I was required to learn by heart I know not how many of Aeneas' wanderings, although forgetful of my own, and to weep over Dido's death, because she killed herself for love, while all the while amid such things, dying to you, O God my life, I most wretchedly bore myself about with dry eyes.[2]

This is a standard an often-quoted passage in the *Confessions*, recounting Augustine's sense of shame at falling victim to the seductive wiles of classical literature. It is followed by another well-known passage enlarging on the danger of "tears for Dido" as a symptom of moral depravity, but I quote it here not for this emphasis but instead to focus on Augustine's elliptical praise for grammar, for reading as a skill. The passage places this humble skill—and it is clearly this limited sense of the *grammatici* that Augustine has in mind—in moral opposition to reading some specific text as a source of pleasure or instruction: rhetoric or logic come to mind as rubrics. To be sure, Augustine here is speaking of pagan literature, but the extenuated pleasure he describes here is a pleasure to be found in any and all texts. For, after dunning himself for weeping, Augustine returns to the subject of literacy:

Sed nunc in anima mea clamet, Deus meus, et veritas tua dicat mihi: Non est ita, non est ita; melior est prorsus doctrina illa prior. Nam ecce paratior sum oblivisci errores Aeneae, atque omnia ejusmodi, quam scribere et legere. At enim vela pendent liminibus grammaticarum scholarum: sed non illa magis honorem secreti, quam tegumentum erroris significant. Non clament adversus me, quos jam non timeo, dum confiteor tibi quae vult anima mea, Deus meus, et acquiesco in reprehensione malarum viarum mearum, ut diligam bonas vias tuas. Non clament adversum me venditores grammaticae vel emptores: quia si proponam eis, interrogans ultrum verum sit quod Aeneam aliquando Carthaginem venisse Poeta dicit; indoctiores se nescire respondebunt, doctiores autem etiam negabunt, verum esse. At si quaeram quibus litteris scribatur Aeneae nomen, omnes mihi, qui haec didicerunt, verum respondebunt; secundum id pactum et placitum, quo inter se homines ista signa firmarunt. Item, si quaeram quid horum majore vitae hujus incommodo quisque obliviscatur, legere et scribere, an poetica illa figmenta; quis non videat quid responsurus sit, qui non est penitus oblitus sui? Peccabam ergo puer cum illa inania istis utilioribus amore praeponebam, vel potius ista oderam, illi amabam. Jamvero unum et unum duo, duo et duo quatuor, odiosa cantio mihi erat; et dulcissimum spectaculum vanitatis equus ligneus plenus armatis, et Trojae incendium, atque ipsius umbra Creusae.

Now let my God cry out in my soul, and let your truth say to me, "It is not so. It is not so." Far better is that earlier teaching. See how I am readier to forget the wanderings of Aeneas and all such tales than to read and write. True it is that the curtains hang before the doors of the grammar schools, but they do not symbolize some honored mystery but rather a cloak for error [*tegumentum erroris*]. Let not men whom I no longer fear inveigh against me when I confess to you, my God, what my soul desires, and when I acquiesce in a condemnation of my evil ways, so that I may love your ways, which are good. Let not these buyers and sellers of literature inveigh against me if I put this question to them: "Did Aeneas ever come to Carthage, as the poet says?" For if I do, the more unlearned will answer that they do not know; the more learned will even deny that it is true. But if I ask them with what letters the name Aeneas is spelled, all who have learned this much will give the right answer in accordance with that agreement and convention by which men have established these characters among themselves. Again, if I should ask which of these would be forgotten with greater inconvenience to our life, to read and write or those poetic fables, who does not discern the answer of every man who has not completely lost his mind? Therefore, as a boy I sinned when I preferred these inane tales to more useful studies, or rather when I hated the one and loved the other. But then, "One and one are two, and two and two are four" was for me a hateful chant, while the wooden horse full of armed men, the burning of Troy, and Creusa's ghost were most sweet but empty spectacles.[3]

The basic distinction which this passage makes, the distinction between reading and writing as useful and practical skills and the study of myth and literature as dangerous vanities, is a familiar one in Augustine, a man who has little use for the Latin classics and a man who has come to painful terms with his own classical rhetorical training and expertise. What is interesting about the passage, then, is not the negative side, not the rejection of the vanities of literature, but Augustine's odd, sincere praise of the simpler, more rudimentary arts of the *grammatici*.[4] At first glance, this looks like a simple anachronism: "grammar" in the Middle Ages referred to a much wider field of study than it does today, making it seem, perhaps, that Augustine is praising grammar and dispraising rhetoric. But this is not what Augustine is doing: he is contrasting simple literacy with the youthful study of classical myth and heroic poetry (though both would have been "grammatical," at least in later medieval curricula). In effect, what Augustine is saying here is that the skill of reading (*uti*) is good, but that reading a text, getting lost in its details and (especially) sympathizing or identifying with a text's characters is not: whenever Augustine recalls himself doing the latter, for example, weeping for Dido while witnessing dry-eyed his own spiritual suicide, he blanches in shame and confesses his guilt. The grammatic arts, especially spelling, are more valuable to Augustine because, although he perceives their obvious conventionality, they are coextensive with all speakers of Latin; the others, being stories, open themselves to debate, opinion, and fantasy. Augustine, therefore, seems to be suggesting here that words and meanings are equally worthless at a divine vantage point (although orthography is more stable than hermeneutics) and that the only worth that inheres in the act of reading is the invisible inner worth of a soul moving imperceptibly to God.

The distinction between intransitive and transitive reading (between "reading" and "reading something") appears again in Augustine, in the *De Doctrina Christiana*, but this time the worthless chaff is not a disreputable pagan poem but, it would appear, Sacred Scripture itself:

> Sic lapidum, sic herbarum, vel quaecumque tenentur radicibus. Nam et carbunculi notitia, quod lucet in tenebris, multa illuminat etiam obscura librorum, ubicumque propter similitudinem ponitur; et ignorantia ber-

ylli vel adamantis claudit plerumque intelligentiae fores. Nec aliam ob causam facile est intelligere pacem perpetuam significari oleae ramusculo, quem rediens ad arcam columba pertulit (Genesis 8, 11), nisi quia novimus et olei lenem contactum non facile alieno humore corrumpi, et arborem ipsam frondere perenniter. Multi autem propter ignorantiam hyssopi, dum nesciunt quam vim habeat, vel ad purgandum pulmonem, vel, ut dicitur, ad saxa radicibus penetranda, cum sit herba brevis atque humilis, omnino invenire non possunt quare sit dictum, *Asperges me hyssopo, et mundabor.* (Psalm 50, 9)

The same thing is true of stones, or of herbs or of other things that take root. For a knowledge of the carbuncle which shines in the darkness also illuminates many obscure places in books where it is used for similitudes, and an ignorance of beryl or of diamonds frequently closes the doors of understanding. In the same way it is not easy to grasp that the twig of olive which the dove brought when it returned to the ark signifies perpetual peace unless we know that the soft surface of oil is not readily corrupted by an alien liquid and that the olive tree is perennially in leaf. Moreover, there are many who because of an ignorance of hyssop— being unaware either of its power to purify the lungs or, as it is said, to penetrate its roots to the rocks in spite of the fact that it is a small and humble plant—are not able at all to understand why it is said, "Thou shalt sprinkle me with hyssop, and I shall be cleansed."[5]

The "knowledge of the carbuncle" or of anything else is, it seems, useless in and of itself; indeed, the passage suggests that "knowledge" or "notitia" can include myths, superstition, folklore or any real or imaginary lore surrounding anything. This "knowledge," which we might be tempted to call "context," understood aright by those with the faith to apply it correctly to the ubiquitous theme of the love of God, becomes a verification of that love abroad in the world. It becomes part of God's "grammar" of the world, a grammar expounded by scores of patristic exegetes. The text of the world, of Scripture, and of all things, is useful (*uti*) only for those who wish to hear once more God's message of love; it is properly enjoyed (*frui*) only as a celebration of this same repeated message. Recalling the issue of Aeneas' possible landfall at Carthage, we can see that the knowledge of the carbuncle separates the ignorant from the learned, but this distinction is finally meaningless, for the ignorant may read with the same *faith* as the learned have and therefore find the same truth verified. Such minutiae are, for Augustine, at best, various integuments hiding-revealing the one and only truth; at worst, they are dangerous, seductive byroads which can lead vain and unwarned readers from their wonted destination. To put it simply, then, for Augustine, intransitive reading is what we do while we are listening to the Father, listening to "my God cry aloud in my soul," and the written, palpable words of the text, finally, need have nothing to do with that internal cry, although they may, if we are not careful, render that cry inaudible.

Like so much of the *De Doctrina Christiana*, this sounds impossibly theoretical, but elsewhere Augustine provides an example of this special, pure, "intransitive" reading. In Book Six, Chapter Three of the *Confessions*, Augustine describes his friend Ambrose in a memorable passage:

> Cum quibus quando non erat, quod per exiguum temporis erat, aut corpus reficiebat necessariis sustenaculis, aut lectione animum. Sed cum legebat, oculi ducebantur per paginas, et cor intellectum rimabatur, vox autem et lingua quiescebant.

> When he was not with them [Milanese who sought his spiritual direction], and this was but a little while, he either refreshed his body with needed food or his mind [*animum*] with reading. When he read, his eyes moved down the pages and his heart sought out their meaning, while his voice and tongue remained silent.[6]

This is more than the first recorded instance of silent reading in Western letters; it is, for Augustine, a profound theological, psychological, and ethical insight. Notice that Ambrose is not reading for meaning or studying—Augustine does not even mention what it is that he is reading—he is, we are told, refreshing his mind as one refreshes his body with food, is reading for enjoyment. His eyes, silently travelling across the page, do not themselves perceive the sense, Augustine says, and neither does his mind: it is his *heart* which *seeks* the sense. In effect, Ambrose is meditating: he is, as Richard of St. Victor and the author of *The Cloud of Unknowing* advise, distracting or occupying his mind while opening his heart and soul to meaning, a meaning that does not necessarily inhere in the text. By reading silently, Ambrose avoids the seductive melodies of classical rhetoric (on which Augustine was an expert) by refusing to perform the text audibly, by reading (intransitive) and attending only to the silent cry of God audible in his soul.

The most striking example of Augustinian intransitive reading is his own experience, the sorites Vergiliana he performed in Alypius' garden at his conversion:

> Et ecce audio vocem de vicina domo cum cantu dicentis et crebro repeten-tis, quasi pueri an puellae, nescio: *Tolle, lege; tolle, lege.*

> And lo, I heard from a nearby house, a voice like that of a boy or girl, I know not which, chanting and repeating over and over, "Take up and read. Take up and read."[7]

The rationalist Augustine assumes the chant to be part of a children's game but, with a moment's thought, can remember no game of which this particular phrase was a part, so

> Repressoque impetu lacrymarum, surrexi, nihi aliud interpretans, nisi divinitus mihi juberi ut aperirem codicem, et legerem quod primum caput invenissem.

> I checked the flow of my tears and got up, for I interpreted this solely as a command given to me by God to open the book and read the first chapter I should come upon.[8]

At this point the narration breaks off as Augustine recounts his memory of the story of St. Anthony's belief that the words of the Gospel he heard one day were a miraculous admonition addressed specifically to him. This short digression, like the momentary thought of the child's game, is an example of Augustine's sense of hermeneutic knowledge, the "knowledge of the carbuncle" or here, of children's games or of hagiography. This knowledge adds nothing whatever to the experience; it serves simply to verify rationally the epiphany that is taking place. And the memory of Anthony does indeed verify and valorize Augustine's own experience, for he remembers that

> . . . tali oraculo confestim ad te esse conversum. Itaque concitus redii ad eum locum ubi sedebat Alypius: ibi enim posueram condicem Apostoli,

cum inde surrexeram. Arripui, aperui, et legi in silentio capitulum, quod primum conjecti sunt oculi mei: *Non in comessationibus et ebrietatibus, non in cubilibus et impudicitiis, non in contentione et aemulatione; sed induite Dominum Jesum Christum, et carnis providentiam ne feceritis in concupiscentiis* (Rom., 13: 13−4). Nec ultra volui legere; nec opus erat.

. . . by such a portent he was immediately converted to you.

So I hurried back to the spot where Alypius was sitting, for I had put there the volume of the apostle when I had got up and left him. I snatched it up, opened it, and read *in silence* the chapter on which my eyes first fell: "Not in rioting and drunkenness, not in chambering or impurities, not in strife and envying; but put you on the Lord Jesus Christ, and make not provision for the flesh and its concupiscences." No further wished I to read, nor was there need to do so.[9] [my emphasis]

The rest, of course, is history. What we need to see in this passage is the precise part that the words of Scripture play in Augustine's conversion. Augustine knew Romans 13: 13−4 well; the words were not new to him. What was special about the experience was that the words were miraculously directed to him and him alone; Augustine intuits that, like St. Anthony, "admonitus fuerit, tanquam sibi diceretur quod legebatur" ("he had been admonished . . . as if the words read were addressed to him").[10] Taken together with the description of Ambrose above, this passage seems to claim that (as the mystics suggest), to read Scripture is to open the heart to the *real* word of God by opening the eyes to His orthographic words. We fail to do this experience justice if we call it merely "identification" or, worse, "taking the words to heart," for what Augustine is describing here is a relationship of reader to text far more radical than identification: "appropriation" might be a term strong enough. For Augustine does not see himself as simply being "like" the original recipients of Paul's letter, and it is not simply that he marvels at God's timeliness in showing him these old but relevant words at this exact moment in his spiritual development: in a miraculous sense, Augustine *is* the recipient of the divine message, is drawn to see that he is part of a special and well-defined community of individuals that is the object of God's discourse through St. Paul.

As Augustine himself observes earlier in the *Confessions*, the psychic appropriation that happens in intransitive reading is not "rhetorical" or even rational in nature. Before his conversion,

> Itaque institui animum intendere in Scripturas sanctas ut viderem quales essent. Et ecce video rem non compertam superbis, neque nudatam pueris; sed incessu humilem, successu excelsam et velatam mysteriis: et non eram ego talis ut intrare in eam possem, aut inclinare cervicem ad ejus gressus. Non enim sicut modo loquor, ita sensi cum attendi ad illam Scripturam sed visa est mihi indigna quam Tullianae dignitate compararem. Tumor enim meus refugiebat modum ejus; et acies mea non penetrabat interiora ejus. Vernum tamen illa erat quae cresceret cum parvulis; sed eqo dedignabar esse parvulis, et turgidus fastu mihi grandis videbar.
>
> I accordingly decided to turn my mind to the Holy Scriptures and to see what they were like. And behold, I see something within them that was neither revealed to the proud nor made plain to children, that was lowly on one's entrance but lofty on further advance, and that was veiled over in mysteries. None such as I was at that time could enter into it, nor could I bend my neck for its passageways. When I first turned to that scripture, I did not feel towards it as I am speaking now, but it seemed to me unworthy of comparison with the nobility of Cicero's writings. My swelling pride turned away from its humble style, and my sharp gaze did not penetrate into its inner meaning. But in truth it was of its nature that its meaning would increase together with your little ones, whereas I distained to be a little child and, puffed up with pride, I considered myself to be a great fellow.[11]

It is important to notice here that Augustine is *not* saying that, in his younger, worldly days, he did not appreciate Scripture rhetorically, though now he does: the tenses and references do not permit this reading. When Augustine describes Scripture as "incessu humilem, successu excelsam et velatam mysteriis" ("humble on entrance, lofty on advance and veiled with mysteries"), he is describing it as he presently appreciates it. The point of the quotation is that the textual experience of Scripture, in contrast to what we would call the rhetorical experience of Cicero or other Latin classics, did not appeal to the young, prideful, and unregenerate Augustine. He says that the experience of Scripture was (on recollection) a humbling one: notice that the text did not repel him but rather *his* unfitness for *it* kept

him from it: "Tumor enim meus refugiebat modum ejus. . . ." The
careful phrasing means that the younger Augustine's failure to appreciate Scripture was one of will, not of intellect or effort. The
experience is thus ethical rather than rhetorical, since the impediment was not the humble text but the prideful reader. Without the
humility to give faith precedence over reason and without the faith
to see what he knows God has written, Augustine saw only the unin-
teresting and inferior rhetorical chaff, "incessu humilem." Later on,
the text and its homely style have not changed at all: Augustine has
changed and now can see the message "neither revealed to the proud
nor made plain to children" but visible only with eyes of faith; "successu excelsam" in this sense suggests not merely "advance" or progress but, once more, "appropriation" or "embrace."[12]

This appropriation or "embrace" of Scripture (or of other special
texts like the dream vision) is an embrace anterior to receiving or
failing to receive a meaning from the text: for Augustine, reading
Scripture is a perception of communion with its divine Author and
not primarily one of communication. Such an intuition or experience of communion precedes any hermeneutic engagement with
the text and is always distinct from appreciation or interpretation;
the experience of the text is either one or the other. On the one
hand, if the reading experience is intransitive and pride does not
repel the reader, the reader will achieve this almost sacramental
communion with the Author of the text. On the other hand, if the
reading experience is transitive and pride and the text as object ob-
struct the communion of reader and Author, then the best the reader
can hope for is interpretation and appreciation.

Thus humility, repulsion, and plainness are not the "defense
mechanisms" of the sacred text whose purpose is to protect it from
the gaze of the unworthy; these emotional responses are *integral
parts of the reading experience*. The factual education of the Christian rhetor as laid down in the *De Doctrina Christiana* does nothing
to diminish the humbling sacramental experience of *lectio divina*,
but neither does it enhance this contemplative, intransitive reading;
the "knowledge of the carbuncle" can only illumine the surface, the

text, and not the Author. At best, such trivia as the properties of beryl or olive oil that Augustine discusses can only verify and celebrate the true message of the text, a meaning discovered in an openness of the mind and a willingness of the heart such as Ambrose's unforced receptiveness, his eyes travelling cross the page, his tongue silent, his heart seeking the sense.

Such a rhetorical orientation is very difficult to find among the rhetoricians of the late classical period and equally rare among the early Fathers of the Church: this participatory sense of the text does not fully re-emerge in Christian thought until the mystical writers of the twelfth century and after. In fact, there is only one other writer who develops a parallel sense of the "special text," a text that does not merely impart information but acts as a means for establishing a communion of spirits, a text that is a celebration of truths already acknowledged, a text for intransitive reading.

The writer is Macrobius. The *Commentary on the Somnium Scipionis* shares all of the notions developed from Augustine. Like Creation, the *Somnium* still bears the marks of its author, and the communion of the reader with Scipio is finally more important than the encyclopedic information encoded in the text. As Scripture is for Augustine, the *Somnium Scipionis* for Macrobius is a transcendent work that contains "the whole body of philosophy," the sum of all knowledge.

Macrobius demonstrates the scriptural nature of his text, its fitness for intransitive reading, by an admittedly artificial expansion of Cicero's narrative. From the smallest details in his original, Macrobius extrapolates entire sciences or bodies of knowledge which he perceives to lie latent in the *Somnium*. Like Scripture for Augustine, however, the *Somnium* for Macrobius is not a textbook from which the sciences can be extracted; on the contrary, the reader must approach the *Somnium* with *prior* encyclopedic knowledge to find all of philosophy verified in Scipio's mystic vision. Again like Scripture for Augustine, the *Somnium* for Macrobius is a celebration of the truth and of that community of believers who apprehend the truth in the text "successu excelsam et velatam mysteriis." The philosopher reading the *Somnium* and identifying with the "rapt" Scipio finds the truths he already affirms—both scientific truths and ethical verities—embodied in the visionary experience of the Roman hero.

But Scipio's dream was a fake and Macrobius knew it. He acknowledges this fact quite early in the *Commentary* in considering the rhetorical choices open to Cicero:

> hanc fabulam Cicero licet ab indoctis quasi ipse veri conscius doleat irrisam, exemplum tamen stolidae reprehensionis vitans excitari narraturum quam reviviscere maluit.

> Cicero, as if assured of the truth of this tale [Plato's "Vision of Er"], deplored the ridicule it received at the hands of ignorant critics and yet, fearful of the unwarranted censure that was heaped upon Plato, preferred to have his account given by a man aroused from sleep rather than by one returned from the dead.[13]

One might assume that such an admission might have a less than salutary effect on Cicero's (and Macrobius') credibility, but such is not the case. Macrobius' response to the problem is to develop a sophisticated sense of truth-in-fiction, a heuristic in which transcendent truths may be—or may only be—expressed in self-consciously fabulous figures or analogies.[14] In the next chapter of the *Commentary*, Macrobius introduces this notion:

> nec omnibus fabulis philosophia repugnat, nec omnibus adquiescit; et ut facile secerni possit quae ex his a se abdicet ac velut profana ab ipso vestibulo sacrae disputationis excludat, quae vero etiam saepe ac libenter admittat, divisionum gradibus explicandum est.

> Philosophy does not discountenance all stories nor does it accept all, and in order to distinguish what it rejects as unfit to enter its sacred precincts and what it frequently and gladly admits, the points of division must needs be clarified.[15]

This process of differentiation, involving distinctions between tall tales and so-called fabulous narratives, with subdivisions upon subdivisions, is a thorny one best represented graphically:

VARIETIES OF FICTION

(after Macrobius, *Commentary on the Somnium Scipionis*, I, ii)

Fabula ——————————— Fictions

wholly fictitious ——————— Narratio Fabulosa

base ——————————— "solid foundation of truth"

seemly

According to Macrobius, only the rightmost, bottommost category, the "seemly *narratio fabulosa*," is fit to serve as a vehicle for philosophic exposition because only such a story is

> sacrarum rerum notio sub pio figmentorum velamine honestis et tecta rebus et vestita nominibus enuntiatur: . . .

> a decent and dignified conception of holy truths, with respectable events and characters, . . . presented beneath a modest veil of allegory.[16]

The next sentence makes the defense of the *Somnium Scipionis* complete by applying the distinction between unseemly fable and seemly fabulous narrative to the present text and to its Platonic forebear:

> cum igitur nullam disputationi pariat iniuriam vel Er index vel somnians Africanus, sed rerum sacrarum enuntiatio integra sui dignitate his sit tecta nominibus, accusator tandem edoctus a fabulis fabulosa secernere conquiescat.

> Therefore, since the treatises of Plato and Cicero suffer no harm from Er's testimony or Scipio's dream, and the treatment of sacred subjects is accomplished without loss of dignity by using their names, let our critic at last hold his peace, taught to differentiate between the fable and the fabulous narrative.[17]

Macrobius next excludes certain subjects which are too lofty for even such decorous tales and then, in a crucial passage, develops an affective rhetoric for the *narratio fabulosa*:

de dis autem (ut dixi) ceteris et de anima non frustra se nec ut oblectent ad fabulosa convertunt, sed quia sciunt inimicam esse naturae apertam nudam que expositionem sui, quae sicut vulgaribus hominum sensibus intellectum sui vario rerum tegmine operimentoque subtraxit, ita a prudentibus arcana sua voluit per fabulosa tractari. sic ipsa mysteria figurarum cuniculis operiuntur ne vel haec adeptis nudam rerum talium natura se praebeat, sed summatibus tantum viris sapienta interprete veri arcani consciis, contenti sint reliqui ad venerationem figuris defendentibus a vilitate secretum.

But in treating of the other gods and the Soul, as I have said, philosophers make use of fabulous narratives; not without a purpose, however, nor merely to entertain, but because they realize that a frank, open exposition of herself is distasteful to Nature, who, just as she has withheld an understanding of herself from the uncouth senses of men by enveloping herself in variegated garments, has also desired to have her secrets handled by more prudent individuals through fabulous narratives. Accordingly, her sacred rites are veiled in mysterious representations so that she may not have to show herself even to initiates. Only eminent men of superior intelligence gain a revelation of her truths; the others must satisfy their desire for worship with a ritual drama which prevents her secrets from becoming common.[18]

Thus, the *narratio fabulosa* is elitist, though not absolutely so. As Augustine says in the *De Doctrina Christiana*, the initiate must be an encyclopedic philosopher to decode the fiction; one must possess all knowledge *to understand*, if this only is the goal. The person of simple faith, however, may embrace and revere the truths *without understanding*, just as Macrobius' "reliqui" ("others") may witness the ritual drama and worship at a distance. Ultimately, such people are probably better off than the "eminent men of superior intelligence" because total understanding—a perfect transitive reading— is an impossibility; both Macrobius and Augustine see their texts as unfathomably rich and teach that the initiate's devotion is sublime not in mere comprehension but "in the embrace."

Macrobius and Augustine differ on the issue of whether the initiates should espouse or pronounce the truths they discover. Augustine's position was, of course, "evangelical," that all doctrine should be universally promulgated, though he seemed to believe that all could never comprehend all. The *De Doctrina Christiana* presupposes that a careful and seemly exposition of the truths of Scripture is possible, though no expert could ever be so universally knowledgeable as to understand all of Scripture's *integumenta*, let alone tell all to the unlearned but faithful populace. Macrobius' view was markedly different. The very purpose of fiction for Macrobius is to insulate truths from ignorance and sacrilege, so it follows that the unworthy should not be made privy to the truth, but should instead worship its fictional representation. This strange notion of worship in lieu of understanding has a curious later history among Christian writers, as Peter Dronke has shown in an edition of a Commentary on Macrobius' *Commentary* by Guillaume de Conches (twelfth century). Going far beyond Macrobius, Guillaume (understandably) perceives the pagan gods themselves as fictions perpetuated to insure the proper behavior in the masses, a control actually endangered by a revelation of the truth:

> Ratio est, quare nuda et aperta expositio est inimica nature deorum: scilicet ut soli sapientes sciant secreta deorum, per interpretationem integumentorum. Rustici vero et insipientes ignorent, sed tantum credant, quia si modo sciret rusticus, quod Ceres non est aliud quam terre naturalis potentia crescendi in segetes et eas multiplicandi, item quod Bacus non est aliud quam terre naturalis potencia crescendi in vineas, non timore Bachi vel Cereris—quos deos esse reputant—retardarent se ab aliqua inhonesta accione.

> There is a reason why naked and open exposition is repugnant to the nature of the gods: namely that only the wise should know the secrets of the gods, (arrived at) through the interpretation of *integumenta*. As for churls and foolish men, let them not know but only believe. For if a churl were but to know that Ceres is nothing other than the earth's natural power of growing into crops and multiplying them, or again that Bacchus is nothing other than the earth's natural power of growing into vines, then fear of Bacchus or Ceres—whom they think to be gods— would no longer keep them back from any dishonorable action in their way of life.[19]

The fictions channel and regulate the actions and beliefs both of the wise who understand and also of the ignorant who do not. Commenting on the Macrobean phrase, "figurarum cuniculus" ("labyrinth of images," quoted earlier), Guillaume meditates:

Cuniculus est via subterranea, per quam homo latenter incedit ab uno
locum ad alium, et inde etiam quoddam animal cuniculus appellatur, quia
scilicet habitat in cavernis terre, qui et cirogrillus dicitur. Hic autem cuni-
culos vocat integumenta, quia quemadmodum in cuniculis latent huiusmodi animalia, ita et in integumentis veritas quasi obscure continetur.

A *cuniculus* is a subterranean passage by which a man walks under
cover from one place to another; so too an animal, a rabbit, is called
cuniculus, because it dwells in the burrows underground. But here it is
integumenta that are called 'labyrinths of imagery'—for as rabbits take
cover in such labyrinths, so truth is enclosed, in darkness as it were, in
integumenta.[20]

This grand image brings together many variegated strands and concepts. The *figurarum cuniculus* is the dark, arbitrary passageway run
by trusting believers in the truth, a track "humble at entrance but
sublime in embrace." This integument or covering is a human creation, worthless in itself but priceless for the truth to which it leads
its trusting runners. To perceive the integument itself, to understand it, is unnecessary to perceive the truth, and the darkness
makes this irrelevant investigation all the more difficult. If one has
only faith, the humble and submissive runner will be led, albeit
blindly, through the maze of the labyrinth. If one has only knowledge, this prideful non-runner will stand and strain to see the construction of the labyrinth, unwilling to submit to its narrow trails,
unwilling to be led to the truth. If one has *both faith and knowledge*,
then this privileged runner will occasionlly glimpse the light that
would blind in excess, even as he runs the *cuniculus*.[21]

It would be inaccurate to call these ideas drawn from Augustine
and Macrobius a "rhetoric," and even less accurate to call them the
rhetoric of the dream vision. It is fair, though, to see in them a
movement, a thrust in two thinkers important for the Middle Ages
that extenuates or even calls into question the traditional sense of
hermeneutics. To sum up the ideas, Augustine and Macrobius both
radicalize the traditional "fruit and chaff" analogy to the extent that
the chaff is at best irrelevant and fabricated and at worst seductive
and misleading. This position may seem a bit extreme in the case of

Augustine, but the *De Doctrina Christiana* contains several passages where Augustine seems to be consciously manufacturing fruit out of the most ridiculous chaff; for example:

> Et tamen nescio quomodo suavius intueor sanctos, cum eos quasi dentes Ecclesiae video praedicere ab erroribus homines, a que in ejus corpus, emollita duritia, quasi demorsos mansosque transferre.

> Nevertheless, in a strange way, I contemplate the saints more pleasantly when I envisage them as the teeth of the Church cutting men off from their errors and transferring them to her body after their hardness has been softened as if by being eaten and chewed.[22]

Augustine (*nescio quomodo*) enjoys this, and it is important to understand just why he does. There is, of course, no legitimate relationship between teeth and the saints according to any human perspective: the point of the comparison is that the creative intellectual exercise of (literally) *making* the comparison is an act of faith which valorizes both the perceptor and the specific detail of the physical world perceived. The exercise would not work, in fact, if a pre-existing logical or iconographic relationship were available: that would not only ruin the fun but would also eliminate the faith-communion between the perceptor and the Author, ruin the exercise of seeking the meaning with the *heart* as opposed to ascertaining it with the intellect.

Elsewhere, Augustine can be heard to announce, in effect, that there is nothing inherently holy in the lexical words of Holy Scripture or even in the word "God" (compare "Yahweh");[23] the words are merely a necessary but contingent system of grunts kindly tolerated by a bemused deity:

> Et tamen Deus, cum de illo nihil digne dici possit, admisit humanae vocis obsequium, et verbis nostris in laude sua gaudere nos voluit. Nam inde est et quod dicitur Deus. Non enim revera in strepitu istarum duarum syllabarum ipse cognoscitur; sed tamen omnes latinae linguae scios, cum aures eorum sonus iste tetigerit, movet ad cogitandam excellentissimam quamdam immortalemque naturam.

> For God, although nothing worthy may be spoken of Him, has accepted

the tribute of the human voice and wished us to take joy in praising Him with our words. In this way He is called *Deus*. Although He is not recognized in the noise of these two syllables, all those who know the Latin language, when this sound reaches their ears, are moved to think of a certain most excellent immortal nature.[24]

In both writers, then, as this quotation from Augustine indicates, the bond between tenor and vehicle is neither inherent, intellectual, nor rational: both rhetorics operate only in faith. Without faith, Augustine's Christian rhetoric falls apart, as does Macrobius' Stoic-Platonic rhetoric: scoffers at the systems—pagans for Augustine, Epicureans for Macrobius—who are unwilling to suspend disbelief and enter humbly into the humble fiction, are forever shut off from the truth. Only the wise may learn all or nearly all there is to *know* of the *veil*, but all of faith can perceive the fitness and seemliness of the *integumentum* or *narratio fabulosa*, believe in the goodness of its craftsman (Craftsman), worship the unseen truths, and travel across the labyrinthine page, their tongues silent, towards ultimate communion with the craftsman in the truth.

We thus have a system that requires a surface or integument that must of necessity be self-consciously and self-evidently fictional or worthless, an artifact created by an individual artificer and designed to embody the truth for the wise and to act as a pathway to that same truth for the less-than-wise. Thus, this fiction is humble and even ridiculous at entrance but sublime in its embrace by faithful readers, a rabbit-run the twists and turns of which are pointless in themselves—though possibly amusing—and valuable only in that they lead finally to an identity or communion with the architect of the *cuniculus*. The end point of the work, this communion or identity, demonstrates to readers that they are part of an elect, a special community which hears the word of the Apostle and intuits it to be addressed specifically to them.

This in turn begins to describe a form. The surface of this form is an inherently worthless projection of an individual human psyche, fit and seemly, perhaps, but revelatory only of the condition of that psyche. While this surface is humble, its contents are sublime, at least for readers whose souls are potentially congruent with that of the fabricator of the labyrinth; for those readers who can transcend the form and embrace the contents—"incessu humilem, successu excelsam et velatam mysteriis" ("humble on entrance, lofty on advance and veiled with mysteries")—the dark labyrinth allows them to see clearly *insomnium*.

Freedom in Parody: The *Roman de la Rose*

The *Somnium Scipionis* was the first dream vision. It was a first-person account of a dream which suggested (but by and large failed to develop) a complex relationship between dream and dreamer. Its exegesis by Macrobius in the fourth century foregrounded the latent ambiguities in the nature of the dream and also, by a strange coincidence, associated Cicero's strange, enigmatic text with a body of protopsychological dream lore that was to become the standard discussion of the topic for a thousand years or more. In the context of an Augustinian rhetoric, the *Somnium Scipionis* and its *Commentary*—the precious allegorical vision of the great *auctor* Cicero and its brilliant expansion by the polymath Macrobius—was obviously assured a special place in late medieval learning. The twelfth and thirteenth centuries were years of dogged search for the literary treasures of the past and, even later, men such as Petrarch and Poggio would embark on veritable expeditions in search of lost fragments of Cicero and other Latin authors, but the *Commentary on the Somnium Scipionis* was already their prized possession. Cicero's *de re publica* had not yet been discovered (nor had Plato's *Republic*, of course), but the *Somnium Scipionis* was already theirs, thanks to the man who explored (and often invented) its profundity, Macrobius. Thus, Cicero, Macrobius, and a thoroughly congruent Augustinian perspective on the *integumenta* of the dream-text: this was a textual nexus ripe for exploitation by poets.

Exploitation came remarkably late in the Middle Ages. In fairness, there were many dream-frame poems before the *Roman de la Rose*—the allegorical spectacles of the Chartrean Naturalists, for example—but these works were in the apocalypse tradition and thus lacked one or more of the distinguishing marks of the dream vision. The Chartrean Naturalists and Dante wrote visions (sometimes waking, sometimes sleeping) which imitated John's vision on Mount Patmos or fed on a separate folkloric tradition of descents into the underworld or raptures into Heaven, while other dream poets before Guillaume de Lorris wrote visions on what should properly be called Boethian models, delicious love-debates presided over by an allegorical figure of authority, the descendant of Lady Philosophy. None of these poets fully exploited the arresting ambivalence of Cicero's *Somnium*; none captured the unique epistemological crux of truth-in-fiction; none troubled themselves to present a distressed, unfit visionary whose vision transcends his unfitness.

None, that is, until Guillaume de Lorris. The *Roman de la Rose* must stand as the first work in a millennium which brings together the disparate rhetorical motifs of Cicero, Macrobius, and Augustine in a framework that captures the ambivalence of the opening of the *Somnium Scipionis*. The claim that the dream is a revelation; the broad hints that it cannot be so; the grounding of the dream-experience in an individual psyche in turmoil or distress; the ultimate, intuitively obvious import of the dream to an elite who have the faith to embrace the work: all is present, for the first time, in the *Roman*.

To illustrate, we need do little more than quote:

> Aucunes genz dient qu'en songes
> n'a sa fables non et mençonges;
> mes l'en puet tex songes songier
> qui ne sont mie mençongier,
> ainz sont apré bien aparent, . . .

> Many men sayn that in sweveninges
> Ther nys but fables and lesynges;
> But men may some swevenes sen
> Whiche hardely that false ne ben,
> But afterward ben apparaunt.[25]

This deft touch takes the reader immediately into the heart of the dream question and speaks directly to the inconsistency between the rational voice of authority (what "men sayn") and the psychological needs and realistic experience of real people (what "men may . . . sen"). While this statement serves at its surface to decide the issue in favor of the prescient dream, the semantic structure of the sentence foregrounds and highlights the medieval ambiguity about dreams rather than smoothing it over. Thus, such an opening should hardly be read as a simple assertion that the sceptical "clerkys" are wrong; if anything, its acknowledgment of what "men sayn" reminds us of the Wife of Bath's Prologue, in which the persona's obsession with authority is as evident as her opposition to it.

The rhetorical complexity increases in the next few lines, as, in seemingly trying to strengthen his case for his own dream as a revelation, Guillaume introduces a decidedly recalcitrant authority:

> si en puis bien traire a garant
> un auctor qui ot non Macrobes,
> qui ne tint pas songes a lobes,
> ançois escrit l'avision
> qui avint au roi Scypion.
> Qui c'onques cuit ne qui que die
> qu'il est folor et musardie
> de croire que songes aviegne,
> qui se voudra, por fol m'en tiegne,
> quar endroit moi ai ge fiance
> que songes est senefiance
> des biens as genz et des anuiz,
> que li plusor songent de nuiz
> maintes choses covertement
> que l'en voit puis apertement.

> This may I drawe to warraunt
> An authour that hight Macrobes,
> That halt nat dremes false ne lees,
> But undoth us the avysioun
> That whilom mette kyng Cipioun.
> And whoso saith or weneth it be
> A jape, or elles nycete,
> To wene that dremes after falle,
> Let whoso lyste a fol me calle.
> For this trowe I, and say for me,

That dremes signifiaunce be
Of good and harm to many wightes,
That dremen in her slep a-nyghtes
Ful many thynges covertly,
That fallen after al openly.[26]

These lines are typically read as an appeal to the authority of Macrobius but, given the sense of Macrobius and of his work that we have developed in the last two chapters, it is hard to read these lines of Guillaume de Lorris in that way. Guillaume cites the authority of Macrobius on only two matters here, and the validity of the citations needs some scrutiny. First, Guillaume correctly attributes to Macrobius the teaching that all dreams are not necessarily false or lying and, second, credits him (as all modern classicists do) with recording and preserving the "avisioun" of Scipio. Both of these acknowledgments are technically righteous but, as we have seen, they are also severely circumscribed and undercut by Macrobius himself, in ways Guillaume and his readers *must* have perceived. First, though indeed he says that all dreams are not false, he does not say by any means that all are true. In fact, Macrobius' favorite example of the worthless somatic dream, the lover's dream of the possession of the beloved, matches the one we are about to hear all too closely, and Guillaume's claim that the *Rose*-dream came true can hardly stand against the explicit disqualification in the very commentary that Guillaume cites. Second, Guillaume's gratitude to Macrobius for recording the *Somnium Scipionis* is complicated, we have seen, by broad hints that the *Somnium* itself is a somatic dream (or, worse, a *narratio fabulosa*, as Macrobius admits). The question then arises, why does Guillaume de Lorris introduce Macrobius here only to do such obvious, intentional violence to his teachings and, effectively, to turn him on his encyclopedic head?

The answer to this question can be found in the next lines of Guillaume's Prologue:

El vintieme an de mon aage,
el point qu'Amors prent le paage
des jones genz, couchier m'aloie

105

une nuit, si con je souloie,
et me dormoie mout forment,
et vi un songe en mon dormant
qui mout fu biaus et mout me plot;
mes en ce songe onques riens n'ot
qui tretor avenu ne soit
si con li songes recensoit.

Within my twenty yer of age,
Whan that Love taketh his cariage
Of yonge folk, I wente soone
To bedde, as I was wont to done,
And faste I slepte; and in slepyng
Me mette such a swevenyng
That lyked me wonders wel.
But in that sweven is never a del
That it nys afterward befalle,
Ryght as this drem wol tel us alle.[27]

These lines maintain the precarious balance established in the preceding ones, a balance between somatic and divine explanations for the dream. Again, Guillaume makes the express claim that the events depicted in the dream subsequently came true, but he also alludes unmistakably to naturalistic explanations, noting that, after all, he has this dream at that time when "Amors prent le paage de jones genz" ("Love exacts his price from young folk"). Such a situation should remind us of exactly the same contradiction in the *Somnium Scipionis*, in which Scipio offers what seems to be evidence of a somatic dream, evidence which Macrobius ignores. Officially, then, this present dream is as indeterminate as that of Scipio, one (this time consciously) suspended between contraries and satisfying the popular need for the relevant dream.

The similarity between Amant's and Scipio's dreams does not end here, for the operation of the God of Love is not simply a localized metaphor confined to the prologue: the figure, of course, becomes a fully-realized personification in the dream. This change in the status of "Amors"—from a conventionalized personification of love languor to a principal allegorical antagonist—deepens and changes the ambiguity of the situation. While the metaphor of love "exacting his price" means one thing at the simple level of personification, it means something radically different if the poem itself is evidence of that exacted price: suddenly, perhaps, this dreamer is not simply in love languor but is actually the recipient of a special revelation, obsessed with divine madness, prophetic frenzy. In short, the deepening complexity of the *Roman* reveals the same mutual valorizing process that operated in the *Somnium Scipionis*: the dream is valorized by the dreamer's great devotion to the deity, while it is clear that such a holy and seemly revelation would only come to a pious follower of Cupid.

Such a reading is the only explanation for the "mes" at line 28: "mes en ce songe ongues riens n'ot qui tretot avenu" ("but in this dream there is nothing that did not later happen"). The concessive suggests that, under these circumstances, we would not normally assume that the dream would be prescient; after all, this dreamer is one of the "jones genz" debilitated by Love. The statement thus maintains the delicate balance between what "men sayn" and what "men sen" at the beginning of the poem and actually capitalizes on the status of the poet-dreamer as courtly lover. As a lover in fact, he is disqualified as a dreamer of *visiones* or *oracula* or *somnia*; as a lover in the mythos of courtly love, he is obviously a worthy contemplative whose temporary *ariditas* (analogous to the mystic's) should cause him to hope for an ultimate revelation. Such a maneuver is a stroke of genius for the courtly love poet Guillaume, who playfully transforms love languor from an obstacle to revelation to a manifestation of the new erotic "piety" that authorizes revelation.

The next lines of the Prologue complete the strategic parallel with the *Somnium Scipionis*, going so far as to imply that Guillaume understood the Macrobean sense of truth-in-fiction:

> Or veil cel songe rimeer,
> por vos cuers plus feire agueer,
> qu'Amors le me prie et comande.
> Et se nule ne nus demande
> comant je veil que li romanz
> soit apelez que je comanz,

107

ce est li *Romanz de la Rose,*
ou l'art d'Amors est tote enclose.

Now this drem wol I ryme aright
To make your hertes gaye and lyght,
For Love it prayeth, and also
Commaundeth me that it be so.
And if there any aske me,
Whether that it be he or she,
How this book, the which is here,
Shal hatte, that I rede you here:
It is the *Romance of the Rose,*
In which at the art of love I close.[28]

Fundamentally, the poem is a divinely sanctioned entertainment: Love commanded that it be so for the enjoyment and instruction of the god's devotees, just as God's book of the world may be legitimately enjoyed by his followers and just as the *Somnium Scipionis* can be reverenced by Macrobius' fellow philosophers. Such an intention de-emphasizes the status of Guilluame's personal revelation and brings the poem into line with the special collapse of *uti-frui* in intransitive reading. The content of the dream—its "factual basis"—is secondary to the truths of the theology of Amors that are contained in its integument. All may read and enjoy the story, and, additionally, the wise will find therein that "l'art d'Amors est tote enclose," that the entire body of philosophy can be found in the text, a claim that directly echoes the *Somnium Scipionis.*

Thus, in remarkable parallels with Macrobius, Guillaume claims that his dream is true, not (importantly) in its events but in its *sentence,* its hidden, scriptural, intransitive truth. While Guillaume certainly claims that his dream is a personal revelation, the force of its principal truth claim is that it is a "ritual drama" produced to lighten the hearts of the followers of Love and, in so doing, to verify and celebrate the truths they already hold in common. The "religious" reader of the *Roman* will be brought by it into that special communion with Amant and will, in embracing the dream, perceive that he too is Amant, is one with the dreamer in his devotion to the God of Love.

The *Roman de la Rose* is thus the watershed text of the dream vision tradition, the singular blasphemous parody that cribbed the rhetorical strategies of Macrobius and Augustine and brought them into the service of secular, popular literature. The ambiguous status of the dream, grounded in the consciousness of the dreamer but ultimately seeming universal in its application, the recognition of truth-in-fiction—all of the motifs recognized by Macrobius are here.

A Psychology and a Metaphysics: Nominalism

The *Roman de la Rose* is very nearly the whole story of the origin of the late medieval dream vision: only one problem remains. Guillaume's persona is still, however metaphorically or blasphemously, an initiate, a saint of the new erotic religion, and it is only in his status as an initiate that his dream can be valorized. In other words, the *Roman* was possible only because courtly love was a mock religion and the "higher truths" buried in its labyrinths are parodic religious truths. To normalize this experience, to allow the dreamer to be truly an everyman and not a man privileged with *raptus Deo*, a revolution was needed, a revolution in metaphysics, epistemology, and psychology. Such a revolution would provide a new sense of the value of the *figmenta* of the human mind and would free these images from the constraining requirement that they adhere to an eternal, universal, and unchanging world of forms. Such a revolution would make the dream vision truly a dream, not a revelation of the higher world but one thoroughly of the inner, individualized world of the dreamer, a world that could only be shared by those who first share in the thoughts, obsessions, and ultimate righteousness of the dreamer.

The revolution is nominalism. Fundamentally, nominalists and conceptualists attacked the ancient Platonic notion that there physically exists a "world of forms," a realm consisting of universal, abstract, incorporeal quiddities on which all phenomenal existence is based. The original concept is probably traceable to the cave metaphor of Plato's *Republic* but, once Christianized, the notion of "extramental universals" became a central tenet of natural philosophy. It was, in fact, on initially theological grounds that Ockham first questioned the extramental existence of universals; if incorruptible and eternal universals exist, Ockham reasoned, then they could not have been created by God. Further, if universals exist, then their very existence constrains God's omnipotence, since He would be able to act on them only in accordance with their universal nature. His first formulation of this position echoes the figmental rhetoric of Macrobius and Augustine:

> Et dico, quod universale non est aliquid reale habens esse subiectivum, nec in anima nec extra animam, sed tantum habet esse obiectivum in anima, et est quoddam fictum habens esse tale in esse obiectivo, quale habet res extra in esse subiectivo.

> I maintain that a universal is not something real that exists in a subject [of inherence], either inside or outside the mind, but that it has being only as a thought-object in the mind. It is a kind of mental picture which as a thought-object has a being similar to that which the thing outside the mind has in its real existence.[29]

This is not the place to assess the impact of this teaching on medieval philosophy;[30] what is relevant to this present discussion is the curious effect that such a teaching has on the rhetorical nexus perceptible in Macrobius and Augustine, one which sees surfaces as vehicles of truth but worthless in and of themselves. In the Platonic system, the status of phenomena is ambivalent: on the one hand, they are but the shadows of noumena, which at best only imperfectly represent them to creatures; on the other hand, phenomenal reality is visible and corporeal, making it hard to remember that these things are the shadows and the invisible entities are the truer reality. The same ambivalence surrounds the "phenomena" of the *Roman de la Rose*: the literal or phenomenal level of the poem, however unaccountable it may appear, serves as the vehicle for a divine revelation and so is insulated from challenge or scrutiny. In other words, the reader of the *Roman* can never declare unilaterally that any given detail of the vision—say, Amant's basting his sleeves at line 100—is totally grounded in the dreamer's own experience because the detail might well be an integument, a vehicle for a hidden allegorical tenor whose meaning has been denied to the reader. As a reading experience, the *Roman* can never fully engage a reader because, given Guillaume's claim that the dream is a prescient revelation—a *somnium*—any given detail or event may operate in a context or at a level unavailable to the reader.

Dualism and its universals exert a pressure on Macrobius and Augustine as well. Despite their rhetorical approaches to their texts, neither exegete is permitted to question the literal truth of the text under analysis. Macrobius especially must balance a sense of the *Somnium Scipionis* as ritual drama with the contradictory claim that it is also literally, naively prescient as well; that, as a revelation, the *Somnium* actually shows a picture of the Platonic cosmos while, as a fabulous narrative, it simultaneously embraces the "entire body of philosophy." Augustine sidesteps this issue by Christianizing the Platonic scheme and claiming that divine artifacts can simultaneously be things and signs (subject to both use and enjoyment, to both intransitive and transitive reading). Effectively, then, in a Platonic framework, the allegorist is always a type of the Creator; his allegorical text is inescapably sacramental, containing representations that are never merely the figments of his own mind.

Ockham's psychology and metaphysics changed this. Without delimiting God's omnipotence or omniscience in any way, Ockham simply claims that human intelligence does not regularly partake of that omniscience. Revelations and prophecies certainly take place but, says Ockham, the normal intellectual process of abstraction is not the result of divine indwelling or of a share in the mind of God. Universals exist, but not outside of the individual mind: they are created by repeated predication (that is, "candiditas" is that quality shared by vanilla ice cream, bond paper, cumulus clouds, etc.). For Ockham, the mental images of which our graphic or oral signs are expressions are grounded in our own minds, not in another realm, and thus are subject to judgments about their validity or righteousness:

> Figmenta habent esse in anima, et non subiectivum, quia tunc essent verae res, et ita chimaera et hircocervus et huiusmodi essent verae res; . . .
>
> . . . fictions have being in the mind, but they do not exist independently

[*subiectivum*], because in that case they would be real things and so a
chimera and a goat-stag and so on would be real things.[31]

In his later writings, Ockham abandoned metaphorical formulations of this doctrine, including the notions of "fictum" or "figmentum," for one more firmly rooted in sign theory. This later formulation identified universals as the basic building blocks of thought, the
nomines or names with which the mind forms propositions:

> . . . ipsae intellectiones animae vocantur passiones animae, et suppo-
> nunt ex natura sua pro ipsis rebus extra vel pro aliis rebus in anima, sicut
> voces supponunt pro rebus ex institutione . . .
>
> The mind's own intellectual acts are called states of mind. By their nature
> they stand for the actual things outside the mind or for other things in
> the mind, just as the spoken words stand for them by convention . . .[32]

Thus, Plato's world of forms exists, but only in Plato's mind, only as
the products of his individual process of abstraction, and only as the
inventory of images with which he constructs propositions and syl-
logisms. They are unique and personal: as each person's experience
of phenomenal reality is different from that of every other person,
so each individual's stock of *intellectiones* will be different from
everyone else's, as different as different languages or as similar as
different pronunciations of "Aeneas."

Thus, the new nominalist orientation was inward, though something short of solipsistic: clearly, worlds of forms still exist and are
still communal if not actually universal, and "psychological" universals like *caninitas* and *candiditas* are probably no less righteous and
accurate categories of *experience* than oral or written names represent. They are based on accrued experience, judgment, wisdom,
learning, and understanding and, though no two corresponding
senses of, say, "virtus," will be exactly synonymous, the senses of
"virtus" developed by most good people will be at least recognizably
similar. Like spoken languages but anterior to them, this interior
language of universals is a useful and necessary vehicle for thought
and communication: useful because conventional, necessary because
everything that is not God is contingent, making knowledge of God

impossible and knowledge of everything else experiential and approximate at best.

Such a rethinking of epistemological and metaphysical problems in the late Middle Ages could not fail to have its effect on literature, especially on allegorical and naively iconic literature. By decapitating a Platonic metaphysics, nominalism turned literature away from a vaguely Neo-Platonic sense of fantasy and allegory as realizations of the world of forms or windows onto a higher realm. Thus, a nominalist allegory, or more generally a nominalist poem, uses imagery not only to communicate (what might be) ultimate realities but also to examine and explore the mind of the image-maker, the poet. A poem such as the *Book of the Duchess*, for example, uses nominalism to have it both ways: the poem can simultaneously mourn Blanche and foreground the intellectual and creative poverty of the narrator and the audience:

> The *ficta* (or *figmenta*) of the brain fail to correspond exactly with the phenomena. It becomes important, then, that man's schemes be interrupted, reassessed, even broken, as they were in the *Book of the Duchess*, so that man, as dreamer, can be rendered naked to start afresh.[33]

Such an observation accounts nicely for the inherent silliness of the obtuse narrator of this stark and serious poem. In this perspective, the *Book of the Duchess* becomes a study in perspective itself, in the contingency of language and in the danger of interpreting phenomena by way of pre-existing generalizations in the interpreter's mind or available to it through books. "Man, as dreamer" becomes the subject of the poem equally with the events dreamed because, just as speech reflects the speaker's thoughts, nominalist universals—realized as dream images—reflect the thinker's soul.

In a more general rhetorical sense, this change in focus from noumenal reality to psychological realities (and the uncertain "communal" reality built from them) served to make nominalism an uncanny backdrop for the medieval dream vision. Recalling Augustine and Macrobius, we should ask what would be the end point of a labyrinth of images that is not merely figmental but which is also the semiotic signature of its architect? In other words, what is embraced by the reader who overcomes the initial humility of another's dream and actually *comprehends* its alien images? The answer is something short of ultimate knowledge or revelation, but something which was, for the logician Ockham, the only human achievement that could transcend the contingency of the phenomenal world. The end point of the dream vision is the communion of two minds, whose *ficta* are astonishingly identical; it is the intuition that the words (or the dream) are not someone else's or anyone's but—"tolle, lege"—mysteriously, specially the reader's coequally with the dreamer. Ockham, of course, saw this communion as possible only in logic, the cold-blooded, abstract system of propositions leading to intellectual or notional assent, but the dream vision extended the possibilities: to read another's dream is to find oneself thinking that person's thoughts, but to embrace that dream, to comprehend or see the justice of its *ficta* or *figmenta*—this is to become one with that dreamer.

Thus, just as the rhetorical goal of reading Scripture is to become one with God in spirit—and not necessarily in mind—the rhetorical goal of reading a dream vision is to become one with the dreamer. The reader actually has shared in the distress, the distraction, and the vision of the dreamer, actually "comes to the place where he is already," as Augustine would say. Such a revelation is certainly less sublime than the one experienced on Mount Patmos but, for the fourteenth century, it was also a more credible and engaging one, one to which a subtle but powerful rhetoric would be brought to bear.

CHAPTER FOUR

STRUCTURE

After considering the contexts of the dream vision and its proximate origins in medieval rhetoric and philosophy, it is finally possible to examine how the poems operate. This examination will be divided into two stages: a formal description of the structure of the dream vision using traditional models and terminology and an affective analysis of this structure. The purpose of this two-stage discussion is to illustrate what I have already suggested about the twofold content of the poems: the poem about a dreamer and a dream, the fabric of the *figmenta* of a troubled dreamer, is simultaneously about the ideas for which those *figmenta* stand and the mind which created the *figmenta*.

The Shape of the Poem

Like any other poem, the dream vision begins by announcing itself to be a certain kind of experience: it does this by introducing a certain sort of persona or speaking voice and determining a specific relationship between that persona and the reader. The text is in the hands of or proceeds from the muse of a specific individual, and all of the words have this person as their ultimate source. Thus, the lyric persona is both the reporter of the narrative (or complex of emotions) and also the text's ultimate (and probably only) subject.

This much is true of all lyric poetry by definition, and the dream vision is a species of the lyric mode. All lyrics are finally about their singers and their subjects—their external topics and the internal responses of the lyric poets to these topics—in ways that frequently make subject and object indistinguishable. The situation in the dream vision, however, complicates even this subtle, often murky configuration because here neither the event nor the reporter are stable, sharply determined entities. The event is ambiguous, of course, because it is a dream and one that is not, in all likelihood, a communication from beyond. Indeed, the "events" reported in dream visions are probably not events at all but, as Augustine and others might have said, are gratuitous, random representations of thoughts and memories given imaginary life in the *figmenta* of the dreamer's brain.

The other element of the lyric mode, the persona, is also especially troublesome and indeterminate in the case of the dream vision.[1] We have noted already that the dreamer is regularly depicted as troubled, depressed, and alienated from the comforts of society: he may be suffering from love languor or be in mourning or he may, like "Long Will" or the dreamer who dreams of the Palace of Fame, be suffering from a deeper, more pervasive anguish or depression. In any case, he is the sort of person who has dreams, the sort of sensibility we might expect in a lyric poet but one in whose hands we might not feel terribly secure.

It could reasonably be objected at this point that the anxious or distracted persona is a feature of all lyric poetry and not unique to the dream vision—after all, why do lyric poets write if they are not moved to do so by some desire to express the overwhelming emotions they feel? The difference, that between the conventional lyric persona and the poet-dreamer, is one of fictive intention: the lyric persona, moved by some emotion to write a poem, goes ahead and writes a poem about that emotion and about the events that engendered it, while the poet-dreamer never sets out consciously to expose his feelings. The elliptical descriptions of dreamers at the beginning of dream visions never include explicit statements about just what is troubling this poor wretch—Geffrey refuses to discuss the question rather brusquely in the *Book of the Duchess* (the "phisicien but oon" passage, lines 30–43). It is thus impossible to begin a dream vision without a sense of intrusion, as when the person sitting next to us on the bus begins to tell us his life story (and we have the window seat); on beginning the poem, the readers discover that all before them promises to be a projection of the troubled mind introduced at the poem's beginning.

These two ambiguities about both halves of the lyric structure—the fantastic event and the unreliable reporter—create *radical lyric expectations* in the reader; however indirectly, the dream report promises to be an expression of emotion like any other lyric except that here the central sentiment is not one about which the poet is being honest and forthright. Such expectations prepare the reader for strange, enigmatic details within the dream reports:

> En icelui tens deliteus,
> que toute rien d'amer s'esfroie,
> songai une nuit que j'estoi.
> Lors m'iere avis en mon dormant
> qu'il iere matin durement;
> de mon lit tantost me levé,
> chaucai moi et mes mains lavé
> lors trés une aguille d'argent
> d'un aguillier mignot et gent,
> si prins l'aguille a enfiler.
> Hors de vile oi talant d'aler
> por oir des oisiaus les sons,
> qui chantent desus les buissons
> en icele saison novele.

> And in this sesoun delytous,
> Whan love affraieth alle thing,
> Me thought a-nyght, in my sleping,
> Right in my bed, ful redily,
> That it was by the morowe erly,
> And up I roos, and gan me clothe.
> Anoon I wisshe myn handis bothe;
> A sylvre nedle forth y drough
> Out of an aguler queynt ynough,
> And gan this nedle threde anon;
> For out of toun me list to gon

117

The song of briddes forto here,
That in thise buskes syngen clere.[2]

What does this mean? The passage seems to violate the rules of logic, sequence, and narrative succession. The very first image of the dream, the wonderfully wrought picture of Amant rising and basting his sleeves with the silver needle, shows by its prominent position in the narrative that it is a crucial motif but offers readers absolutely no clue as to what that motif or image might mean. Explanations for the detail abound in editions of the poem, but none fully accounts for the extraordinary vividness and power of this striking, truly dreamlike image. To say that this intense picture of Amant basting his sleeves in advance of his meeting with *le Dieu d'Amors* captures the real experience of dreaming is fine and true, but such an appreciation does not begin to account for its power and enigma.

The meaning of the passage, of course, is secondary to this rhetorical power: if the basting of the sleeves has any *meaning* at all, this meaning is obviously suppressed to allow the image to remain a radically lyric enigma. Guillaume shows us his dream-self basting his sleeves with the silver needle as the birds sing to underscore the total conflation of text and persona here and to reinforce the sense of enigma and intrusion already felt by readers at the opening of the poem. In this radical lyric situation at the beginning of the dream report, the image is tauntingly enigmatic for readers who are not privy to the dreamer's secret distress; the image calls forth a reaction of hushed, respectful ignorance like that of the *rustici* watching a Macrobean "ritual drama." Like parallel opening enigmas in many other dream visions—the whelp (*Book of Duchess*), the "huyl" (*Pearl*), the "shroudes" (*Piers Plowman*), and the daisy (*Legend of Good Women*)—this image shouts its meaningfulness but remains silent on its meaning. It is an image, sure enough, but one presented to demonstrate to readers that the ritual drama of this text is, so far, beyond the ken of the uninitiated.

This relationship can be neatly expressed in terms of Viktor

Shklovsky's concepts of "story" and "plot," a pair of terms he first used to analyze *Tristram Shandy*.[3] By "story," Shklovsky means the real chronological and external events that are the subject of a narration; by "plot" he means the verbal or stylistic character, pace, and progress of the narrative. Applying the terms to the rhetorical situation at the beginning of the dream vision, with its enigmatic but hypnotic images, we could say that story and plot are indistinguishable, for it is clear from the prologue of the poems that the efficient subject of the poem is to be the dreamer, which makes the dream, the representation of the dreamer's inner life, the "story." At the same time, however, the character and development of the text—the "plot"—are equally reflections or representations of that same subject. Thus, as we might expect in a lyric, the dream vision begins by asserting its expressiveness, though it soon demonstrates the practical inexpressibility of its story; the poem effectively declares that the narrative it is to tell is really no narrative at all but the *insomnium* of one who has refused to name the vexation that caused it. This means, therefore, that both the text and its content are equally the personal products of the distressed dreamer—that story is indistinguishable from plot—and that both are insulated from the readers' comprehension by their fundamental lack of communion with the dreamer. In other words, basting the sleeves must mean something to Guillaume de Lorris (the origin of the dream of Amant), but this meaning is unavailable to all who do not share in Guillaume's unidentified distress.

Perhaps the best example of this initial conflation, of dream and dreamer, of story and plot, occurs early in the *Book of the Duchess*:

> I was go walked fro my tree,
> And as I wente, ther cam be mee
> A whelp, that fauned me as I stood,
> That hadde yfolowed, and koude no good.
> Hyt com and crepte to me as lowe
> Ryght as hyt hadde me yknowe,
> Helde doun hys hed and joyned hys eres,
> And leyde al smothe doun hys heres.
> I wolde have kaught hyt, and anoon

Hyt fledde, and was fro me goon;
And I hym folwed, and hyt forth wente
Doun by a floury grene wente
Ful thikke of gras, ful softe and swete.

(lines 387–99)

There are few more traditionally lyric moments in all of Chaucer. The whelp is all but pure symbol, a little unit of passionate lyric expression that is allusive without reference, all vehicle and no tenor. In the hands of the courtly lover-persona of the *Book of the Duchess*, the whelp is little more than sentimental window dressing, an occasional emblem of love and fidelity to warm the questionable heart of Madame Eglantine. The whelp surfaces and disappears without a trace in the space of only thirteen lines, leaving behind the sense that it has no place in a rational allegorical or narrative structure. Yet, in this radical lyric opening of the dream vision, where all is quite palpably the mindscape of the distressed dreamer, the errant image seems perfectly congruent. Were such an "event" to happen, say, in Spenser, we would demand a meaning (and sooner or later would get one); here, we hardly even wonder, for this is not a narrative and the voice is not that of a rational, meticulous allegorist: this is the fevered lyric expression of poor, love-languishing Geffrey, in which text is teller, story is plot.

As the dream report continues, however, this identity of story and plot, this conflation of dream and dreamer, begins to break down in a process we might call "narrative normalization." At a distance from the dream prologue (where the lyric sense of the poem is the strongest), two subtle changes occur which begin to shift the dream report out of its lyric mode: the splitting of the dreamer and the foregrounding of the iconography of the text.

The first of these changes, the splitting of the dreamer, is less a change than a manifestation of a state of affairs that has obtained from the beginning of the poem. At the start of the dream report, the reader tacitly accepts the identity of the poem's persona with the "I" of the dream report. A passage from the *Roman de la Rose* should illustrate:

120

Et li dex d'Amors m'a seü
endementieres aguetant
con li vanieres qui atant
que la beste en bon leu se meite
por lessier aler la saeste.

And thus while I wente in my play,
The God of Love me folowed ay,
Right as an hunter can abyde
The beest, tyl he seeth his tyde
To shoten at good mes to the der,
Whan that hym nedeth go no ner.[4]

Because of the fundamentally lyric situation at early stages such as this in the *Roman*, there is no particular reason to make nice distinctions between the character in the dream and the narrator of the poem: in this case, since this is manifestly a poem about Guillaume's experiences in love, it is entirely reasonable that he should portray himself as being stalked by *li Dieu d'Amors*. Nonetheless, it is Amant the dreamer-character that sees the God of Love stalking him as his prey; it is Guillaume the dreamer-narrator that supplies the detail.

Such a point may seem tedious and over-subtle, but the fact is that the "two Amants," the dreamer-character and the dreamer-narrator, become thoroughly distinct—split—in the very next lines of the poem, as the omniscient narrator records a mistake made by his fallible alter-ego in the dream:

Dedenz une piere de mabre
ot Nature par grant mestrise
soz le pin la fontaine asise;
si ot desus la pierre escrites
el bort amont letres petites,
qui disoient, ilec desus
estoit morz li biau Narcisus.

And springyng in a marble ston
Had Nature set, the sothe to telle,
Under that pyn-tree a welle.

> And on the border, al withoute,
> Was written in the ston aboute,
> Letters smal, that sayden thus,
> "Here starf the fayre Narcisus."[5]

The one-line inscription on the well diverts the text into a new, didactic mode. For the next seventy-odd lines, the physical narrative is deferred as Guillaume rehearses the story of Narcissus from *Metamorphoses*. The rehearsal is brisk, accurate, and entertaining, but the digression distracts the reader's mind (and certainly Amant's) from the physical object to its mythological history as interpreted by this new, detached persona. The interpretation of the legend (and, thus, of the well), is made explicit in the final lines of the digression:

> Dames, cest essample aprenez,
> qui vers vos amis mesprenez;
> car se vos les lessiez morir,
> Dex le vos savra bien merir.

> Ladyes, I preye ensample takith,
> Ye that ageyns youre love mistakith;
> For if her deth be yow to wite,
> God can ful well youre while quyte.[6]

The warning is racy and urbane—to the point of a possible pun on "full well" in the translation—and the meaning it imposes on the image is not applicable to any but "proude-hertid" loved ones such as Amant's.[7] Specifically, the interpolated gloss fails to suggest that the well represents any danger to Amant:

> Quant li escrit m'ot fet savoir
> que ce estoit trestot por voir
> la fontaine au bel Narcisus,
> je me suis trez un poi ensus,
> que dedenz n'ousai esgarder,
> ainz comançai a coarder,
> que de Narcisus me sovint
> cui malement en mesavint.
> Mes me pensai que a seür,
> sanz peor de mauvés eür,

a la fontaine aler pooie;
por folie m'en esloignoie.

Whanne that this lettre, of which I telle,
Hadde taught me that it was the welle
Of Narcisus in his beaute,
I gan anoon withdrawe me,
Whanne it fel in my remembraunce
That hym bitidde such myschaunce,
But at the laste thanne thought I,
That scatheles, full sykerly,
I myght unto the welle goo.
Wherof shulde I abasshen soo?[8]

This carefully wrought passage allows Guillaume to have it both
ways. The first six lines (1543–48) tease the reader with a cautious,
sensible reaction to the well of Narcissus. The dreamer-character
has not noticed (recall) that the God of Love has been stalking him
all this while, but the readers and the dreamer-narrator have noted
this. Readers, I suspect, know "full well" that the well represents a
danger to Amant, and these first few lines of the passage allow readers to savor the danger. Lines 1549–52, however, show that the
dreamer-character does not realize the danger and, following the
cue of the rehearsal of the Narcissus legend and its sanguine *sentence*, Amant approaches the well, looks in, and falls under the spell
of the lady's eyes, represented by the crystal stones.

Thus, the dreamer-character has made a mistake. He has misinterpreted the meaning of the well, with the help of the "glossator,"
whose redaction of *Metamorphoses* suggested that it represented no
danger. On the rhetorical level, story has diverged from plot, first,
since images have been introduced into the vision that the dreamer-
character has misinterpreted and second, since this misinterpretation is immediately manifest to the readers. The two dreamer-
figures have been split—into an omniscient dreamer-narrator and a
naive dreamer-character, one who knows what the well holds in
store and one who cannot predict this.

This splitting "normalizes" the text by freeing the readers from
the exclusive perspective of the dreamer-character's consciousness.

More than this, by giving readers a perspective on the action that is superior to or at least different from that of the dreamer-character, this splitting also frees the text from the lyric mode, in which the meaning of an image is never totally independent of the lyric "I." Instead, the splitting of the dreamer seems to place the readers in a classic narrative structure in which no character is favored and in which the readers and the narrator are the final arbiters of the sequence of events and their meaning.

It is difficult to find this peculiar arrangement anywhere in literature outside of dream-poetry, in which the mistakes of the dreamer-character (a pseudo-eyewitness) are quite common and conventional. A list of such "authorial" miscues might begin with the jeweler's misapprehension of the status of his pearl (*Pearl*), Drede's misplaced trust of his shipmates (*The Bouge of Court*), and Geffrey's fabled obtuseness towards the Black Knight (the *Book of the Duchess*).

The second movement towards "narrative normalization" is the foregrounding of iconography. This typically occurs simultaneously with the splitting of the dreamer, but it is a sufficiently important feature to warrant notice on its own. The foregrounding is, put simply, the readers' growing intuition that the events and images, the details and the situations of the dream narrative are symbolic *and that their symbolism is comprehensible to the readers without the intervention of the dreamer-narrator.*[9] This sense, in effect a sense of the divergence of story and plot, is a sort of confidence or familiarity with the scenes and images of the dream, which, just perhaps, may not be inscrutable, enigmatic functions of the psyche of the dreamer. In the extreme, this foregrounding happens when the dreamer-character shows himself incapable of interpreting his own dream or becomes himself an object of interpretation ("Amant," "Drede," and so on, as personifications as well as personae). Even when this does not happen—even when the dreamer-character has not been separated from the dreamer-narrator—the conventional or self-evident imagery of the dream report still comes to militate against the radical lyric expectations of the beginning of the poem, still suggests that there is something of this *insomnium* that is comprehensible to the readers. A case in point is the fair field of folk in *Piers Plowman*:

> Thanne gan I to meten a merueilouse sweuene,
> That I was in a wildernesse, wist I neuer where.
> As I bihelde into þe est, an hiegh to þe sonne,
> I seigh a toure on a toft trielich ymaked;
> A depe dale binethe, a dongeon þereinne
> With depe dyches and derke and dredful of sight.
> A faire felde ful of folk fonde I there bytwene,
> Of alle maner of men, þe mene and þe riche,
> Worchyng and wandryng as þe worlde asketh.
> Somme putten hem to þe plow, pleyed ful selde, . . .[10]

There is nothing in this panoramic image to suggest that it is a dream image, nothing peculiar or personal about it, nothing to suggest that its thrust is different from that of the social panoramas of the morality plays from which it is derived. The effect of such a passage (and of a great deal of the *Visio*) is to orient the reader in a familiar allegorical framework and then, in time, to call that familiarity into question. Such a familiar orientation invites readers to forget that this is a somatic dream, to embrace the righteousness of the text as a figurative narrative and not as the dream-projection of Long Will.

A final case, in which splitting and foregrounding occur together, is that of *Pearl*. Early in the dream report, the narrator catches sight of the Pearl maiden on the verge of Heaven and proceeds directly to ask her all the wrong questions:

> 'O perle', quod I,'in perleȝ pyȝt,
> Art þou my perle þat I haf playned,
> Regretted by myn one on nyȝte?
> Much longeyng haf I for þe layned,
> Syþen into gresse þou me aglyȝte.
> Pensyf, payred, I am forpayned,
> And þou in a lyf of lykyng lyȝte,
> In Paradys erde, of stryf vnstrayned.

> What wyrde hat₃ hyder my iuel vayned,
> And don me in þys del and gret daunger?
> Fro we in twynne wern towen and twayned,
> I haf ben a joyle₃ jueler.[11]

Unlike the readers, who have already guessed that this is to be an apocalyptic revelation, the narrator does not appreciate or even understand the privilege that has been accorded him and, ignoring the possibilities for beatific eschatological knowledge to be learned from the Pearl maiden, begins immediately to chastise her for leaving him back on earth to mourn her passing. As in the next few stanzas the dreamer-character attempts to elicit an invitation to cross the river into Heaven and to stay there with her forever, both the splitting and the foregrounding become more obvious. *Pearl* even reaches the point where readers begin to wish that this supernal vision might have been granted to one with more foresight and less self-interest, one who, if offered intelligence about the next world, would not play courtly lover and complain of his lady's "daungere."

So the second stage or phase of the dream vision is a sort of narrative normalization in which various forces work together to submerge the essential lyric mode of the dream report and to encourage narrative expectations (to the extent that, in *Pearl* and the *Book of the Duchess*, the *dreamer* is often perceived to be impeding the progress of the epiphany). The dream vision typically remains in this stage nearly until its conclusion. For evidence of this we need only turn to secondary sources, to critical books and articles on specific poems, which attest eloquently to the fact that the body of the dream report is, or seems to be, interpretable independent of the dream frame. The *Piers Plowman Visio* might serve as an example here, for it is taken in large measure from antifraternal and Wycliffite sources and so seems to have a life of its own apart from the dreaming mind of Long Will, a "life" so vivid that many a commentator on *Piers Plowman* all but forgets that the poem is a dream report. The *Book of the Duchess* is an even clearer case: narrative normalization virtually turns this poem against its own dreamer-persona, the man who cannot see what the dream makes so patently obvious—that the Black Knight has lost his lady Blanche through death. In this case, as in that of *Pearl*, critics of the poem have actually become impatient with the dreamer, calling him boorish, insensitive, cruel, or at least obtuse. This long-standing view of Chaucer's character "Geffrey"—a perfectly accurate character description—is the mark of Chaucer's success in normalizing the lyric experience of the *Book of the Duchess*, for it shows that readers feel perfectly competent to judge the actions and reactions of the dreamer in what is, remember, *his* dream.

This second phase typically ends with the conclusion of the dream report (if not of the poem), at which a third and final stage is reached. The end of the dream vision always includes a reminder—sometimes explicit, sometimes tacit—that this was, after all and all expectations to the contrary, this one fellow's dream. The poems frequently employ a "reawakening device" which serves nicely to remind readers that the narrative (or seeming narrative) they have read is and has always been a dream. The best known such device is to be found at the conclusion of the *Book of the Duchess*:

> Ryght thus me mette, as I yow telle,
> That in the castell ther was a belle,
> As hyt hadde smyten houres twelve.—
> Therwyth I awook myselve
> And fond me lyinge in my bed; . . .
>
> (lines 1321–25)

The bell reminds the reader quite neatly that both of the dreamer figures—the dreamer-character who hears the bell and the dreamer-narrator who awakens, "Ryght thus me mette," to nocturnal "houres twelve"—are the same person, at least in some important ways. They are both clearly the same Geffrey who suffers the eight years' sickness, both the same disappointed courtly lover. The device, and thus the third stage, reassert the identity of the two dreamer-figures and with it the identity of story and plot. In effect, the third stage restores the integrity of the dream vision: it is not

127

and never was a narrative with an eyewitness, but from first to last it has been a lyric experience.

A similar device concludes *Pearl*'s dream report:

> I þo3t þat noþyng my3t me dere
> To fech me bur and take me halte,
> And to start in þe strem schulde non me stere,
> To swymme þe remnaunt, þa3 I þer swalte.
>
> (lines 1157–60)

He jumps into the river, begins to swim, and, it seems, the very futile exertion of the attempt awakens him:

> For, ry3t as I sparred vnto þe bonc,
> þat brath þe out of my drem me brayde.
> þen wakned I in þat erber wlonk;
> My hede vpon þat hylle wat3 layde
> þer as my perle to grounde strayd.
> I raxled, and fel in gret affray,
> And, sykyng, to myself I sayd,
> 'Now al be to þat Prynce3 paye'.
>
> (line 1169–76)

The physical exertion of the dreamer-character in trying to cross the river—tossing and turning, as it were—awakens him and discovers him to be the same man with the same enigmatic longing, though now less enigmatic, now identifiable with the orthodox Christian's longing for communion with the "Prince." At the same time, readers are made to see that the dreamer-character's futile exertion is analogous to their own futile attempts to put Heaven in earthbound terms, an intellectual thrashing about in a foreign medium that is equally exhausting and equally doomed to fail.

The conclusion of the dream vision (the third phase) thus marks the reunion of the dreamer-character and the dreamer-narrator and with this reunion the reassertion of the lyric mode in place of the symbolic pseudonarrative which the readers have been following: the conclusion of the poem shows that the experience is and always was located in the mind of a dreamer whose secret longing, distress, or distraction has caused his dream. In other words, story and plot have once more come together as well, since, at the conclusion of the dream report, the story (the seeming narrative of events in the dream report) has been exposed as no "sequence of [external and reported] events" at all but a sequence of internal psychic events—the plot, in Shklovsky's terminology—which took place only in the mind of the dreamer.

This structure may be represented graphically thus:

Stage	Mode	Events in the Text	Reader Role	Formalist Description
1. prologue	lyric	introduction of the dream as a symptom of distress	simple lyric perception: diagnosis	story=plot
2. early in the dream report	narrative	the dreamer-character makes a mistake; imagery becomes self-evident to the readers	illusory narrative perception or pseudonarrative; "narrative normalization"	story diverges from plot
3. end of the dream report (or epilogue)	lyric	reassertion of the dream report as a symptom	complex lyric perception; communion with the dreamer	true or redefined story=plot

This table suggests the typical movement of the dream vision, one definable within fairly traditional bounds. The principal movement is one from an initial lyric perception at the beginning of the poem where the dream is introduced as an *insomnium*, through a second, finally illusory stage in which the dream report takes on the features of a narrative free from any special relationship with the psyche of the dreamer, to a final reassertion of the lyric identity of the whole experience. In effect, this movement is a strategy of misdirection: a lyric experience masquerades for a time as a narrative one only to reveal at its conclusion that it is not and never was a narrative in any traditional sense. Allegory often behaves this way, but seldom does allegory retreat at its conclusion from the tacit admission or intuitive truth that it represents a universal experience. The dream vision, in its conventional epilogue-reminder that it is a dream, always effects this retreat, always therefore undercutting and devaluing its body. The reasons for this three-part movement, this attempt to mask and then to reassert the lyric integrity of the poem, can now be considered.

The Poem and the Readers

We have been able to describe, in the terms of traditional literary criticism, "what happens in a dream vision": put simply, the poems' essentially lyric identity becomes submerged in what seems to be a typical figurative or allegorical narrative. The dream reports are usually long and paratactic enough to allow and even encourage readers to forget that the poems are the reports of dreams, or, more accurately, to encourage readers to try to make sense of the narrative of "events" independent of the dream nature of those events. The illusion of eyewitness narrative is lifted at and by the poems' conclusion, as the readers are reminded—either explicitly or tacitly—that the dream images are and always have been the interior imaginative events of the still-troubled dreamer.

But this is not all and, in fairness, there are those who would claim that this sort of formal description is nothing at all, is itself illusory. Proponents of affective stylistics, for example, can claim that there is no "in a text" because there is no text, because, finally, a text is nothing other than a reader's experience of it. We have seen that there existed a medieval version of this position, found chiefly in Augustine's *De Doctrina Christiana*, and that this "affective" rhetorical stance is at the heart of the appeal of the dream vision. A glance at Augustine shows that this theory differs from modern ones only in Augustine's avowal of a level of communication or communion anterior to human language, a meaning to be sought with the heart, not expressed in words.

This notion of a text somehow communicating at a level beneath its graphic words is strengthened by the impact of nominalism and its effect on medieval ideas of abstraction. While Ockham was no existentialist or agnostic, his critique of the Platonic notion of extramental universals does represent a movement away from the text as naively didactic—of books as analogues to the Book of the World. The movement is towards a text that is interactive and experiential: the *ficta* or *figmenta* of the brain record or show the character of the maker, even more credibly than these images represent their phenomenal originals. To use an example which Ockham might have considered, when we read five or six *Commentaries* on the *Sentences* of Peter Lombard—a required exercise for masters of philosophy at Oxford in Ockham's day—do we learn more about Peter Lombard or more about the five or six commentators? The answer is the paradox of pluralism: in reading one or two such commentaries, we see most clearly the characters of the writers, and can trust our sense of the makers' signatures more than we can trust their individual sense of the *Sentences*. Afer several commentaries, however, we can begin to see what the diverse individual minds of the various commentators perceived together and can begin to make judgments when the commentators differed—in short, we can begin to learn something of Peter Lombard. Thus, to read is to experience both subject and object, to see both the maker and, through the maker's eyes (and *nomines*), the object of the discourse. Writing can only be trusted as this complex of representations.

The dream vision can be called "affective" in this broad, Augustinian-nominalist sense. The form operates as a giant trope or scheme which initially taunts readers by its artifice and irrelevance to their experience—for what, after all, could be less relevant than another person's *insomnium*? Properly "alienated" from sympathy with the experience, readers discover in the dream report that the images and events it records are *not* quite so alien (foregrounding of iconography) and that the perspective of the pseudo-eyewitness is not always correct in its interpretation or construction of the events (splitting of the dreamer). Finally, at the conclusion of the poem, readers are reminded that this is a dream and thereby that they are in a peculiar communion with the dreamer insofar as they share that person's *insomnium*, share that person's *ficta* or *figmenta*.

The best example of initial, radically lyric alienation in the dream vision is the infamous crux at the beginning of the *Book of the Duchess*:

> But men myght axe me why soo
> I may not sleepe, and what me is.
> But natheles, who aske this
> Leseth his asking trewely.
> Myselven can not telle why
> The sothe; but trewly, as I gesse,
> I holde hit be a sicknesse
> That I have suffred this eight yeer,
> And yet me boote is never the ner;
> For there is phisicien but oon
> That may me hele; but that is don.
> Passe we over untill eft;
> That wil not be mot nede be left; . . .

(lines 30–42)

Arguments on the passage's courtly reticence notwithstanding, the inarguable effect of this passage on the reader is one of total and unequivocal alienation. Men might ask "what me is" and, in a private lyric designed to illuminate this very point, the question would be entirely proper, but its answer here is not forthcoming. Instead of an explanation, the reader is given a teasing reference to a mysterious "phisicien," the identity of whom could be the now-absent Blanche, Jesus Christ, the comfort of death which comes when it will, or perhaps Joan of Kent or some other lady to whom young Geoffrey Chaucer paid the respects of the courtly lover.

But enough, Chaucer says: "That wil not be mot nede be left." By these lines, the reader is decisively shut off from the experience that forms the basis of the dream that follows. *Pearl*'s "huyl," Long Will's disguise, and even the blather of lore that begins the *Hous of Fame* achieve the same effect. Alienated from the persona of the poem and able to look forward to nothing other than this mysterious figure's day residue dream, the reader is forced effectively into a "diagnostic" relationship with the text; knowing Macrobius and the rest, this reader may only hope to be able to uncover the dreamer's distress by examining the imagery and structure of the dream, thereby affirming the lyric expressiveness of the artifact. By reading the dream as a symptom, the reader can hope to discover the lyric thrust of the poem and see the dream as an objective or somatic correlative of the dreamer's unnamed and unshared distress.

This alienated diagnostic kind of reading, a "simple lyric perception" of the text as the expression of a powerful authorial emotion, continues as long as the dream report remains solely the proprietary creature of the dreamer. The tacit reduplication of the dreamer into two figures, the dreamer-narrator and the dreamer-character, does nothing to eliminate or reduce the alienation of the reader as long as these two dreamer-figures, between them, seem to be invested with reportial and interpretive omniscience, that is, as long as story does not diverge from plot. If the poems were to continue in this mode, they would be little more than weird, random collections of images that, at best, might satisfy only this diagnostic urge in readers, little medieval detective stories with the glandular appeal of, say, Browning's "Porphyria's Lover." They would be experiences like Pertelote's of Chaunticleer's dream in the *Nun's Priest's Tale*, empty somatic experiences referable only to the pathology of the dreamer.

But the medieval dream vision does not typically end this way— no more than does the *Nun's Priest's Tale* end with Pertelote's sense of Chaunticleer's dream. The splitting of the dreamer and the foregrounding of imagery or inconography, in the service of "narrative normalization," crucially though subtly change the reader's experience of the dream report. Considering the effect of the first change, when the dreamer-character makes a mistake or otherwise is shown to be differentiable from the dreamer-narrator, the reader's perception of the text changes from that of the pre-emptive lyric experience of the dreamer to one in which the reader's palpable representative in the text (the dreamer-character as erstwhile eyewitness) is capable of error. This demoting of the dreamer-character from pseudo-narrator to fallible "hero" does not require a blatant or critical error such as that of Amant; a subtle, barely perceptible naiveté or failure of insight such as displayed by Long Will or Geffrey in the *Hous of Fame* is sufficient to split the dreamer-character off from the narrator and to establish the former as normative narrative protagonist of the dream report. This splitting of the dreamer into one who writes the poem and another who lives in the dream world serves to complicate the initial lyric expectations. The change makes it clear that the poem is other than the report of a personal internal experience of a single integral consciousness: Geffrey in the *House of Fame* seems shaken by the discrepancy of Vergilian and Ovidian views of Dido; the *Pearl*-narrator seems surprised that he cannot cross the river of mortality and visit the Pearl maiden; another Geffrey wonders what the Black Knight is doing in *his* love vision. Such events in dream narratives seduce their readers away from diagnostic reticence and deference to the controlling consciousness of the dream-experience and awaken a confidence in their own ability to understand the dream for themselves. In formalist terms, this phenomenon is the divergence of story from plot, of the narrative of events (presumably objective, like the chronology of Tristram Shandy's life) from plot, the authorial imprint on the narrative (highly subjective, like Tristram's digressive rehearsal of his life story). In the dream vision as in *Tristram Shandy*, this divergence effectively releases the reader to examine and investigate the narrative, to separate it (it would seem) from the obtrusive shape given it by the narrator and to discover, for example, that Tristram was illegitimate or that this Black Knight is John of Gaunt or that the Pearl maiden's enigmatic statements about the Heavenly hierarchy mean this or that.

Simultaneous with this splitting is the foregrounding of imagery or iconography. This feature, the introduction of scenes or images or exchanges which are either conventional or are naively interpretable without reference to the somatic framework, completes the process of narrative normalization. No longer able to rely on the dreamer-character's internal commentary to interpret the text, the reader suddenly discovers that this lost crutch is no longer necessary and begins to recognize, even in the unlikely venue of another person's *insomnium*, images and scenes which make sense and ultimately begin to describe or suggest a theme. Estates satire, conventional hints of raptures into Heaven, or even the recognizable figure of the melancholy John of Gaunt begin to appear, making this *insomnium* the impossible relevant dream, something more, perhaps, than the anxious somatic experience of a distressed individual. As the dream report continues in this normalized narrative mode, the readers become increasingly confident in their own interpretive abilities and even begin to feel superior to the dreamer-character as analysts of the poem, an urge to competition easily found in the criticism of the *Book of the Duchess* or *Pearl*, for example. This is not a dream but a poem, the reader feels; an understandable poem, a poem about universal or at least communal problems or emotions or concerns. Elizabeth Kirk makes the point nicely:

> The self-contained dream-world, that artifact accessible and intelligible only in terms of the greater reality beyond on which it is dependent, has turned out to be "real life"; it is human society in all its concreteness, human existence susceptible of the pattern and significance characteristic of art or of religious and philosophical systems but with the pattern suspended until we have been immersed in the reality.[12]

The salvation of baptized infants, the sorrow of England over the death of the Duchess Blanche, the inequities of a society polluted by Lady Meed—the more central such issues become in the dream report, the less relevant the dream frame seems to become and the more universal or apocalyptic becomes the status of the text. This is no mere *insomnium*, those few might say who even consciously remember that it was so introduced.

But it is an *insomnium*, always was and always will be, and the reawakening of the dreamer, that same fallible, mysterious fellow, demonstrates this and thus explodes the illusion of narrative. Of course the dreamer-character is not an eyewitness; of course this figure is a character in the "story," but the other "I" of the dream report, the other consciousness that has lurked in the background all this while—the dreamer-narrator—*is* a witness, a privileged interpreter, and the ultimate lyric subject-object of the poem. This inescapable fact, obscured from readers since the opening frame, returns

135

to the foreground at the end of the poem and demands a giant adjustment, a major rethinking of the significance of the experience of the dream report.

This rethinking is usually not painless. The reappearance of the dreamer-narrator at the conclusion of the dream vision reasserts more than the fundamental lyric nature of the whole poem, for this figure appears *ipso facto unchanged by his experience.* He could not be changed, of course, because—lyric mode—he has written this poem after the fact: he is the "reawakened dreamer" in the prologue, after all. The fact that we tend to forget this, forget that the Geffrey who bemoans the chaotic state of oneiromantic learning or the Geffrey who suffers an "eight years' sickness" is the same Geffrey throughout the poem, is a testament to the power of the form's narrative normalization. The experience should change the dreamer, we think: what experience? which dreamer?

This perception is true even for poems like *Pearl,* the prologue of which describes the state of mind of the dreamer before his dream. The conclusion of *Pearl* (or of *Piers Plowman* or of the *Bouge of Court* or of the *Legend of Good Women*) does not show readers a rehabilitated dreamer but only one whose problem or distress has been *redefined* by the experience of the dream.[13] Specifically, the *Pearl*-narrator is still longing for his "perle," though this image seems now to refer to his own place in Heaven and not to the earthly "Pearl maiden" which he has "lost"; the *Book of the Duchess*-narrator still has, we assume, his eight years' sickness, though now it is put into a larger perspective and compared with more realistic sorrows and losses; Long Will is still an outcast in society, though now, perhaps, he begins to understand that alienation is the only possible relationship a right-minded person can have to a society that is itself so distant from the City of God.

So the reappearance of the dreamer-narrator does not suggest that his dream has been recuperative of anything more than his perception, his perspective. The real import of this re-emergence, this reassertion of the lyric mode, is for the community of readers, who are suddenly required to accept the impossible contradiction: they have been seduced into experiencing another man's *insom-*

nium, and the experience has changed from an odd diagnostic and alienated one at its inception to one which they have understood, comprehended, or "embraced," as Augustine would have said. In short, the readers have discovered themselves enrolled in the experience, and this enrollment, this communion, entails enrollment in the "dreamer's distress" as well: in order to have embraced the *insomnium,* the readers must necessarily have shared—unwittingly at first—in the emotional knot, the distraction, the perturbation that produced the dream experience. In one sense, the dream vision is nothing more than the impossible *insomnium* that truly speaks to human needs and concerns; in a more important sense, it is the medieval poet's special vehicle for generating a recognition of communion in the truth.[14] The dream vision is the wonderful, impossible *insomnium* of all those who feel, of all those who speak the special language, all those who dream the dream, creatures who may have failed to comprehend but who have run together the *cuniculus figurarum* and have completed a journey as humble as a meaningless dream in the reading but as sublime as their common human spirit in the embrace.

A second chart might summarize:

Stage	Mode	Events in the Text	Reader Role	Formalist Description	Literary Context	Scientific Context	Reader Relationship
1. prologue	lyric	introduction of the dream as a symptom of distress	simple lyric perception: diagnosis	story=plot	dream as narrative event	*insomnium*	alienation from the dreamer
2. early in the dream report	narrative	the dreamer-character makes a mistake; imagery becomes self-evident to the readers	illusory narrative perception or pseudonarrative; "narrative normalization"	story diverges from plot	apocalypse	*somnium*	comprehension of the dream report
3. end of the dream report (or epilogue)	lyric	reassertion of the dream report as a symptom	complex lyric perception; communion with the dreamer	true or redefined story=plot	anomalous final literary context	anomalous final scientific context	special identification with the dreamer

CHAPTER FIVE

APPLICATIONS: THREE DECONSTRUCTIVE DREAM VISIONS

oes form prescribe content? Does the shape of a poem or argument determine or even affect the theme or point or concept being presented or argued? Do novels, lyrics, epics, and other literary forms tend towards certain themes to the exclusion of others? Or are form and content completely separate, the former simply the vehicle by which the latter is expressed? Specifically, does the peculiarly interpersonal strategy of the dream vision, which devalues the discursive component of its dream report for the purpose of establishing a special sort of psychic communion between reader and dreamer, necessarily cause the poetic form to gravitate toward certain themes and away from others?

The answer to this is a qualified yes, at least for the dream vision. Medieval dream visions tend to be about the same things and consider the same topics, provided we maintain a loose, relatively abstract sense of words like "theme" and "topic." Poems as different in their announced subjects as the *Roman de la Rose*, the *Dream of the Rood*, the *Hous of Fame*, the *Book of the Duchess*, and *Pearl* all treat, in the last analysis, questions of epistemology, of perspective, of ways of knowing, and of the relationship between words and the truth these words seek to express. Deferring the *Book of the Duchess*, *Pearl*, and the *Hous of Fame* for later in this chapter, consider for a moment the other poems in this list and note their common interest in knowing, in language, and in the verities language attempts to express. The *Roman de la Rose*, especially as conceived by

Jean de Meun, is a thoroughly epistemological poem whose ultimate concern is with the cosmic implications of human life, a satire on learning that slowly chips away at the medieval edifice of lore. The poem concludes, in the address of Genius, that the fundamental and natural generative urges, which seemed so foolish when all that was at stake was Amant and his rose, are the basis of human existence, are truer and more real than all the contingent verbiage that surrounds them. The graven message on the Well of Narcissus, taken at face value without any attempt to twist or gloss or determine it, is the final message graven on the reader at the conclusion of the *Roman*: "here starf the faire Narcisus."

The *Dream of the Rood* is more obviously an exercise in perspective. The narrator of this dream vision, a person "stained with sins, wounded with stains," encounters the Rood, a physical object that, historically, is more reprehensible than he but which has been transformed by the Redemptive Act into an object of veneration, a golden, jewel-bedecked "beacen" or sign of hope. The encounter, it seems, teaches the dreamer that, although he is morally flawed and unworthy, God's redemption operates on an unearthly and irrational level, transforming these very flaws into signs of divine love and forgiveness. *Piers Plowman* shows a remarkably similar movement, presenting in the *Visio* what seems to be the villainous figure of Lady Meed, expelling her, and finally discovering that, without her, humanity is denied access to the holy "meed" of salvation. The words of the pardon that appears in the climactic scene of the *Visio* constitute the chief impediment to an understanding of meed *in bono* and, in a strangely liberating act, Piers tears up the pardon and frees the folk from the limitations inherent in human formulations of divine verities.[1]

This similarity of theme in dream visions is not accidental but inherent, a function of the poems' common form. We have seen that the dream vision as a rhetorical nexus was born of late medieval scepticism, a scepticism that questioned dream lore, the relationship between truth and its semantic representations, and ultimately the ancient and pervasive Platonic dualism of the Scholastic period. It is only logical and reasonable to assume that the same philosophical impulses that quickened the form might also find their way into the poems as contents.

These impulses did find their way into the poems. The three dream visions discussed in the next few pages all share a profound distrust of language and its ability to represent phenomenal reality (to say nothing of the other world), and an equal distrust of the knowability of that reality. In positing and then denying the possibility of supernal knowledge, the *Book of the Duchess*, *Pearl*, and the *Hous of Fame* each offer for purposes of examination a "discourse," test out the discourse in a dream setting, then finally awaken their readers to critique the possibility of using words to access the realities that have lain behind them. The *Book of the Duchess* is a creative exercise in the "discourse of sentiment," which discovers that the relationship between emotions and their verbal expressions is artificial, ambivalent, and contingent; *Pearl*'s dialogue subsumes its many topics into a grand demonstration of the "discourse of eschatology," showing at its conclusion that (if nothing else) the realm of Heaven is beyond representation in earthbound terms; the *Hous of Fame*, in its Proem and three books, considers the discourses of science, history, rhetoric, and philosophy and shows that all are finally equally contingent, equally functions of humankind and of the here and now.

It is in this spirit that I call the discussion that follows "deconstructive." While deconstruction as a clearly recognizable antirhetoric is a product of eighteenth and nineteenth century thinking, deconstruction as a basic social impulse has existed and must exist in every culture insofar as and as soon as that culture is articulated. Far from being a tool of literary criticism, another new way to get at a text, deconstruction is the necessary obverse of any culture-as-system, the ubiquitous urge to untangle, untie, unravel, and demythologize any intellectual system that comes to be replaced by its semantic formulations, any system whose primitive communal sense becomes—literally—"lost in transmission." Thus, we should not be surprised to find deconstruction in places other than in Derrida or Rousseau or Nietzsche or Levi-Strauss; it ought positively to be expected in the fourteenth century, in the obsolescence of old ways of knowing but before the bright reasonableness of new ones. Thus, if our sense of content is broad enough to include such notions as "thrust," "purpose," "movement," or, perhaps best, "program," then the dream vision, born in the gaps of medieval taxonomies and realized in a rhetoric that is based on the contingent and even illusory relationship of words and things, does prescribe its content. This can happen because (to risk circularity) the content prescribed is, finally, that contents *are* functions of form: dream visions are about the obstructive nature of language and its troublous relationship to the world. Thus, what we might otherwise be tempted to call the topics of the poems—Blanche's death, the loss of the "perle," the search for tidings—become in this case constitutive vehicles analogous to words and sentences. Just as Augustine's discussion of hyssop or Marcrobius' of the stars show that they are not really talking about either plants or stars—even as symbols—but instead are presenting a discourse to celebrate the communion of souls predisposed to communion, the dream vision uses its literal contents as morphemes in the expression of its higher "content" or "program." In other words, the dream vision is about *aboutness*; it explores the problematics of reference; it begins as an *insomnium*, an experience by definition lyrical rather than discursive, then masquerades for a time as discourse, and then finally undercuts this discourse while affirming the emotions or dispositions or perceptions that generated it. It is an *insomnium*-revelation, a somatic event that reveals, first, that personal or somatic experiences are the only true experiences, and second, that the emotional or spiritual ground of these experiences, when felt and shared, is the only true, holy, and worthy response to the ritual drama of human life.

The *Book of the Duchess* and the Discourse of Sentiment

The subject of the *Book of the Duchess* is, to use Chaucer's own carefully chosen word, "routhe." It is not in any traditional sense an *elegy* on the lately deceased wife of John of Gaunt, Blanche of Lancaster, although her passing and the feelings of those left behind are surely its occasion. Instead of being an explicit memorial, the poem is a meditation on the problems of the language of sentiment on such occasions, a subtle examination of one of the crucial spheres in which language fails to represent the motives and the will behind its articulation.[2] Thus, the *Book of the Duchess* is a deconstructive poem the program of which is to show language at work, to show it failing to meet the investigative, expressive, or rhetorical intentions for which it was invoked, and, finally, to show that its very failure affirms the commonality of intention that underlies it, affirms a community of individuals who together hold beliefs or values inexpressible in words.

It is this final plank in the program, the dream vision's tacit and indirect assertion that there exists a feeling or belief in the poet and in the right readers of the poem of which the artifact is a failed expression, that technically disqualifies the dream vision as truly or thoroughly deconstructive, but the defect is not a serious one. This unspoken thematic core—"routhe" in the *Book of the Duchess*, "faith" in *Pearl* and in the *Hous of Fame*—is more a movement of the soul than a topic or a content. In keeping with a deconstructive program or movement, this thematic core is enacted rather than referenced: only one of the *Book of the Duchess'* 1333 lines is "thematic" in even this broad sense. Line 1309, "Is that youre los? By God, hyt ys routhe!" enacts the inadequacy of all that has gone before it: it asks a simple question about reality—a rhetorical question representing Geffrey's[3] sudden intuition of the Black Knight's sorrow—and then responds with a simple, unadorned assertion of the will to sympathy. The line is not elaborate: its only figure, the oath "By God," invokes the Deity as witness to Geffrey's sincerity in a discourse from which all rhetorical or ornamental artifice has been stripped. All of the other lines of the poem (too numerous to quote) prepare the reader for this shattering moment by methodically deconstructing the discourse of sentiment, leaving Geffrey and the readers with a failed artifact, a *cuniculus figurarum* whose failure and foolishness—and whose success—are perceptible only at its terminus.

The term "discourse of sentiment" deserves some brief elaboration before I continue. By "discourse of sentiment" I mean language produced to express emotion *and* to betoken sympathy, two intentions which are closely related but surely very different. As anyone knows who has written a letter to a friend who has lost a parent or child or spouse (for example), the *expression* of grief or sympathy is very easy and made even easier by the many universal clichés and conventional phrases guaranteed to send the appropriate signals. Paradoxically, it is this very ease of expression that makes it proportionally difficult to broadcast or betoken sincere sympathy in the expression. To turn to another sentiment for a moment, the availability of mass-produced Christmas cards—with preprinted signatures—devalues them as successful tokens of good wishes for the holidays. In the discourse of sentiment, it is almost worse to be a poet, a word crafter, one whose tools and currency are self-conscious and artifical expression and, worse yet, to be a medieval poet, one whose words and phrases nearly never ring with the simple expression of sincere feelings. In the age of Froissart and Machaut and Guillaume de Lorris and Petrarch, how does a poet both express emotion and betoken sympathy? In an age where the greatest poetry consists of passionate love protestations to women often unknown to the poets, full of artifical and grotesquely inflated *expressions* of sentiment, how does Chaucer write a poem to his patron and friend John of Gaunt on the occasion of Blanche's death?

This is Chaucer's challenge in the *Book of the Duchess*. Faced with this impossible task, Chaucer hit upon a novel and daring strategy: to write not an expression of sympathy but a demonstration of the hopelessness of such an expression, a poem that enacts the hollowness of language and its inextricable entanglement in paradoxes of expression, intention, effect, and entailment.[4] Taken as such a demonstration, the *Book of the Duchess* exposes the discourse of sentiment—all of it, the Black Knight's as well as Geffey's—for all its foolishness and inefficacy: all that survives the *Book of the Duchess'* indictment of the discourse of sentiment is, captured in the gruff, old-fashioned "My God, hyt ys routhe,"[5] the will to express emotions forever imprisoned in inadequate language. To reach this still, tense moment of recognition, Chaucer the journeyman poet constructs a subtle structure which, in holding religiously to the conventions of contemporary French poetry, undermines those conventions.

This feature, the conscious imitation of a set of conventions to expose those conventions and their shallowness, is one which Chaucer will exploit for comic and other purposes later in his career in *Sir Thopas* and in other of the *Canterbury Tales*—the tales of the Clerk, the Pardoner, and the Prioress come to mind—but here Chaucer's exploitation of conventional language and form reflects his sense of the operation of the dream vision, with its fabulous, labyrinthine, and finally pointless surface which nonetheless leads to an ultimate revelation of an identity between dreamer and reader. The *Book of the Duchess* illustrates nearly all of the structural and affective features of the form: the modal movement from lyric to narrative and back to lyric; the failed attempt to identify the dreamer by his distress; the splitting of the dreamer into a fallible character and a mysterious narrator; narrative normalization; and finally the reunification of the dreamer figures and the identification of the dreamer and readers in their common sympathy for John of Gaunt.

This procedure must therefore begin with the introduction of a dreamer-narrator, one with a problem, setting up the poem's radical lyric expectations:

> I have gret wonder, be this lyght,
> How that I lyve, for day ne nyght
> I may nat slepe, wel nygh noght;
> I have so many an ydel thoght,
> Purely for defaute of slep,
> That, by my trouthe, I take no kep
> Of nothing, how hyt cometh or gooth,
> Ne me nys nothyng leef nor looth.
> Al is ylyche good to me—
> Joye or sorowe, wherso hyt be—
> For I have felynge in nothyng,
> But, as yt were, a mased thyng,
> Alway in poynt to falle a-doun;

> For sorwful ymagynacioun
> Ys alway hooly in my mynde.
>
> (lines 1–15)

Chaucerians have long recognized the conventionality of this opening, especially its near-translation of Froissart's *Le Paradys d'Amour*. In his contribution to *Chaucer and Chaucerians*, D.S. Brewer reproduces the two texts side by side, italicizing examples of what he sees as Chaucer's "Englishness"; for similar purposes but different conclusions, compare the lines above with Froissart:

> Je sui de moi en grant merveille
> Comment je vifs quant tant je veille
> Et on ne point en veillant
> Trouver de moi plus traveillant,
> Car bien sacies que par veillier
> Me viennent souvent travillier
> Pensees et merancolies
> Qui me sont ens au coer liies
> Et pas ne les puis deslyer,
> Car ne voeil la belle oublyer
> Pour quele amour en ce travail
> Je sui entres et tant je veil.

> I am in great wonder about myself,
> how I yet live, I've been awake so long.
> One couldn't find anyone more belabored
> than I in my long sleeplessness.
> Know well that thoughts and sadnesses
> often come to torture me;
> they are bound inside my heart.
> I cannot loose them
> because I do not wish to forget that beauty.
> For such a love, I am in this travail
> and stay awake so long.[6]

Brewer's point in comparing the two passages is to emphasize Chaucer's stylistic departure from his French original, the fact that he adds distinctly English, conversational, or idiomatic "doublets and alternatives, asseverations that are mild oathes, expletives and parentheses."[7] Brewer is certainly correct in seeing these features as adding an English flavor to the poem—"routhe" in line 1309 comes to mind again—but what is the final rhetorical effect of these changes, the impact on the artifact of replacing the highly stylized French courtly idiom with something more closely resembling the idiom of everyday speech? Far from heightening the drama of the passage, the addition of phrases like "wel nygh noght," "by my trouthe," and "leef nor looth" tends to devalue the passage as an expression of sentiment by rendering it less taut, less hushed, less "pained." Without making a value judgment here (for emotional "realism" is rarely a virtue in this tradition), I believe we can say that Froissart sounds more *realistically languishing* than Chaucer does. In fact, this opening, like the unfinished *Sir Thopas*, is an example of Chaucer's adoption of a persona who knows and can imitate a set of conventions but who cannot quite reproduce them to the desired effect. To put it another way, Geffrey can use the discourse of sentiment for expressive purposes but cannot use it to betoken sincere sympathy. The addition of the conversational phrases, far from giving the passage color and character, mottle and flaw it as a conventional and therefore legitimate expression of shared emotion.[8]

This notion, by no means a new one, valorizes a long-standing negative judgment on the opening of the *Book of the Duchess*. The sleeplessness, the famous eight years' sickness, and the sentimentalized redaction of the story of Ceys and Alcion are all evidence for the belief that this is a totally conventional love allegory which includes all of the necessary details and makes all the right moves (though making them very flatfootedly). Geffrey's point in recalling the Ceys and Alcion story, it seems, is the magnitude and poignance of Alcion's grief and uncertainty, along with the boon granted her by the gods: he seems to miss the fact that the story ends rather unhappily.[9] After telling her that he is dead, Ceys' ghost counsels her to be of good cheer:

> "And farewel, swete, my worldes blysse!
> I praye God youre sorwe lysse.

> To lytel while oure blysse lasteth!"
> With that hir eyen up she casteth
> And saw noght. "Allas!" quod she for sorwe,
> And deyede within the thridde morwe.
> But what she sayede more in that swow
> I may not telle yow as now;
> Hyt were to longe for to dwelle.
> My first matere I wil yow telle, . . .
>
> (lines 209–18)

This "first matere," of course, is the favor granted to Alcion by the gods, the dream-visitation by her husband's spirit (or rather by Morpheus clothed in Ceys' "dreynt" body). Like a Browning persona, Geffrey skates blithely over the pathetic story of the queen's death to get to more important business, ignoring life and death in his obsession with his "sicknesse." This is the same Geffrey, we shall see, who can hear the Knight's lament in a few lines and simply not attend to the fact that the fellow is mourning a death. Alcion's death is, for Geffrey, not the crucial part of the story: what is important is that Morpheus granted her a resolution of her distress through sleep and dream and, impressed though dubious, Geffrey prays for a similar visitation though he "knew never god but oon" (237).[10]

Geffrey's prayer to Morpheus (or to "som wight elles, I ne roghte who" [244]) is one of the funniest passages in the poem. The gross, mercantile description of the bribe of the featherbed and the obvious, clanking progress of the prayer is, more than any other passage in the poem, the broad comedy of *Sir Thopas*.[11] Like that tale, the parody is funny in being both excessive *and* accurate, holding true to the prescribed conventions but botching their execution through tastelessness and excess:

> I wil yive hym a fether-bed,
> Rayed with gold, and ryght wel cled
> In fyn blak satyn doutremer,
> And many a pilowe, and every ber
> Of cloth of Reynes, to slepe softe;
> Hym thar not nede to turnen ofte.
>
> (lines 251–56)

Though there is precedent for such a gift—that of Machaut's *La Fontaine Amoureuse*—Geffrey's bourgeois advertisement seems silly next to the exotic bed of gyrfalcon feathers that Machaut offers. The additions here to the offer, specifically Geffrey's assurances of the high quality of the materials and his prediction that Morpheus will sleep surpassingly well, cross the line into parody. The thrust of such an opening is, clearly, to create radical lyric expectations in the reader. It is patently, even embarrassingly obvious from even the first twenty lines of the *Book of the Duchess* what sort of poem it is to be: the broad comic parody announces itself to be a poem after the French school and invites—rather desperately—the reader to see its dream as the conventional lover's *insomnium* described disparagingly by Macrobius, an *insomnium* that will take, perhaps, the form of a love *debat* (after Machaut's two *Jugement* poems) in which two aggrieved lovers present their sorrows before a figure of authority who decides who suffers the most.[12]

The early stages of the dream report reinforce these perceptions of bankrupt conventionality. Early in the dream, the whelp appears and disappears, a gratuitous, sentimental image:

> I was go walked fro my tree,
> And as I wente, ther cam by mee
> A whelp, that fauned me as I stood,
> That hadde yfolowed, and koude no good.
> Hyt com and crepte to me as lowe
> Ryght as hyt hadde me yknowe,
> Helde doun hys hed and joyned hys eres,
> And leyde al smothe doun hys heres.
> I wolde have kaught hyt, and anoon
> Hyt fledde, and was fro me goon;
> And I hym folwed, and hyt forth wente
> Doun by a floury grene wente
> Ful thikke of gras, ful softe and swete.
>
> (lines 387–99)

While intended, I believe, to be seen as a clumsy transitional device, the whelp does serve nicely as an emblem of the generic identity of the poem to this point, an identity that must be held clearly in mind if the next few crucial lines—the encounter with the Black Knight—are to be understood correctly.[13] As I argued above, the whelp is pure and radical lyricism like the basting of the sleeves in the *Roman*; in the discourse of sentiment, the image is a qualified failure both as an expression of emotion (for, what does it mean?) and also a failure as a token of true and sincere feeling (in its artless conventionality). Nonetheless, the little dog succeeds in reinforcing the lyricism of the passage, as opposed to, say, its discursive possibilities: it is a clear signal that this is a love elegy, even a love *debat*, to the forum of which Geffrey is led by this pallid little descendent of the lion in Machuat's *Dit*. The consciously awkward, even bumbling exposition and expression to this point strain the readers' patience (as they do in *Sir Thopas*), as the readers surmise all too easily the tenor for which this dream vision is the vehicle.[14]

And sure enough, the doggy leads Geffrey to the Black Knight, the figure surely meant to be his interlocutor in the *debat*:

> But forth they romed ryght wonder faste
> Doun the woode; so at the laste
> I was war of a man in blak,
> That sat and had yturned his bak
> To an ook, an huge tree.
> "Lord," thoght I, "who may that be?
> What ayleth hym to sitten her?"
> Anoon-ryght I wente ner;
> Than found I sitte even upryght
> A wonder wel-farynge knyght—
> By the maner me thoghte so—
> Of good mochel, and ryght yong therto,
> Of the age of foure and twenty yer,
> Upon hys berd but lytel her,
> And he was clothed al in blak.
>
> (lines 443–57)

This moment is the first turning point in the *Book of the Duchess*, the beginning of "narrative normalization," the second stage of the dream vision structure. Beginning with the introduction of this central figure, the *mode* of the poem begins to change from the essentially lyric situation of the lover's *insomnium* to a narrative one in which events take place or images are introduced which the reader can interpret independent of the dream frame.

This stage is typically signalled by a mistake or misinterpretation on the part of the dreamer-character, and the *Book of the Duchess* is no exception to this rule. The mistake, of course, is Geffrey's failure to understand (hear?) that the loss which the Black Knight mourns is the death of his good Lady White, which he seems to make so abundantly clear:

> "I have of sorwe so gret won
> That joye gete I never non,
> Now that I see my lady bryght,
> Which I have loved with al my myght,
> Isfro me ded and ys agoon.
>   Allas, deth, what ayleth the,
> That thou noldest have taken me,
> Whan thou toke my lady swete,
> That was so fair, so fresh, so fre,
> So good, that men may wel se
> Of al goodnesse she had no mete!"
>   Whan he had mad thus his complaynte,
> Hys sorwful hert gan faste faynte,
> And his spirites wexen dede;
> The blood was fled for pure drede
> Doun to hys herte, to make hym warm—
> For wel hyt feled the herte had harm—
> To wite eke why hyt was adrad
> By kynde, and for to make hyt glad;
> For hit ys membre principal
> Of the body; and that made al
> Hys hewe chaunge and wexe grene
> And pale, for ther noo blood ys sene
> In no maner lym of hys.

(lines 475–99)

This is the key to the *Book of the Duchess*. Deferring for a time a discussion of the Black Knight's lament, consider the dreamer-character's outrageous reaction to the song. After hearing the complaint, Geffrey spends fully thirteen lines in an accurate but inane dissertation on the physiology of the swoon, detailing the descent of the blood into the heart and reflecting with unbelievable coldness on the Knight's green coloring and eventual unconsciousness. His reaction, to anticipate the argument a bit, is analogous to the readers' reaction to Geffrey's own languor: we recognize these symptoms, we know what is going on here—oh yes, this person is lovesick. For Geffrey, the Knight's lament is half-successful as discourse of sentiment. As far as Geffrey goes, the song is sincere without being expressive: Geffrey is clearly able to see that something is bothering the Black Knight but he can't figure out what that something is. This means that this song is exactly the opposite of Geffrey's prologue, which was expressive but not credibly sincere, conventional but not genuine.

Such thoughts begin to explain Geffrey's curious and obtuse response:

> "Me thynketh in grete sorowe I yow see.
> But certes, sire, yif that yee
> Wolde ought discure me youre woo,
> I wolde, as wys God helpe me soo,
> Amende hyt, yif I kan or may.
> Ye mowe preve hyt be assay;
> For, by my trouthe, to make yow hool,
> I wol do al my power hool.
> And telleth me of your sorwes smerte;
> Paraunter hyt may ese youre herte,
> That semeth ful sek under your syde."

(lines 547–57)

The critical literature abounds on this strange speech, with ingenious explanations why Geffrey does not understand or hear or react humanely to the Knight's wretched situation. It is possible, for example, that Geffrey is playing dumb here, only tipping his hand slightly at lines 545–47, which could look forward to the balance of the poem.[15] The perspective from which we are viewing the poem, however, offers only one sensible explanation for this crux. This is the pre-eminent moment of narrative normalization, at which the dreamer-character makes a mistake which is recognizable by readers in their newly won independence from the interpretive prerogative of the "eyewitness." Given Geffrey's clear predilection for the love *debat* to this point, he assumes that the Black Knight is simply the other principal in the contest of sorrows to follow and, as such, the very last thing that this mysterious figure would be doing while leaning mournfully against his tree is telling the exactly literal truth.[16] Geffrey's reaction to the story of Ceys and Alcion in the prologue has demonstrated that death to this dreamer is a sentimental, even bathetic experience, either a hyperbolic metaphor for a beloved's scorn or a boring and irrelevant detail in a love story. It seems perfectly natural, then, to assume that Geffrey would hear the Knight's lament and conclude that it is of the same courtly, figurative patois that he himself uses.

The readers, of course, know better. They have been wondering for five hundred lines or so what is to become of this odd, truant little poem, and now the answer becomes clear: this is not Geffrey's languishing love elegy, written in artificial homage to Joan of Kent or to whomever. It may still be a love *debat*: Machaut contrasted the sorrows of death and *"daunguere"* in the *Jugement du Roy de Behaigne* and, in the *Jugement du Roy de Navarre*, even concluded that a beloved's death is the greater sorrow.

So the appearance of John of Gaunt here reassures the reader that the *Book of the Duchess* is, if peculiar, perhaps not unprecedented. Perhaps Geffrey's mistake is not so much one about the content of the poem but rather one about the *point* of the poem, a mistaken view which the readers can now understand. Thus, Geffrey's request for plain talk after the Knight's complaint is based on the belief that the purpose of the dream is to compare two sorrows, two sentimental catastrophes, and the readers are now positioned to reject this view and to decide that the *Book of the Duchess* is a funereal elegy on Blanche of Lancaster, that Geffrey's *insomnium* is puff, and that this will be the emblematic story of the love of John and Blanche. For the record, remember that Geffrey is right and the readers are wrong (of which more later).

What is quite neatly set up in these lines is a clear-cut opposition between what seems to be the Black Knight's "real" sorrow and consequently righteous discourse of sentiment and Geffrey's artificial, ridiculous sorrow and faulty discourse. Forgetting the frame and the fact that this is, after all, Geffrey's dream, the reader embraces this opposition and so feels considerable pain as Geffrey says all the wrong things (such as, above, offering to make it all better). Unaware (as readers are not) that his questioning is painful to the Black Knight, the dreamer-character tries repeatedly to draw the figure out and learn the cause of his sorrow. The Knight for his part obliges, offering as explanation the famous metaphor of the chess game with Dame Fortune (perhaps drawn from the Zodiac) and the long, rather stylized rehearsal of his meeting and courtship with the lady. The Knight's discourse of sentiment, it seems, succeeds both expressively and affectively, for the readers both know and sympathize with the pain he suffers. Ignoring Geffrey's obtuseness—*we* are not obtuse—the poem has a completely new locus (the Black Knight) and, as Chaucerians are fond of remarking, he is a far better poet than Geffrey.

This last judgment, that the Black Knight's sorrow and discourse are inherently more worthy than Geffrey's, needs examination. In the spirit of many a naive reader of Chaucer who simply *can't see* that the Knight is a better poet, it needs to be said that he is not, or at least that he is not less mannered, artificial, and conventional than Geffrey. The Knight's heavily stylized imagery and diction may be better executed than Geffrey's, but they are not different in kind; for example:

"But swich a fairnesse of a nekke
Had that swete that boon nor brekke
Nas her non sene that myssat.
Hyt was whit, smothe, streght, and pure flat,
Wythouten hole; or canel-boon,
As be semynge, had she noon.
Hyr throte, as I have now memoyre,
Semed a round tour of yvorye,
Of good gretnesse, and noght to gret.

154

> "And goode faire White she het;
> That was my lady name ryght.
> She was bothe faire and bryght;
> She hadde not hir name wrong.
> Ryght faire shuldres and body long
> She had, and armes, every lyth
> Fattyssh, flesshy, not gret therwith;
> Ryght white handes, and nayles rede,
> Rounde brestes; and of good brede
> Hyr hippes were, a streight flat bak.
>
> (lines 939-57)

This is fine poetry, but it is every bit as conventional as Geffrey's; it *appears* more excellent, perhaps, because it lacks some of Geffrey's "Englishness" and because its topic is "real,"not artificial. Still, Blanche's exemplary bone structure and her arms, "fattyssh, flesshy, not gret therwith," could easily have come from the muse that offered the black satin bedclothes to Morpheus. Yet it is somehow heretical—and rightly so—to make this point, to compare the Black Knight's diction with Geffrey's, or at least to do so at this stage of the poem. The recognition of John of Gaunt and his "goode faire White" (948) and the comparison of her death with the eight years' sickness of Geffrey make such discriminations all but impossible at this point in the *Book of the Duchess*. An objective consideration of the Black Knight's discourse of sentiment literally cannot be made at this juncture, for any such judgment would be clouded by the readers' appreciation or apprehension of the good reasons for the Black Knight's grief. As I suggested above, the Black Knight's sorrow is "real" while Geffrey's is "only conventional," a pair of interpretations that will not be challenged until the conclusion of the *Book of the Duchess*.

The remainder of the poem is an excellent illustration of narrative normalization, the pseudo-narrative in which the dreamer-character is divested of any special interpretive prerogative and one in which readers feel competent and comfortable. It is, we remember, a virtual monologue on the part of the Black Knight, punctuated only occasionally by wrongheaded conclusions of the dreamer-character:

"But wherfore that y telle my tale?
Ryght on thys same, as I have seyd,
Was hooly al my love leyd;
For certes she was, that swete wif,
My suffisaunce, my lust, my lyf,
Myn hap, myn hele, and al my blesse,
My worldes welfare, and my goddesse,
And I hooly hires and everydel."
   "By oure Lord," quod I, "y trow yow wel!
Hardely, your love was wel beset;
I not how ye myghte have do bet."
"Bet? ne no wyght so wel," quod he.
"Y trowe hyt, sir," quod I, "parde!"
"Nay, leve hyt wel!" "Sire, so do I;
I leve yow wel, that trewely
Yow thoghte that she was the beste,
And to beholde the alderfayreste,
Whoso had loked hir with your eyen."
"With myn? nay, alle that hir seyen
Seyde and sworen hyt was soo.

(lines 1034–53)

Passages such as this are typically seen as examples of the pain to be felt in the *Book of the Duchess*, the pain inflicted on the suffering Knight by the obtuse Geffrey. The dreamer-character can seemingly say nothing right: in lines 1042–44, he agrees with the Knight, saying that he cannot imagine him doing "bet" than the Lady White, to which the Knight responds in anguish and distraction that, indeed, no man could hope to do so well. Next come a few lines of throat-clearing, after which (lines 1047–51) Geffrey attempts to initiate the *debat* format. He begins by courteously acknowledging that the Lady White was the "alderfayreste" to all who saw her through the Black Knight's eyes; to say more for Geffrey would be to admit that the Knight's lady was superior to his own. The Knight will have none of this, of course (lines 1052–53), and, refusing to play along, denies Geffrey any framework for comparing White to any other woman. Thus, Geffrey's "naive" attempt to impose the *debat* frame on the exchange intensifies the Black Knight's pain, while the

Knight's refusal to respond courteously to a brother-sufferer frustrates Geffrey.

Frustrates him, and worse. Affecting sympathy with the dreamer-character for a moment, we can easily see that, far from allowing room for Geffrey and his empty, conventional love languor, the Black Knight gives the poor fool no chance even to try and be sympathetic or companionable to him: he constantly and sharply corrects Geffrey's attempts to restate his ideas and gives him no credit for trying, according to his lights, to understand. Alongside fitful bursts of dialogue such as lines 1034–53, just quoted, we should consider the discourteous refrain of the poem:

> "Thow wost ful lytel what thow menest;
> I have lost more than thow wenest'—
> (lines 1305–06 and elsewhere)

The reader who has embraced the Black Knight's perspective on the poem must certainly agree with this judgment: the dreamer-character does not know what the Knight is talking about while the readers do. At the same time, however, from a longer perspective we should see the lines as a titillating and noncommunicative figure of speech, either aposiopesis, significatio, or innuendo, a locution to exactly the same effect as Geffrey's elliptical "physicien but oon That may me hele" (lines 39–40). Both statements, recalling my notion of the discourse of sentiment, fulfill the second requirement while failing utterly to address the first, for both statements betoken sentiment without expressing or specifying it; both statements assert that the speaker is suffering grievously while also asserting that the nature of that suffering is beyond the hearer's ken. The fact that the reader is generally unable to make comparisons such as this one between Geffrey and the Black Knight is testimony to the success of the dislocation of the reader and of the power of narrative normalization in the *Book of the Duchess*: at no point at which both characters are on stage does the text allow the reader sufficient distance to see that the Black Knight and Geffrey are comparable or that their comparison has any relevance or validity except to Geffrey, in his frustrated expectations of a love *debat.*

When the spell is broken at the end of the poem, the "Game is doon," as Geffrey says. When Geffrey finally gets the Black Knight to repeat explicitly the cause of his distress—that "she ys ded"—several perspectives shift suddenly and radically. In the stark and beautiful exchange of artless sympathy,

> "She ys ded!" "Nay!" "Yis, be my trouthe!"
> "Is that youre los? Be God, hyt ys routhe!"
>
> (lines 1309–10)

the reader is (or should be) challenged to rethink all earlier judgments about griefs and their expression in the poem.[17] In light of such a humble, human empathy, we are made to see that, while Geffrey's discourse of sentiment is expression without sympathy, the Black Knight's was (at least for Geffrey) a "betokening" without expression and, in fairness, rather perversely teasing to the dreamer-character. The final explicit expression of the Black Knight's grief, by shocking Geffrey out of his courtly miasma, precludes the possibility of a love *debat*—no man could contest with such a griever—but, more important, the simple statement also forces a realignment of the relationships among the reader, Geffrey, and the Black Knight, relationships that have obtained throughout the poem. In truth, the reader has failed to appreciate (or even perceive) Geffrey's loss just as Geffrey failed to perceive the Knight's. Both failures—Geffrey's and the reader's—were due to the speakers' conventional, artificial language, discourse that is sincere in inverse proportion to its expressiveness.[18] As Geffrey feels with (and his always felt with) the Black Knight's loss without knowing it, the reader has known all along but has not felt with Geffrey's distress. When the Knight's loss is finally revealed to him, Geffrey's sympathy is natural and automatic, but, insofar as he was able, he has sympathized throughout. Readers of the *Book of the Duchess* cannot say this, however, for they have cast aside Geffrey's conventionalized distress because it seemed so trite, so conventional. So the *Book of the Duchess* reveals its readers to be caught in a trap, the trap of judging the discourse of sentiment by a double standard: dismissing Geffrey's discourse because it is trite while accepting the

Black Knight's discourse because what it describes is famous and worthy.

Ultimately, all human grief, we learn, is as impossible to express or to judge as Geffrey's eight years' sickness. We sympathize with the Black Knight because we know he is John of Gaunt; we fail to sympathize with Geffrey because we do not know the real grief of which his words are the expression or, even worse, brush aside that sorrow because its expression is so sloppily conventional.

Both of these responses are central to the experience of the *Book of the Duchess*, which is finally a poem which expresses grief by proving that successful such expressions are impossible. The good, solid Anglo-Saxon word "routhe"—not "pitee," mind you—is the artless predicate that destroys all that has gone before it. Its artful but empty environment has invested it, paradoxically, with great rhetorical power because, when the discourse of sentiment has been examined and its two requisites set in unbreakable opposition to one another, that is all that can be said. "Is that youre los?" (recognition); "Be God, hyt ys routhe!" (sympathy): the discourse of sentiment is an excrescence, at best trite (Geffrey's) or egregious (the Black Knight's), at worst an obstruction to the wordless, interior, spiritual sympathy that makes the dream's noon bell our own midnight bell.

Pearl and the Discourse of Eschatology

Pearl is surely the Middle English poem least understood by modern critics, or at least the poem confidently understood. In more genteel days, Sir Robert Cotton's librarian catalogued the poem as

Vetus poema Anglicanum, in quo sub insomnii figmento, multa ad religionem et mores spectantia explicantur.

An old English poem wherein, under the fiction of a dream, many things concerning religion and morals are expounded.

Modern criticism has done very little to enlarge on this simple but accurate formulation. While scholars have detailed the many specific doctrinal points raised in the poem and have identified them variously with contemporary orthodox and heterodox teachings, we have neglected in large measure the nature of the medium in which "multa ad religionem er mores" are presented in the poem. We have yet to begin to appreciate how the poem is about "mores" as well as being about "religionem," about conduct as well as doctrine. Finally, we have not settled the issue of *explicandum* by way of a *figmentum*, in a sphere in which both Macrobius and later Christian theorists alike frowned on the use of fabulous narratives.

In other words, *Pearl* is an important test case of the sense of the dream vision developed in these pages. Unlike the *Book of the Duchess*, the *Hous of Fame*, the *Parlement of Foules*, and even *Piers Plowman*, *Pearl* is, from first to last, a serious doctrinal poem concerned with nothing other than crucial truths of eschatology. If anywhere, the Macrobean sanctions against the use of the fabulous narrative in discussions of the highest truths ought to apply here. If anywhere, the argument that the dream vision is a fictive apocalypse should prevail here, in a poem that concludes with a vision of the Procession of the company of the Lamb in Heaven. If anywhere, the sense of the dream vision as a perceptual puzzle issuing in community, not revelation, should *not* apply here.

The seriousness of these challenges is, I believe, a mark of the depth of our misunderstanding of *Pearl*. *Pearl* is not an exposition of the mysterious hierarchy of Heaven; not a presentation of the notion of democratic royalty (every man a king, every woman a queen in Heaven); not an argument on the salvation of baptized (or unbaptized) infants. It is not a Michelin guide to the other world, not a reasoned and logical disputation of theological controversy, and certainly not an elegy written by a wayward priest on his dead daughter Margery.[19] What *Pearl is* is a deconstruction of the discourse of eschatology: a sophisticated presentation of a human discourse the purpose of which is to demonstrate the complete inefficacy of that discourse. Like the *Book of the Duchess* and the *Hous of Fame*, *Pearl* attempts to bring human discourse to bear on a subject, only to discover human discourse to be inadequate as a medium.

Though this position is new and radical, it has its roots, not only in my own view of the dream vision and its background, but also in two sensitive attempts to remove *Pearl* from the worn-out elegy-doctrine controversy and to place it in relevant medieval contexts. The most extensive such attempt is a long chapter in A. C. Spearing's *The Gawain-Poet: A Critical Study*, the style and manner of which tend to belie its importance in the history of *Pearl* criticism.[20] Amplifying Schofield's remark that the pearl-image is "Protean" in its reference, Spearing suggests what is effectively a new reading of the poem, one which might truly be called "dramatic" rather than "elegiac" or "didactic" or doctrinal. In the subtle manipulation of the image of the pearl in the dialogue between the Pearl maiden and the narrator, Spearing sees a conscious movement from initial elegiac expectations to the wider perspective of the religious vision, a movement both masked and intensified by the conventional naive narrator of the medieval dream vision.[21] In an important article in *Traditio*, Louis Blenker characterizes a similar movement from a personal to an eschatological orientation, as he notes three stages in the poem analogous to the three stages of contemplation.[22]

What these two very different perspectives on *Pearl* share is a *dynamic* sense of the progress of the poem, a sense of movement from the personal, local, phenomenal, or sensory to the communal, universal, supernal, or spiritual. Both Spearing and Blenker are correct in their identification of the ground of this movement: the poem works on both levels, moving simultaneously outward and upward, away from the self and the world and mutability and the senses and toward "unknowing."

What neither writer suggests, however, is that the poem ultimately critiques this dynamic itself. In the last analysis, *Pearl* is not even an eschatological poem: its intent or purpose or program is to undermine the discourse of eschatology through an exposition of its dependence on human language and human reason, and from this to encourage in place of such notional comprehension of Heaven a simple relationship with God based on faith and trust, not on thoughts and words. Such a sense of the poem eliminates the need for choosing between elegiac and didactic readings because it effectively identifies *Pearl* as both and neither: by arguing that eschatology is as misguided as a survivor's tears, such a reading turns *Pearl*'s two interpretive poles into extremes, both of which are (similarly) improper human responses to the facts of mortality and of the gratuitous, irrational meed of salvation. This presentation of funereal grief as an analogue to eschatological speculation also brings the poem into line with the persistent medieval doctrina themes of personal slavation and the imcomprehensibility of redemption. Like *Piers Plowman* and other religious poems of the period, *Pearl* perceived as an anti-eschatological poem becomes a profound statement about the inescapable simplicity of the relationship between God and humanity, a relationship beclouded, not elucidated, by the discourse of eschatology.[23]

Considering *Pearl* as a deconstruction also enables us to come to terms with the often contradictory contents of the poem. The doctrinal points made in *Pearl* are, as has often been noted, alternatively conservative and radical, ranging from the fact of the Pearl maiden's salvation (conservative) to her unaccountably high position in Heaven (radical). The only way these stances can be reconciled is in rejecting them as contents and considering them as strategies: all of the narrator's attempts to come to rational terms with the organization of Heavenly society are thwarted by the (often snappish) rejoinders from his "daughter," who challenges him and the readers to put by the mysteries of eschatology and to embrace the single mystery that lies behind them and that makes consideration of them foolish and even sinful. The "message" of *Pearl*, then, is the Pearl maiden's persistent theme of Heavenly "cortaysye," the sweet, mysterious *gentilesse* that, understood and embraced, constitutes the poem's attack on the discourse of eschatology.

The Pearl maiden approaches this effective goal through the carefully planned pattern of perceptions, hints, explanations, and denials that make up the body of the dream-vision dialogue. In about the middle of the poem, for example, the Pearl maiden makes the superficially outrageous claim that she is the Bride of the Lamb and thereby Queen of Heaven. The narrator, who has been resting comfortably in the realization that this visionary lady is his long lost "pearl," responds to her claim quite predictably, seeming a little scandalized and answering that he had always understood the Virgin Mary to be the one and only Queen of Heaven. This common sense response to the paradox is based, of course, on sound doctrine and tradition, and also on the presumably stable denotations of words like "queen":

> 'Blysful', quod I, may þys be trwe?
> Dyspleseȝ not if I speke errour.
> Art þou þe quene of heueneȝ blwe,
> þat al þys worlde schal do honour?
> We leuen on Marye þat grace of grewe,
> þat ber a barne of vyrgyn flour;
> þe croune fro hyr quo moȝt remwe
> Bot ho hir passed in sum fauour?[24]

In other words, the narrator reasons, owing to the nature of queenship, that there may be only one queen per realm, and doctrine teaches us that the Queen of this Realm is the Virgin Mary.

The Pearl maiden responds to this with a short prayer of Marian praise and then the crucial explanation of the "cortaysye" of Heaven:

> The court of þe kyndom of God alyue
> Hatȝ a property in hytself beyng:
> Alle þat may þerinne aryue
> Of al þe reme is quen oþer kyng,
> And neuer oþer ȝet schal depryue,
> Bot vchon fayn of oþereȝ hafyng,
> And wolde her corouneȝ wern worþe þo fyue,
> If possyble were her mendyng.
> Bot my Lady of quom Jesu con spryng,
> Ho haldeȝ þe empyre ouer vus ful hyȝe;
> And þat displeseȝ non of oure gyng,
> For ho is Quene of cortaysye.

(lines 445–56)

If this explanation seems hairsplitting or even casuistical, the fault, the Pearl maiden would say, is in our fallen minds and our fallen language: she has succeeded in removing the narrator's puzzlement by affirming the doctrine of the queenship of Mary alongside the doctrine of celestial courtesy at (for her) the negligible expense of the efficacy of language and logic. Effectively, the Pearl maiden says here that the courtesy of Heaven is a contradictory one in which everybody is a monarch, Mary is a "meta-monarch," and, most importantly, everybody is totally satisfied with his or her royal prerogative over no one.

Given the courtly diction of the poem and especially given the blithe tone and homely vocabulary of the Pearl maiden's answer, then, this is not much of an explanation. What she says is true, of course, and has a rich history in Christian apocalyptic writing, but we should not lose sight of the fact that what she says is also exceedingly odd; especially considering the literalist, courtly preconceptions of the narrator, this "explanation" seems intended more to confound by irrationality than to satisfy with simplicity. Like Orwell's dictum that all pigs are created equal but that some are more equal than others, the Pearl maiden's assertion of universal queenship is really a tease, a form of verbal unknowing that enacts the fact that, with the language at our disposal, explaining is the last thing that will explain.

Perhaps guessing that the dreamer is not yet ready for such a frontal attack on sublunar logic and semantics—the discourse of eschatology—the Pearl maiden restates the paradoxical courtesy of Heaven in the next stanza, avoiding overt verbal paradox and alluding to St. Paul's metaphor of the mystical body of Christ:

> 'Of courtaysye, as saytȝ Saynt Poule,
> Al arn we membreȝ of Jesu Kryst:
> As heued and arme and legg and naule
> Temen to hys body ful trwe and tryste,
> Ryȝt so is vch a Krysten sawle
> A longande lym to þe Mayster of myste.
> þenne loke what hate oþer any gawle
> Is tached oþer tyȝed þy lymmeȝ bytwyste.
> þy heued hatȝ nauþer greme ne gryste,
> On arme oþer fynger þaȝ þou bere byȝe.
> So fare we alle wyth luf and lyste
> To kyng and quene by cortaysye.

(lines 457–68)

Once more, it is important to see these lines dramatically as well as

164

didactically. At the level of doctrine, Paul's corporeal metaphor is a perfect emblem of Christian unity and Heavenly parity, but, for the narrator, whose question was "sensible" in at least two senses of the word, the answer seems platitudinous and mildly evasive, not serving to answer a material question in material terms.[25] Recall that the original concern was the Pearl maiden's obtrusive reference to herself as a queen and to a courtesy or courtliness that seemingly exists without the principles of monarchy and hierarchy on which every court is based. Courtesy is, after all, a function and an acknowledgment of rank, and, without rank, the narrator *reasons*, there can be no courtesy. Thus, the Pauline metaphor of the mystical body of Christ serves to authorize or insulate the Pearl maiden's principles of royal parity and uncourtly courtesy, but it does not explain these mysteries in terms which are either coherent or comprehensible.

The Pearl maiden's last attempt to characterize Heavenly "cortaysye" is by a direct and extended allusion to the New Testament, a degree of authoritarian evidence to which she has not resorted before. At the effective center of the poem, she rehearses and interprets the parable of the vineyard workers from Matthew 20: 1–16 and, true to the spirit of the parable, uses it not as an explanation of but as a celebration of God's irrational love for humankind. A gloss she offers toward the end of the discussion gives a good sense of the meaning that she draws from the narrative:

> More haf I of joye and blysse hereinne,
> Of ladyschyp gret and lyue ʒ blom,
> þen alle the wyʒeʒ in þe worlde myʒt wynne
> By þe way of ryʒt to aske dome.
> Wheþer welnygh now I con bygynne—
> In euentyde into þe vyne I come—
> Fyrst of my hyre my Lorde con mynne:
> I wat ʒ payed anon of al and sum.
>
> (lines 577–84)

Not even the long redaction of the parable—occupying nearly a hundred lines in the text—seems to satisfy the narrator's curiosity about the social architecture or protocol of the Heavenly society for, ignoring the hortatory tone of the lines just quoted, he continues to treat the Pearl maiden's exhortations to peace and courtesy as positions to be understood and judged rationally and not merely to be accepted. At this point in the poem (if not much earlier), the two functions of narrative normalization, the splitting of the dreamer and the foregrounding of imagery, have acted to separate the dream-experience from its somatic frame, and the readers begin (wrongly, as always) to believe that they understand what is going on in the text. Even if the Pearl maiden were *once* a human individual to whom this boorish narrator had some tie, she is certainly something else, something more, now. The Pearl maiden offers, it seems, a glimpse of Heavenly bliss and precious eschatological information, but the narrator, the readers' frustrating representative, refuses to learn what is to be learned about the world of light and argues with his visionary interlocutor. This misperception—that there is something new and true to be learned at all here—is a trap, as I suggested earlier, but traps are the result of narrative normalization, and the readers' hunger for eschatology will soon be proven to be as wrongheaded as the narrator's elegiac pouting.

Nonetheless, the marked change in tone to be noted in the Pearl maiden at this point in the poem—just after the vineyard workers redaction—seems righteous, signalling her strategic shift from the relatively mild and patient invitation to accept the irrationality of her position to more aggressive tactic designed to undermine the narrator's stubborn, prideful rationality. The tonal change can be seen in the following lines, which appear about three stanzas after those quoted above ("More haf I of joye and blysse hereinne," etc.), but they are decidedly more shrill and their contents downright accusatory:

> Bot now þou moteȝ, me for to mate,
> Þat I my peny haf wrang tan here;
> þou sayȝ þat I þat com to late
> Am not worþy so gret fere.
> Where wysteȝ þou euer any bourne abate,
> Euer so holy in hys prayere,
> þat he ne forfeted by sumkyn gate

> þe mede sumtyme of heueneȝ clere?
> And ay þe ofter, þe alder þay were,
> þay laften ryȝt and wroȝten woghe.
> Mercy and grace moste hem þen stere,
> For þe grace of God is gret innoȝe.
>
> (lines 613–24)

At first glance, these lines seem a startling violation of the very "cortaysye" that the Pearl maiden has been advocating; her notion that the older one gets, the more one sins is, though uncourteous, the perfect rejoinder to the narrator's position that long struggle is more meritorious than innocence. The last line of the Pearl maiden's attack, however—the tag line for this set of stanzas—will ultimately help readers put her indictment of adult holiness into perspective. If, as she says, "þe grace of God is gret innoȝe," that is, sufficient in itself to save anyone, then all talk of merit and deserts is foolish and misdirected.[26] The Pearl maiden's attack, then, shows readers that we may justly (but pointlessly) attack the merits of anyone, even of the saints, because none of us actually *merits* Heaven.

In specific doctrinal terms, this obsession with justice and merit is the error of the Bradwardinians, who taught that unbaptized infants received a Heavenly reward perceptibly inferior to that of those who led complete lives of piety.[27] In a larger sense, however, the error of the narrator (and ultimately the error of readers as well), who has concluded or judged anything at all about his pearl's fitness for her rewards, is the error of eschatology in general, the error inherent in seeking to comprehend the eternal and supernal joy of salvation in rational, logical terms. The wisdom of God (which may or may not be foolishness to men) is nowhere more evident than in His granting the gift of eternal salvation: both Piers the Plowman and the Pearl maiden take care to call it a "mede" or unwarranted gift, as opposed to a payment for services rendered.[28] Such a notion certainly corrects the Bradwardinians, but it also challenges and invalidates all other eschatological positions as well: insofar as we are intellectually curious about the shape of the Heavenly society, this poem suggests, we imperil our eventual enjoyment of the simple peace and happiness implicit in faith and hope, the joy in which is the source of the Pearl maiden's "cortaysye."

This conflict, between courtesy and *curiositas*, is the central dramatic tension of the poem and, before examining its resolution through the dream vision form, we may digress momentarily to consider the background of the tension in contemporary mystical writings. At base, as Blenker points out, the positions of the dreamer and the Pearl maiden represent, respectively, meditation and contemplation. Blenker's source for this distinction, Hugh of St. Victor's *Nineteen Homilies in Salomonis Ecclesiasten*, makes the point nicely:

> Tres sunt animae rationalis visiones, cogitatio, meditatio, contemplatio. Cogitatio est, cum mens notione rerum transitorie tangitur cum ipsa res, sua imagine animo subito praesentatur, vel per sensum ingrediens, vel a memoria exsurgens. Meditatio est assidua et sagax retractatio cogitationis, aliquid, vel involutum explicare nitens, vel scrutans, penetrare occultum. Contemplatio est perspicax, et liber animi contuitus is res perspiciendas usquequaque diffusus.

> There are three modes of cognition (*visiones*) belonging to the rational mind: cogitation, meditation, contemplation. It is cogitation when the mind is touched with the idea of things, and the thing itself is by its image presented suddenly, either by entering the mind through sense or by rising from memory. Meditation is the assiduous and sagacious revision of cogitation, and strives to explain the involved, and penetrate the hidden. Contemplation is the mind's perspicacious and free attention, diffused everywhere throughout the range of whatever may be explored.[29]

Blenker argues that each of these three stages is represented sequentially in the poem in something close to the (chronologically) later Ignatian pattern of meditation of place, meditation of participation, and final contemplation. We have already seen, though, that this program is not precisely true to the dynamic of the poem: the conversation between the Pearl maiden and the narrator is anything but a smooth straight ascent and is only nominally a conventional oracular instruction by a figure of authority.[30] The pair vigorously dispute in human and realistic ways, which suggests that the *Pearl* vision is actually something closer to a struggle *between* meditation (or eschatology, represented by the narrator and the readers) and contemplation (or humble, graceful acquiescence, represented by the Pearl maiden). In English contemplative writing of this period and especially in the naive, populist tradition, this tension between meditation and contemplation was far more important than the less challenging "step approach" offered by Blenker and more closely associated with later continental writers. In *The Cloud of Unknowing*, for example, meditation is described as an impediment to rather than as a stage of contemplation:

> Be sure that if you are occupied with something less than God, you place it above you for the time being and create a barrier between yourself and God. Therefore, firmly reject all clear ideas however pious or delightful. For I tell you this, one loving blind desire for God alone is more valuable in itself, more pleasing to God and to the saints, more beneficial to your own growth, and more helpful to your friends, both living and dead, than anything else you could do. And you are more blessed to experience the interior affection of this love within the darkness of the *cloud of unknowing* than to contemplate the angels and saints or to hear the mirth and melody of their heavenly festival.[31]

In this text and elsewhere in mystical writings, contemplation of "the angels and saints" and of "their heavenly festival" of exactly the sort that the narrator and the readers seek from this dream is treated merely as a special case of the vain imaginings which prevent the soul's mystic union with God:

> These originate in a conceited, curious, or romantic mind whereas the blind stirring of love springs from a sincere and humble heart. Pride, curiosity, and daydreaming must be sternly checked if the contemplative work is to be authentically conceived in singleness of heart.[32]

Such perception of the "conceited, curious" *and* "romantic" dreamer (and reader) of *Pearl* redefines the poem's fundamental tension and makes it virtually a new poem, a poem full of self-consciously insoluble intellectual puzzles. Throughout the vision, the dreamer and the readers he represents treat these puzzles as challenges: the narrator attempts to gather information from the Pearl maiden toward their solution and assumes that his eschatologist's mind is sufficient to unlock their mysteries. This attitude, a stubborn unwillingness simply to rest in the presence of God, is treated with growing contempt by the Pearl maiden, who first seeks to amend the narrator's mind but finally comes to the more aggressive strategy of teaching humility by confounding intellectual pride with the wonderful irrationality of God. This later strategy, seen first in her rhetorical attack on adult holiness, reappears as she recollects her own call to Heaven:

> 'My makeleȝ Lambe þat alle may bete',
> Quod scho, 'my dere destyné,
> Me ches to hys make, alþaȝ vnmete
> Sumtyme semed þat assemblé.
> When I wente fro yor worlde wete,
> He calde me to hys bonerté:
> "Cum hyder to me, my lemman swete,
> For mote ne spot is non in þe."
> He gef me myȝt and als bewté;
> In hys blod he wesch me wede on dese,
> And coronde clene in vergynté,
> And pyȝt me in perleȝ maskelleȝ.
>
> (lines 757–68)

But this appeal, like all those that went before it, falls on deaf ears, or rather on ears that might as well have been deaf, for the narrator fails to appreciate the Pearl maiden's insistence on her humble unworthiness for brideship and, worse, mishears her crucial distinction between "makeleȝ" and "maskelleȝ":

> Quat kyn þyng may be þat Lambe
> þat ȝe wolde wedde vnto hys vyf?
> Ouer alle oþer so hyȝ þou clambe
> To lede wyth hym so ladyly lyf.
> So mony a comly on-vunder cambe
> For Kryst han lyued in much stryf;
> And þou con alle þo dere out dryf
> And fro þat maryag al oþer depres,
> Al only þyself so stout and styf,
> A makeleȝ may and maskelleȝ.
>
> (lines 771–80)

Clearly, the narrator still fails to understand that Heaven is beyond earthly conventions (such as merit or monogamy), but more important at this later stage of the poem is his mistaken predication of both adjectives, "makeleʒ" and maskelleʒ," to the Pearl maiden. In her response, she makes the difference between the two clear:

> "Maskelles" quod þat myry quene,
> "Vnblemyst I am, wythouten blot,
> And þat may I wyth mensk menteene;
> Bot 'makeleʒ quene' þenne sade I not."
>
> (lines 781–84)

The distinction, now underscored by the dangerous similarity of the two words, is one of the crucial ones of the poem: superior goodness or sanctity, indicated by "makeleʒ," has no significance, is an empty eschatological fiction, while absolute goodness, the state of being untainted absolutely or "maskelleʒ" ("immaculate"), is the mark of the saved soul and especially of the soul that enters Heaven without having had even the opportunity to know sin. It is such souls that the Pearl maiden has in mind as ideals, souls that escaped unavoidable sin by their early absention from physical life, when she introduces the most famous pearl of the New Testament, the *margarita pretiosa*:

> "Iesus con calle to hym hys mylde,
> And sayde hys ryche no wyʒ myʒt wynne
> Bot he com þyder ryʒt as a chylde,
> Oþer elleʒ neuermore com þerinne.
> Harmleʒ, trwe, and vndefylde,
> Wythouten mote oþer mascle of sulpande synne,
> Quen such þer cnoken on þe bylde,
> Tyt schal hem men þe ʒate vnpynne.
> þer is þe blys þat con not blynne
> þat þe jueler soʒte þurʒ perré pres,
> And solde all hys goud, boþe wolen and lynne,
> To bye hym a perle watʒ mascelleʒ.
>
> "This makelleʒ perle, þat boʒt is dere,

> þe joueler gef fore all hys god,
> Is lyke þe reme of heuenesse clere:
> So sayde þe Fader of folde and flode;
> For hit is wemleȝ, clene, and clere,
> And endeleȝ rounde, and bly þe of mode,
> And commune to alle þat ryȝtwys were.
> Lo, euen inmyddeȝ my breste hit stode."
>
> (lines 721–40)

The beauty of this passage lies in the way it brings together disparate allusions from Scripture with motifs in the poem itself to deconstruct eschatology and to assert the courtesy of Heaven. Jesus'
injunction to become "as a chylde" (Mark 10: 15, etc.) recalls the
various senses of childhood in the poem: initially considered unworthy of eminence in Heaven (by the narrator), the child is now
seen as having the essential purity that will "þe ȝate vnpynne."
The play on "makeleȝ" and "maskelleȝ" in these lines looks forward to the narrator's problem with these words a few lines later,
but the confusion—essentially a semantic one—can already be seen
as destroying the discourse of eschatology by showing (as the notion
of common queenship did) that eschatology is finally beyond discourse. The pearl (here suggesting personal salvation) is "maskelleȝ" by virtue of the soul's fastidiousness and also "makeleȝ" or
incomparable to any other possible reward for the avoidance of
"sulpande synne." As if to underscore the inadequacy of the discourse of eschatology, note the recurrence of an earlier paradox implicit in lines 721 and 739, the pearl's being both "makeleȝ" and
also "commune to alle þat ryȝtwys were," that is, the badge of
membership in a peerless community of equals.

Such is the nature of Heavenly courtesy, a special, ecstatic courtesy that exists among the elect without the earthly prerequisites of
rank and hierarchy. And this "cortaysye" is *Pearl's* critique of eschatology, a critique of meditation, intellection, and even of earthly
dreams which conceptualize the afterlife in insufficient human
terms. That the dreamer fails to learn this within the dream is evident from the dream's interruption: the dreamer's final act in the

dream is the fundamental violation of courtesy, a radical breaking of the rules specifically laid down by the Pearl maiden:

> Delyt me drof in yȝe and ere,
> My maneȝ mynde to maddyng malte;
> Quen I seȝ my frely, I wolde be þere,
> Byȝonde þe water þaȝ ho were walte.
> I þoȝt þat noþyng myȝt me dere
> To fech me bur and take me halte,
> And to start in þe strem schulde non me stere,
> To symme þe remnaunt, þaȝ I þer swalte.
>
> (lines 1153–60)

The narrator's attempt to cross the river is in direct defiance of the third of the Pearl maiden's injunctions, the "three errors" specified in lines 289–300. Moreover, the dreamer's emphasis on his delight and his following of his curious "maneȝ mynde" suggest that his awakening at this point is a signal of his unworthiness to cross. His desire to know, in place of what should be his desire to be, expels this still-ignorant intruder.

It is only on awakening that the narrator's perspective of the vision begins to change from human to celestial:

> To paye þe Prince oþer sete saȝte
> Hit is ful eþe to þe god Krystyin;
> For I haf founden hym, boþe day and naȝte,
> A God, a Lorde, a frende ful fyin.
> Ouer þis hyul þis lote I laȝte,
> For pyty of my perle enclynin,
> And syþen to God I hit bytaȝte
> In Krysteȝ dere blessyng and myn,
> þat in þe forme of bred and wyn
> þe prest vus scheweȝ vch a daye.
> He gef vus to be his homly hyne
> Ande precious perleȝ vnto his pay.
> Amen. Amen.
>
> (lines 1201–13)

As with those of the *Book of the Duchess*, these final lines require readers to readjust their allegiances. Until this point, the narrator has been the fool who was offered a vision of the afterlife and ignored it, the boor who was offered a sense of Heavenly courtesy and challenged and repudiated it. The poem's conclusion, however, gives evidence that the dreamer-poet—as opposed to the dreamer-character—understands the courtesy of Heaven full well and knows it to be available in this world through humble service to the Prince and through sacramental intermediaries. This shift in perspective within the poem, discovering the tenor of the pearl-image (or at least its final tenor) to be salvation and not some little girl, redefines the anxiety or longing of the dreamer at the beginning of the vision, showing it to be the laudable and holy desire for membership in the community of the elect. That the dreamer was unable to comprehend this until this late point is not as important as the readers' analogous failure to recognize—again, before this—the futility of such dreams of the afterlife. Such are, *Pearl* teaches, as misdirected as the search for baby Margery, the attempt to make human sense of Heavenly society, and the desire to "preview" what is open and comprehensible only to those loosed from the discourse of eschatology.

The *Hous of Fame* and the End of Lore

I claimed above that the *Book of the Duchess* is a poem which says impossible words, a poem that expresses grief without succumbing to the trivial locutions required for such expression. The *Hous of Fame* expresses the inexpressible as well, for it is a poem that demonstrates that poems lie.

This is not by any means a new reading of the *Hous of Fame*; from among the many others who have shared some of the following perceptions, I should single out Sheila Delany's *The House of Fame: The Poetics of Skeptical Fideism* as an important source for this present discussion.[33] After treatments of sceptical fideism and its poetics in early chapters of her book, Delany moves sequentially through the poem and traces a progressive dismantling of received wisdom in its Proem and three books. Defining fame as "the body of traditional knowledge that confronted the educated fourteenth-century reader," Delany perceives Chaucer to be fundamentally anxious about the contingency of this body of knowledge but unable to perform the logical gymnastics necessitated by the late medieval crisis of authority:

> Despite its benefits, the distinction between kinds of truth was one which Chaucer was unable fully to accept as the basis for literary practice. The *House of Fame* shows that while Chaucer felt the dilemma which made the separation of truths necessary, he still preferred to transcend the choice between traditions rather than to commit himself wholeheartedly to a single intellectual position or consistent point of view.[34]

Delany is certainly correct in identifying the *Hous of Fame* as a sceptical poem, but her book leaves unanswered many crucial questions about Chaucer's perspective on this medieval scepticism and, in subtle but important ways, misjudges the poet. The anxiety of the *Hous of Fame* is unmistakable, but it is still a work of art produced not by its anxious dreamer but by its less anxious artist. We must take care not to confuse the two: it is Geffrey the dreamer-character who prays,

> "O Crist!" thoughte I, "that art in blysse,
> Fro fantome and illusion
> Me save!"
>
> (lines 492–94)

and Chaucer the maker who writes these lines for him. The distinction, of course, is as old as Kittredge but, we shall see, the working distance between the dreamer-character and the dreamer-poet— and the distance between these two figures and Chaucer—is especially difficult to maintain in this, Chaucer's greatest dream vision.

These slippery distinctions suggest the purpose or program of this poem, the undermining of lore itself, the deconstruction of, perhaps, discourse itself. To do this, Chaucer must produce a poem that implicates lore and poems, a very different project than that of merely decrying their contingency; to do this, Chaucer must use lore to its own destruction, use writing to deconstruct the tyranny of the written word. What must survive the *Hous of Fame* is a community whose perception of the contingency of this world and whose distrust of human language and human rational formulations are their common bonds. This is a much more ambitious program than that of the *Book of the Duchess* or of *Pearl*, which attacked only very limited discourses; the strategy, however, is the same. What the *Hous of Fame* will do is make its dreamer's *insomnium* our own *insomnium* as well and then wake us up.

The poem begins with what seems a striking departure from convention, a departure which, I suspect, has led Curry, Lewis, Koonce, and others to see the *Hous of Fame* as a *somnium coeleste*, a revelatory dream and no *insomnium* at all.[35] Instead of elliptical autobiography or hints at the dreamer's distress as in *Pearl* or the *Book of the Duchess* and other dream visions, the Proem to the *Hous of Fame* offers a long, rather panicked synopsis of dream lore:

> God turne us every drem to goode!
> For hyt is wonder, be the roode,
> To my wyt, what causeth swevenes
> Eyther on morwes or on evenes;
> And why th'effect folweth of somme,
> And of somme hit shal never come;
> Why that is an avisioun
> And this a revelacioun,
> Why this a drem, why that a sweven,
> And noght to every man lyche even;
> Why this a fantome, why these oracles,
> I not; but whoso of these miracles
> The causes knoweth bet then I,
> Devyne he; for I certeinly
> Ne kan hem noght, ne never thinke
> To besily my wyt to swinke,
> To knowe of hir signifiaunce
> The gendres, neyther the distaunce
> Of tymes of hem, ne the causes,
> Or why this more than that cause is;
> As yf folkys complexions
> Make hem dreme of reflexions;
> Or ellys thus, as other sayn,
> For to gret feblenesse of her brayn,

By abstinence, or by seknesse,
Prison, stewe, or gret distresse,
Or ellys by disordynaunce
Of naturel acustumaunce,
That som man is to curious
In studye, or melancolyous,
Or thus, so inly ful of drede,
That no man may hym botc bede;
Or elles that devocion
Of somme, and contemplacion
Causeth suche dremes ofte;
Or that the cruel lyf unsofte
Which these ilke lovers leden
That hopen over-muche or dreden,
That purely her impressions
Causen hem to have visions;
Or yf that spirites have the myght
To make folk to dreme a-nyght;
Or yf the soule, of propre kynde,
Be so parfit, as men fynde,
That yt forwot that ys to come,
And that hyt warneth alle and some
Of everych of her aventures
Be avisions, or be figures,
But that oure flessh ne hath no myght
To understonde hyt aryght,
For hyt is warned to derkly;—
But why the cause is, noght wot I.

(lines 1–52)

While many claim that these lines are a tour de force reflecting Chaucer's wide knowledge of oneiromancy, this is clearly not their dramatic, radical lyric force.[36] The lines bespeak familiarity with dream lore sure enough, but they emphasize this lore's eclectic, inconclusive, and aimless expanse and not its (arguable) status as a coherent body of knowledge. We have seen that such a sense of medieval oneiromancy is justified—as righteous as the almost exclusive emphasis here on pathological or somatic causes for dreams—but we should nonetheless beware of taking this precision and show of knowledge too seriously, for the passage as a whole shows that Geffrey's bewilderment is at least equal to his expertise. Taken as an example of the radical lyricism that begins the dream vision, the Proem is more outburst than dissertation, a frantic, rambling speech enunciated by a nervous persona who has read the authorities and has discovered that they cannot be made to agree. The long passage just quoted, a single 296-word sentence in the Robinson edition, hardly suggests the calm, measured, confident style of the author of the *Treatise of the Astrolabe* or the *Equatorie of the Planets*. The repeated prayer, "God turne us every dreme to goode!" which frames the Proem like praying hands bookends, adds to the sense that this is a dramatic production, the monologue of a "mased thyng" who (for once) is bewildered *and* anxious, even unnerved. To recall Delany's title, "fideism" here brackets "scepticism" and the structure holds only by the grace of God. And Geffrey asks God, not for inspiration, guidance, or wisdom in interpreting dreams, but only, naively, that He turn all our dreams to good event. He is thus far more serious than his namesakes in the *Book of the Duchess*, whose concerns seem banal by comparison: the stakes are much higher, somehow, here.

Thus, the Proem to the *Hous of Fame* is actually not a departure from the convention of introducing the dreamer as distressed or anxious; it simply establishes this element through dramatic monologue rather than through explicit statement or innuendo. After reading the Proem, the reader knows, just as surely as if Chaucer has said so outright, that this fellow has problems. Far from suggesting a Dantesque apocalypse or a *somnium coeleste*, this errant, quirky proem presents readers with a worried, confused persona who has discovered to his dismay just what we discovered for ourselves in chapter 2 above—that the dream authorities cannot be made to make any practical, usable sense. The nightmare has begun.

Its end is not in sight. The three books that follow this proem constitute a steady, unrelenting accretion of evidence for a conclusion that is, perhaps, inherent in that proem: that truth in this world is either unavailable or indeterminate.[37] Like the nightmare experience of fleeing an enemy but finding him again and again at every turn, or like the nightmarish experience of learned men of the fourteenth century like Ockham or Abelard who found contingency in every branch of knowledge, this poem is a fictive record of Geffrey's dream of history, philosophy, and science, rehearsing his repeated attempts to find solid foundations for these three *artes*. Like all nightmares, this is a personal, even idiosyncratic vision; like all visions, its personal perspective comes to be fully shared by all who read and see aright.

Book One of the *Hous of Fame* is an exercise in textuality, a revelation of the contingency of history, a deconstruction of the discourse of history. In the temple of glass, Geffrey comes upon a text:

> But as I romed up and doun,
> I fond that on a wall ther was
> Thus writen on a table of bras:
> "I wol now singen, yif I kan,
> The armes, and also the man
> That first cam, thurgh his destinee,
> Fugityf of Troy contree,
> In Itayle, with ful moche pyne
> Unto the strondes of Layvne."
> And tho began the story anoon,
> As I shal telle yow echon.

(lines 140–50)

As the quotation suggests, history, the record of the adventures of Aeneas as inscribed by Vergil ("*Arma virumque cano . . .*") has become a story, one subject to rehearsal or retelling, one that can now be "told" yet again by Geffrey. Its stability seems, as it begins, to inhere both in its familiarity—no author is attached to the text— and equally by its being engraved in brass, solidity symbolizing stability.

This very stability is immediately called into question in the next lines, as Geffrey's relationship with his source becomes less clear:

> First sawgh I the destruction
> Of Troye, thurgh the Grek Synon,

179

> That with his false forswerynge,
> And his chere and his lesygne,
> Made the hors broght into Troye,
> Thorgh which Troyens loste al her joye.
> And aftir this was grave, allas!
> How Ilyon assayled was
> And wonne, and kyng Priam yslayn
> And Polytes, his sone, certayn,
> Dispitously, of daun Pirrus.

(lines 151–61)

The crucial question here is how we are to take the verb "sawgh."[38] Whether it is simply shorthand for "read" or a reference to representational carvings is not clear, though if it is the latter, it is peculiar that Chaucer fails to tell us directly. Whatever the correct sense may be, though, the word "sawgh" moves the narrative of events of the *Aeneid* away from Vergil's text. What is reported here is, to say the least, at several removes from the events being described: the destruction of Troy (through, notice, the *lies* of Sinon) as recorded by Vergil, as, it seems, reinterpreted by the mysterious artisan of the temple, as described by Geffrey. But this is a dream and, as such, the mind of Geffrey is the ultimate source of all he reports. Thus the double contingency of history is introduced: history (and especially medieval history) is a sequence of representations, each dependent on the accuracy of its predecessors and all dependent on the integrity of the human mind, here represented at its least trustworthy through the dream frame.

The second, anterior contingency is emphasized more and more in the rehearsal of the Troy story in Book One, as Geffrey introduces value judgments and emotional expletives:

> And I saugh next, in al thys fere,
> How Creusa, daun Eneas wif,
> Which that he lovede as hys lyf,
> And hir yonge sone Iulo,
> And eke Askanius also,
> Fledden eke with drery chere,
> That hyt was pitee for to here;

> And in a forest, as they wente,
> At a turnynge of a wente,
> How Creusa was ylost, allas!
> That ded, not I how, she was;
> How he hir soughte, and how hir gost
> Bad hym to flee the Grekes host,
> And seyde he moste unto Itayle,
> As was his destinee, sauns faille;
> That hyt was pitee for to here,
> When hir spirit gan appere,
> The wordes that she to him seyde,
> And for to kepe hir sone hym preyde.
>
> (lines 174-92)

The random, nonsequential character of the narrative is evident from these lines; through Geffrey, Chaucer is intentionally giving readers a partial, impressionistic picture of a scene inspired by the *Aeneid*, a far cry from "I wol now singen" much closer to "yif I kan." The intrusive "That hyt was pitee for to here" (lines 180 and 189), like the intrusive "yif I kan," are emblems of contingency, of history's dependence on fallible human historians. More than this, the mystery surrounding Creusa's death demonstrates that history is always subject to gaps and lacunae, which may be silently supplied, like emotional responses or moral judgments, by individual talents in the tradition.

Inclusions and exclusions figure prominently in the climax of the *Aeneid* redaction—if it is still accurate to call it this—as the story of Aeneas suddenly takes on a decidedly un-Vergilian project, the rehabilitation of Dido:

> But let us speke of Eneas,
> How he betrayed hir, allas!
> And lefte hir ful unkyndely.
> So when she saw al utterly,
> That he wolde hir of trouthe fayle,
> And wende fro hir to Itayle,
> She gan to wringe hir hondes two.
> "Allas!" quod she, "what me ys woo!

> Allas! is every man thus trewe,
> That every yer wolde have a newe,
> Yf hit so longe tyme dure,
> Or elles three, peraventure?
> As thus: of oon he wolde have fame
> In magnifyinge of hys name;
> Another for frendshippe, seyth he;
> And yet ther shal the thridde be
> That shal be take for delyt,
> Loo, or for synguler profit."
>
> (lines 293–310)

This speech is one of the most interesting in the *Hous of Fame* because it shows so clearly the nightmarish quality of this strange vision of contingency. First, of course, Dido never speaks these words in the *Aeneid*: Vergil is quite unforgiving to this woman who turned his hero's head. This, therefore, is a reprise of the "source problem"—words or sights?—introduced earlier. Where does this Dido come from? How is Geffrey hearing her? Whose words is she saying?[39] Second, Dido's words themselves are subtly troublesome. The three women to whom she alludes can be safely identified as Creusa (fame), Dido herself (friendship, etc.), and lastly Lavinia (delight and profit)—of the last of whom Vergil's Dido was obviously unaware. This "Dido" whose complaint Geffrey duly records is, thus, a strangely ahistorical creature, not wholly Vergil's Dido by virtue of her foreknowledge (and her "freedom of speech") but not wholly un-Vergilian by virtue of her biography. In some ways, she is Ovid's Dido, of course, but if she is, she still is so in a redaction of the *Aeneid* and not of the *Heroides*, an alternate "authority" Geffrey will not mention until it is too late.

As if to emphasize this very problem of sources and especially of the apparent sourcelessness of this prescient Dido, Geffrey interrupts her speech at this very point to offer a curious but not terribly reassuring disclaimer:

> In suche wordes gan to pleyne
> Dydo of her grete peyne,

> As me mette redely;
> Non other auctour alegge I.
>
> (lines 311–14)

Such a statement dramatizes the readers' ambivalence with the mode of the dream vision, which hovers between lyric and narrative, between dream as emotional correlative and dream as story. This statement of "authority" is, by this point in the text, both true and false. It is true, of course, because, when all is said and done, this *is* Geffrey's *insomnium*, an experience for which there can be no "auctour" or source other than the *figmenta* of the dreamer. It is simultaneously false, however, because this Dido—any Dido—is not wholly a creature of Geffrey's imagination: she is a creature of history given by Vergil to the world (and therefore an example of narrative normalization, in that she is identifiable independent of the dream frame). She has never spoken these words before—"non other auctour alegge I"—but the matter of her complaint is just and familiar, at least to readers of the *Heroides.* Thus, Dido is a creature sprung contradictorily to life, a character seemingly free from textual contingency but in fact free only to bemoan that contingency:

> "O, wel-away that I was born!
> For thorgh yow [Aeneas? Vergil?] is my name lorn,
> And alle myn actes red and songe
> Over al thys lond, on every tonge.
> O wikke Fame! for ther nys
> Nothing so swift, lo, as she is!
> O, soth ys, every thing ys wyst,
> Though hit be kevered with the myst.
> Eke, though I myghte duren ever,
> That I have don, rekever I never,
> That I ne shal be seyd, allas,
> Yshamed be through Eneas,
> And that I shal thus juged be—
> 'Loo, ryght as she hath don, now she
> Wol doo eft-sones, hardely;'
> Thus seyth the peple prively."

> But that is don, is not to done;
> Al hir compleynt ne al hir moone,
> Certeyn, avayleth hir not a stre.

(lines 345–63)

It is to the point here to mention that Dido is factually incorrect when she claims that her side of the story is untold. Aside from the *Heroides* (which *Geffrey* will mention at line 379), she is allowed her day in court in this present text, a fact which makes her complaint untrue by virtue of its utterance. More than this, Dido is actually complaining not against Aeneas or even against Vergil but against Fame, an antagonist she unsuccessfully attempts to apostrophize in lines 349–50: because Vergil, the agent of Fame, has immortalized her villainy in verse, she is doomed forever to do again what she did before (each time the *Aeneid* is opened and read) and so doomed to ever-renewed ill Fame.[40]

Such maddening contradictions take their toll on poor Geffrey, who seems here to be searching for a stable ontological basis for his art of versecraft and for the source of the putative solidity of "tydinges" among the "lesynges" of men's mouths. The bewildering experience with Dido calls even the sainted Vergil into question and, forsaking him who was Dante's first guide and master, Geffrey responds to the perplexity with calculated uncertainty:

> When I had seen al this syghte,
> In this noble temple thus,
> "A Lord!" thoughte I, "that madest us,
> Yet sawgh I never such noblesse
> Of ymages, ne such richesse,
> As I saugh graven in this chirche;
> But not wot I whoo did hem wirche,
> Ne where I am, ne in what contree.
> But now wol I goo out and see,
> Ryght at the wyket, yf y kan
> See owhere any stiryng man,
> That may me telle where I am."

(lines 468–79)

The "rich and noble images," so awesome and yet so problematic, make the question of their authority and source all the more crucial to Geffrey, who flees the temple to get his bearings. Outside, he finds a trackless wasteland, the emblem of the contingent web of lore. Without markings or landmarks, either geographic or textual, Geffrey panics:

> "O Crist!" thoughte I, "that art in blysse,
> Fro fantome and illusion
> Me save!" and with devocion
> Myn eyen to the hevene I caste.
>
> (lines 492–95)

In true nightmare fashion, this prayer for truth amid contingency is answered, not by the Second Coming of the Logos, but by the second coming of Dante's eagle, another contingent creature truant from its text.

Book Two of the *Hous of Fame* is a new beginning, complete with a new invocation designed to leave behind the confusing clash of authorities manifest in the Dido debacle:

> Now faire blisfull, O Cipris,
> So be my favour at this tyme!
> And ye, me to endite and ryme
> Helpeth, that on Parnaso duelle,
> Be Elicon, the clere welle.
> O Thought, that wrot al that I mette,
> And in the tresorye hyt shette
> Of my brayn, now shal men se
> Yf any vertu in the be,
> To tellen al my drem aryght.
>
> (lines 518–27)

Leaving behind Vergil, Ovid, and the myths of history, Geffrey grounds his vision once more in his own mind: in the dream, in what he "mette," and in his conscious mind, "thought," which records and processes his memories. The quest remains the same, but now, turning away from the unstable authority of old books, Geffrey flies toward a personal revelation.

And this revelation can be found in Book Two in the words of the eagle, who begins his chirping dissertation with the significant command, "Awak!" The eagle calls on Geffrey to awaken indeed: to awaken from the dreamlike belief in words, to awaken to the cold light of reason and the axia of science. The eagle's carefully wrought disquisition on "kyndely enclynyng" (lines 729–864) is the perfect methodological counterpart to the chaotic experience of the temple of glass, throwing a stark backlight on the grim lessons learned in the confrontation with Dido.

The revelation comes innocently enough. In explaining how the Palace of Fame can be the repository of all sound and thus of all speech, the eagle demythologizes verbal noise, reducing it to its unimpressive essence:

> "Soun ys noght but eyr ybroken,
> And every speche that ys spoken,
> Lowd or pryvee, foul or fair,
> In his substaunce ys but air;
> For as flaumbe ys but lyghted smoke,
> Ryght soo soun ys air ybroke.
> But this may be in many wyse,
> Of which I wil the twoo devyse,
> As soun that cometh of pipe or harpe.
> For whan a pipe is blowen sharpe,
> The air ys twyst with violence
> And rent; loo, thys ys my sentence;
> Eke, whan men harpe-strynges smyte,
> Whether hyt be moche or lyte,
> Loo, with the strok the ayr tobreketh;
> And ryght so breketh it when men speketh.
> Thus wost thou wel what thing is speche."
>
> (lines 765–81)

This "proves" inductively how it can be that all speech might reside in the Palace of Fame, but it does so at great cost. The cost, of course, is the truth that speech is nothing more than noise, a breaking of air

no different from the noise of the harp, the insensible accompani-
ment to the "noise" of the singer-poet. This explanation may eerily
recall a passage from *De Doctrina Christiana*:

> Sed quia verberato aere statim transeunt, nec diutius manent quam so-
> nant, instituta sunt per litteras signa verborum. Ita voces oculis ostendun-
> tur, non per seipsas, sed per signa quaedam sua.

> But because vibrations in the air soon pass away and remain no longer
> than they sound, signs of words have been constructed by means of let-
> ters. Thus words are shown to the eyes, not in themselves but through
> certain signs which stand for them.[41]

When we recall that the resident of the Hous of Fame is the goddess
who *uses* the craftsmen of the written word to lend solidity to the
broken air of speech, we can see that the eagle is a true Augustinian
who has simply replaced Augustine's written signs "instituta . . .
per litteras" with the goddess who orders these engravings of the
stammerings of fallible humans.

In concluding his explanation, the eagle asks Geffrey if he is convinced, not by rhetoric and figure but by the sheer logic and reasonableness of the argument:

> "Telle me this now feythfully,
> Have y not preved thus symply,
> Withoute any subtilite
> Of speche, or gret prolixite
> Of termes of philosophie,
> Of figures of poetrie,
> Or colours of rethorike?
> Pardee, hit oughte thee to lyke!
> For hard langage and hard matere
> Ys encombrous for to here
> Attones; wost thou not wel this?"
> And y answered and seyde, "Yis."

(lines 853–64)

The muttered "Yis" speaks volumes. In convincing Geffrey that the
Palace of Fame is his wonted destination, the eagle has completely
devalued the object of Geffrey's quest. Speech (true or lying speech)

is mere sonic stuff and hidden behind that quiet "Yis" is perhaps Geffrey's realization that the tidings for which he searches will not be quite so easy to find.

In keeping with this sense of Book Two as the book of awakening, it contains several references to apotheoses and to the structure of the Platonic universe. From their shared vantage point, the eagle and Geffrey recall Alexander and, of course, Scipio:

> "Seest thou any toun
> Or ought thou knowest yonder doun?"
> I seyde, "Nay." "No wonder nys,"
> Quod he, "for half so high as this
> Nas Alixandre Macedo;
> Ne the kyng, Daun Scipio,
> That saw in drem, at poynt devys,
> Helle and erthe and paradys;
> Ne eke the wrechche Dedalus,
> Ne his child, nyce Ykarus,
> That fleigh so highe that the hete
> Hys wynges malt, and he fel wete
> In myd the see, and ther he dreynte,
> For whom was maked moch compleynte."
>
> (lines 911–24)

Echoing a now-familiar phrase from St. Paul, Geffrey expresses his new belief in the apotheoses of his fellow *literati*:

> Thoo gan y wexen in a were,
> And seyde, "Y wot wel y am here;
> But wher in body or in gost
> I not, ywys; both God, thou wost!"
> For more clere entendement
> Nas me never yit ysent.
> And than thoughte y on Marcian,
> And eke on Anteclaudian,
> That sooth was her descripsion
> Of alle the hevenes region,
> As fer as that y sey the preve;
> Therfore y kan hem now beleve.
>
> (lines 979–90)

To which the eagle responds pointedly, " 'Lat be,' quod he, 'thy fan-tasye!' " (992). The references to Scipio, Martianus Capella, Alanus, and so on should not suggest that this is a Chaucerian apotheosis or a feigned *somnium coeleste*; the eagle's rebuke and especially his call-ing these musings "fantasye" preclude this. In referring all that he sees to books he has read, Geffrey shows that, like the *Pearl* narra-tor, he has failed to learn the fundamental message of this expe-rience, has *not* awakened from the dream of earthly truth and au-thorial authority. To the eagle's offer to name the stars for him, that is, to tell him their *true* names, Geffrey demurs, leaving such mat-ters to earthbound "authorities" inferior to his guide in intelligence as well as in vantage point:

> "No fors," quod y, "hyt is no nede:
> I leve as wel, so God me spede,
> Hem that write of this matere,
> As though I knew her places here;
> And eke they shynen here so bryghte,
> Hyt shulde shenden al my syghte,
> To loke on hem."
>
> (lines 1011–17)

To which the eagle, again reassessing his ward, replies quietly, "That may wel be" (1017). Throughout this second book, Geffrey remains the naive, bookish fellow staring straight at the truth and refusing to recognize it or, as here, averting his eyes in fear that its brilliance will blind him. Like the dreamer of the *Book of the Duch-ess* and even more of *Pearl*, this dreamer can be seen to lag far behind the readers, who have embraced the pseudonarrative and, at this stage, recognize John of Gaunt or desire to see the Procession of the Elect or yearn for knowledge of the "true" names of the stars. In repeated such moments of narrative normalization, Geffrey is con-fronted again and again with the contingency of earthly knowledge, in which history is as transitory as Augustinian "vibrations of the air" or in which this world is as a mote in the universe and yet, at an epistemological distance at which even "touns" are no longer recog-nizable, Geffrey fails to draw the Stoic lessons of Boethius or Troilus, turns his back on the truth, squints towards earth, and longs to get home to his old books.

Book Three of the *Hous of Fame* begins with yet another prologue, yet another attempt to reground the vision in the radical personal authority of the dream. Reminding readers rather backhandedly of his profession (and possibly echoing the eagle's humbling judgment on his artistry), Geffrey prays:

> O God of science and of lyght,
> Appollo, thurgh thy grete myght,
> This lytel laste bok thou gye!
> Nat that I wilne, for maistrye,
> Here art poetical be shewed;
> But for the rym ys lyght and lewed,
> Yit make hyt sumwhat agreable,
> Though som vers fayle in a sillable;
> And that I do no diligence
> To shewe craft, but o sentence.
> And yif, devyne vertu, thow
> Wilt helpe me to shewe now
> That in myn hed ymarked ys—
> Loo, that is for to menen this,
> The Hous of Fame for to descryve—
> Thou shalt se me go as blyve
> Unto the nexte laure y see,
> And kysse yt, for hyt is thy tree.
> Now entre in my brest anoon!
>
> (lines 1091–1109)

By this point, intentions such as these (and an orientation towards discourse such as this) should have a decidedly hollow ring. Chastened by his experiences with Dido and the eagle, Geffrey now has a more radical view of the poetic art and will now be content if the form is only "agreable" provided the *sentence* is accurate.[42] This noble intention is devalued, however, as we remember that—"non other auctour alegge I"—the source of the vision and all its *sentence* is none other than Geffrey's dream. As if to underscore this increasing hollowness of the authorial voice as the final vision of Fame and

Rumour approach, notice, as in the opening of the *Book of the Duchess*, Chaucer's careful, self-effacing use of quotation here. Here, Chaucer's (or perhaps Geffrey's) source is *Paradiso* I (lines 13–27) and the translation is accurate but punctuated with asides and other elements which deflate its original high seriousness. Specifically, lines 1104–05, a stumbling appositive explaining to Apollo what he means, are an emblem of Geffrey's and the poem's increasing nervousness with discourse, with the poetic art, and even with simple reference. Further, like "I have gret wonder, be thys lyght," in the *Book of the Duchess*, this eclectic moment in the *Hous of Fame* bungles its lush source with excess and indecorous detail: while Dante says that he will make himself a laurel crown in honor of Apollo, Geffrey promises to kiss the tree.

Moments like these are not examples of Chaucer's fabled default of high seriousness: they are serious indeed, though their seriousness derives from *Chaucerian sentence* and not "craft," a poetic art that uses the dreamer-persona as a foil for the reader and not as a representative. Such moments are, again, moments of narrative normalization, moments when the perspective of the poetic persona is gently subverted to involve the reader fully in the developing *drama* of the dream vision.

It is hard to tell whether Apollo answers Geffrey's prayer here, but it is easy to see that the object of Geffrey's description is not conducive to pithy rime emphasizing *sentence*. Atop the mount of icy words—a perfect emblem for the contingency of language— Geffrey beholds the palace, itself *all* craft *no sentence*:

> And eke in ech of the pynacles
> Weren sondry habitacles,
> In which stoden, al withoute—
> Ful the castel, al aboute—
> Of alle maner of mynstralles,
> And gestiours, that tellen tales
> Both of wepinge and of game,
> Of al that longeth unto Fame.
>   Ther herde I pleyen on an harpe
>   That sowned bothe wel and sharpe,

> Orpheus, ful craftely,
> And on his syde, faste by,
> Sat the harper Orion,
> And Eacides Chiron,
> And other harpers many oon,
> And the Bret Glascurion;
> And smale harpers with her gleës
> Sate under hem in dyvers seës,
> And gunne on hem upward to gape,
> And countrefete hem as an ape,
> Or as craft countrefeteth kynde.
>
> (lines 1193–1213)

The word "craft" here, which appeared with negative connotations only a hundred lines earlier in the Invocation (line 1100), emphasizes the richness and splendor of the palace, but it should also represent a caution to the reader. In each of the "pynacles" craft is visible counterfeiting not "kynde" but more craft—recall the several removes at which Geffrey received the *Aeneid* story. Further, it is relevant to note that the "smale harpers" of line 1209, playing the very instrument that the eagle used to illustrate the insubstantiality of sound, look up to and "ape" not real historical characters but Orpheus, Orion, Chiron, and Glascurion, figures from myth and literature.

The events of Book Three, while spectacular, need not detain us here. They are, once more, a continuous emblem of the contingency and capriciousness of written, literary discourse, which bestows authority on Augustine's "vibrations of the air" simply when the oral, airy words are written down, "authored." This intimation of the truth that has lain latent throughout the poem brings the *Hous of Fame* to a thematic, though not dramatic, climax. The descriptions of the Domus Dedaly and of the goddess Fame, with their rich and wondrous detail, are final proof for the reader that Fame is a capricious lady who regales true or false noise as she will (the lesson of Book One), and that the raw material for such "befaming" is the sonic flotsam and jetsam merrily warehoused across the road from her palace (the lesson of Book Two).[43]

In the end, the *Hous of Fame* transcends even its own form. The poem ends, not with the reawakening of the dreamer and the consequent return to the lyric mode, but with an ellipsis within the dream, making this poem quite literally the dream vision from which we do not awaken. Many argue sensibly that the poem is merely unfinished and there is not solid evidence to settle the issue finally, but I am forced to side with those who see the poem as a complete work of art, even if it is unfinished grammatically:

> I herde a gret noyse withalle
> In a corner of the halle,
> Ther men of love-tydynges tolde,
> And I gan thiderward beholde;
> For I saugh rennynge every wight,
> As faste as that they hadden myght;
> And everych cried, "What thing is that?"
> And somme sayde, "I not never what."
> And whan they were alle on an hepe,
> Tho behynde begunne up lepe,
> And clamben up on other faste,
> And up the nose and yën kaste,
> And troden fast on others heles,
> And stampen, as men doon aftir eles.
> Atte laste y saugh a man,
> Which that y nevene nat ne kan;
> But he semed for to be
> A man of gret auctorite. . . .

> (lines 2141–58)

I need not rehearse the several theories raised to explain these lines or, more improbably, to identify the "man of gret auctorite"; the controversy will endure as long will the *Hous of Fame* itself.[44] I wish only to suggest a rhetorical force for the lines, not a meaning but a strategy. As we have seen, the *Hous of Fame* is a series of failed attempts to locate fruit amidst the chaff, truth within the welter of authorities and, throughout, Geffey has been the naive, troubled but always intrepid searcher for these. We have watched his face fall as the Dido authorities dismantled themselves before his eyes, shared his morbid curiosity as the eagle demythologized human language, and watched in knowing amusement his futile search for a stable basis for fame. The lessons have all been negative, and the reader has learned them all.

Has Geffrey? The answer must be no. Disappointment after disappointment has not daunted him: he has pressed on despite our growing surety that his search for stability amid contingency will be a failure. At the end of the poem, Geffrey is literally and figuratively incarcerated in his own nightmare world—the poem does not allow him to awaken—for Geffrey's dream of final authority and unpolluted truth in this world is one from which the mind does not allow escape.

Awakening and escape can only come through the will, and the choice offered the free will of readers of the *Hous of Fame* can best be expressed in the terms that I introduced in chapter 4 above. The *Hous of Fame* has no third stage, no ultimate return to the lyric mode and reassertion of the identity of the two dreamer-figures. Thus, if a reader sees this poem as unfinished, then this reader is incarcerated, like Geffrey, in the dark irrelevancy of the *cuniculus figurarum*, trapped in the bowels of the poem instead of being liberated at the terminus of the maze.[45] Like Geffrey, this reader is doomed forever to follow the mob in the Domus Dedaly in search of the *recognizable* word of truth in all that noise.

So the choice is to "stay" in the poem with Geffrey or to "Awak!" as the eagle commanded, to impose one's own personal lyric closure on this dream vision, to recreate Geffrey the dreamer and to understand the futility of the quest, to forsake forever the search for truth among *men*, even those of "gret auctorite . . . ."

194

EPILOGUE: "IT WAS NO DREME: I LAY BRODE WAKING"

F or a variety of reasons, the dream vision is a late medieval phenomenon: while poems of this form can be found in ancient and modern literature alike, they lack for the most part the vigor and immediacy of those written in the fourteenth century.

In part, as I have argued, this flowering of the form is the result of a confluence of literary and philosophical currents, notably the maturity of the notion of the fabulous narrative, the derivative nature of medieval dream lore, the rise of conceptualism. These factors came together in the later Middle Ages to offer new challenges and new freedoms to poets. Most crucial to dream vision poets, however, was the freedom to depict simultaneously the way of the world and the way of the mind, to offer a *speculum mundi* whose images were dangerously ambivalent. Were these images true reflections of the world observed and captured in the consciousness of the dreamer-poet? Or are they waves and imperfections in the glass and thus revelatory more of the glass' character than of the scene reflected?

The dream vision was a way to exploit this ambivalence and, as we have seen, the great dream visions of the fourteenth century returned insistently to this theme of authority and vision, reflection and refraction, personal and universal revelation. Chaucer especially found in the dream vision a useful device for evading authorial authority: his Geffreys speak with the authority only of dreamers, and require their readers to decide whether they have any claim to broader revelations. We must decide in part by intuiting how like we are to these Geffreys (is this glass imperfect as ours is?) and in part by judging how well the vision coheres with ours (is the scene viewed through the glass familiar to us?).

Seen in this way, the fourteenth century dream vision is a wondrous authorial disappearing act, the sceptical poetic form which requires readers to pass simultaneous judgment on vision and visionary. Unlike the traditional allegorical forms of the Middle Ages, the dream vision made the personality (and occasionally the pathology) of the poet-dreamer as central to the experience as the iconographic terrain of the vision. This insistence—on the imperfections in the *speculum*—is what gives the dream vision its stunningly circular experience: we can know the vision only if we accept the dreamer, while we can know the dreamer only in accepting the dream (see above, pp. 9 and 14).

Apart from its rhetorical effectiveness, this interdependence of dream and dreamer is a profound gesture of respect for readers, invited but not required to partake of the visions of *Pearl* or of the fair field full of folk or of the palace of fame. As I have suggested above, the evasive lyricism of the form is the source of this liberation: neither quite a narrative nor quite a lyric, the dream vision draws drama and objectivity from the former, passion and involvement from the latter, and allows the reader to choose which responses—which mode, in effect—to accept.

This subtlety, even fragility, of the dream vision is the subject of this epilogue. I will examine here a very few late medieval and postmedieval poems which seem to have lost or misplaced some of the energy we have seen in the form. This examination may then suggest reasons why the form's flowering was so short-lived, and specifically why Renaissance dream visions and related poems seem pale and errant compared to the masterpieces of the fourteenth century. These exemplary theses can only suggest and illustrate—not demonstrate—the erosion of the form: the currents under discussion here are too broad to permit a thorough examination.

The anonymous satire "Mum and the Sothesegger," written probably within ten years of the death of Chaucer, strikingly illustrates the fragility of the form. The dream vision included in the poem begins at line 875, after a lengthy debate between the narrator and "Mum," a personification of silence in the face of abuses in the Henrican court. Weakened by the confrontation, the narrator wanders until he nearly drops from exhaustion:

> Yit was I not the wiser for way that I wente,
> This made me all mad, as I moste nede,
> And well fleuble and faint, and fell to the grounde,
> And lay down on a linche to lithe my bones,
> Rolling in remembrance my renning aboute
> And alle the perillous pathes that I passed had,
> As priories amd personages and pluralités,
> Abbayes of Augustin and other holy places,
> To knightes courtes and crafty men many,
> To mayers and maisters, men of high wittes,
> And to the felle freres, alle the foure ordres,
> And other hobbes a heep, as ye herd have,
> And nought the neer by a note! This noyed me ofte,
> That thurgh construing of clerkes that knewe alle bokes
> That Mum sholde be maister most upon erthe.[1]

The weight of these thoughts induces sleep and the dream of the Sothesegger:

> And ere I were ware, a wink me assailled,
> That I slepte sadly seven houres large.
>   Thenne mette I of mervailles mo than me luste . . .
>   (lines 869-71)

These "mervailles" ultimately center on the "Truthteller" who, like Justinus in the Merchant's Tale, can say what needs to be said, and whose example inspires the narrator to disclose his "bag of truths" to the king.

Even given the fact that the dream frame is here only part of a larger and looser satiric framework, we can clearly see that "Mum and the Sothesegger" is out of touch with the subtlety and complexity of the Chaucerian dream vision. Most obviously, personification and realism interpenetrate the dream-world and the waking world:

the disputation with Mum precedes the dream, a nicety forgivable in political satire certainly, but one not to be found in *Pearl* or *Piers Plowman*. This detail—which shows that the dream does not represent a modal shift from the phenomenal to the figmental—is a crucial one. If Mum is recognizable in the waking world, then there is no psychological or artistic reason requiring the dream frame for the introduction of the Sothesegger. More than this, the dream frame here lacks the ambivalence of the more traditional pattern: because Mum is our waking experience in common with the dreamer's, we have no reason to entertain suspicions that the Sothesegger is a *figmentum*, that momentary uncertainty that is so central to the dream vision. If, simply depressed at the corruption of the court, the narrator dreamed of the Sothesegger, the reader could wonder for a moment if the dream were a wish fulfillment. We are not allowed that moment here.

Further, the crucial motif of the "dreamer's distress" is, paradoxically, missing here. The diatribe of lines 854–68 certainly indicates distress, but the dreamer's discomfiture has none of the psychic energy that empowers the classical dream vision. Closest to the surface, this passage differs from the "dreamer's distress" in that the source of the distress is identified: unlike readers of the *Hous of Fame* or the *Book of the Duchess*, for example, we know precisely what is troubling this narrator because he tells us. As I have argued above, the mystery surrounding the introduction of this "dreamer's distress" is central because it isolates the dreamer-poet from the reader and creates the tensions that motivate the dream vision. Because the "dreamer's distress" here is indistinguishable from reasonable and laudable political diatribe, the passage does not separate the dreamer from the readers as do the mysterious ailments of Long Will, the jeweler, or the various Geffreys: because it is specified *and righteous*, the distress actually unifies the dreamer and the reader. This man's sensibilities are ours.

I am not suggesting here that "Mum and the Sothesegger" is a bad poem or that it would have been a better poem if it were a more classic dream vision. I am suggesting that it is a poem whose author was acquainted with the dream vision *but who was out of sympathy with it.* There are easily enough traditional motifs here to illustrate that the poet of "Mum and the Sothesegger" knew *Piers Plowman* (for example); the *use* of these motifs here shows equally clearly that the poet did not appreciate the subtle conceptual hold which *Piers Plowman* exerts on its readers. For this satirist, the dream is simply a vehicle for solving his narrator's problem: there is no hint here of the ambivalence that haunts the *Hous of Fame* or *Piers Plowman.* Like *The Kingis Quahir* (the *Parlement of Foules*) or Lydgate's "Complaynt of a Loveres Lyfe" (the *Book of the Duchess*), this poem seems inarguably inspired by a dream vision but only in the most superficial ways. The complex arrangement of parts and the fragility of their operation are lost on this poet, for whom they have become merely traditional or conventional motifs.

As a second example of the obsolescence of the dream vision, we can turn to *The Temple of Glass,* a poem religiously adherent to the conventions of the form and to its undisguised model (the *Hous of Fame*), but for all this, a poem unable to capture the spirit and com-plexity of its original. *The Temple of Glass* begins with a virtual precis of the state of the dreamer in the *Hous of Fame*:

> For thou3t, constreint and greuous heuines,
> For pensifhede, and for hei3 distres,
> To bed I went nov þis oþir ny3t
> Whan þat Lucina wiþ hir pale li3t
> Was ioyned last wiþ Phebus in Aquarie,
> Amyd Decembre, when of Ianuarie
> Ther be kalendes of þe nwe yere,
> And derk Diane, ihorned, noþing clere,
> Had hir bemys vndir a mysty cloude . . .[2]

The difference between this opening and "God turne us every drem to goode" nicely typifies the difference between medieval and Renaissance dream visions. Chaucer's character embodies what Lydgate's only describes: Lydgate's opening strains to include all of the salient diagnostic details at the expense of a credible patient, while Chaucer, fully in touch with his form, simply allows his dream-er to take shape on his page. The real problem with the Lydgate

dreamer is thus his meticulousness: with a stunning vocabulary and
nicely measured phrases, he declares in stark, objective, clinical
terms that he is beset to the point of distraction. The point of the
"dreamer's distress" is, again, to awaken suspicions as to his credibility and visionary fitness: this dreamer sounds, his assertions notwithstanding, just fine, nothing like the haggard Geffrey, blessing
himself and rambling about the uncertainty of dreams. Lydgate stud-
ied the form so well that he missed its point.

But Lydgate continues his imitation of the *Hous of Fame*:

> Wiþin my bed for sore I gan me shroude,
> Al desolate for constreint of my wo,
> The longe nyʒt waloing to and fro,
> Til atte laste, er I gan taken kepe,
> Me did oppresse a sodein dedeli slepe,
> Wiþin þe which me þou ʒte þat I was
> Rauysshid in spirit in a temple of glas—
> I nyste how, ful fer in wildirnes—
> That foundid was, as bi liklynesse,
> Not opon stele, but on a craggy roche,
> Like ise ifrore.

(lines 10–20)

And so the dream begins, indistinguishable from the popular iconographic visions, waking and sleeping, that are so common in fifteenth century English poetry. There are neither characters nor dialogue for over three hundred lines, at which the Lady, involved in an
adulterous love triangle, begins an ornate appeal to Venus. In the
course of the entire poem, the narrator remains an observer, anxious only that he might forget crucial details of the vision (lines
1369–77).

In many ways, *The Temple of Glass* is the subtlest and most faithful of the fifteenth century dream visions: its only departure from
the paradigm is in its one-dimensional narrator, a figure all but forgotten once the dream begins. There is in Lydgate none of the lyricism of the Chaucerian personae, for, in truth, the poems are no
longer about these figures and their relationship to the readers.

These poems and the visions of Hoccleve, Henryson, Dunbar, and Spenser are truly obsolescent dream visions, poems that keep alive the forms of the old poetic kind without the energy that produced it. Why did the dream vision grow so old, look so tattered, so soon? Among the reasons we could consider might be the rise of science and the parallel collapse of Scholasticism and the oneiromantic tradition which was a part of it. The Renaissance was, if anything, more inquisitive and credulous about dreams, visions, and the occult than the fourteenth century sceptics were and, with the withdrawal of a church which forbade revelation in dreams, the Renaissance could fantasize more freely than the Middle Ages did.[3] A related cause is the rapid decline in speculative philosophy, especially conceptualism. We have seen that the dream vision works only within a very carefully articulated psychology, one associated with only the first and second generation or conceptualists and nominalists in the thirteenth and fourteenth centuries. As Gordon Leff and others have shown, later developments in conceptualist or nominalist thought, those of Nicholas of Autrecourt or John of Mirecourt, for example, degraded what was initially a carefully conceived critique of Platonism into riddles, conundra, and attacks on the possibility of a divine nature. Fifteenth century nominalists at the universities, speaking their own language of contradiction and absurdity, become the butts of student satires and ultimately, the personifications of a senescent theology ridiculed, attacked, and finally forsaken by the Reformation.

With conceptualism, the Renaissance lost the conceptualist image of communion or communication as the synonymy of two persons' *figmenta*, and without this notion, there is no drama in another man's dream. In the instant when one mind embraces the icons of another, the conceptualists revealed a sympathy more powerful than any that mere rhetoric could produce. Without this psychology of the individual, the by-product of Scotus and Ockham, the dream vision had no purpose.

The most compelling reason for the dramatic disappearance of the dream vision was not political or philosophical or psychological: it was a literary reason. Put simply, the Renaissance rediscovered lyricism, the immediate depiction of powerful emotions in verse, a discovery which made the fragile, complex, allusive structure of the old dreams useless. Of what use are feints and slights, self-effacement and misdirection, frames and persona, in an age whose poetic herald is Thomas Wyatt:

> They fle from me that sometyme did me seke
> With naked fote stalking in my chambre.
> I have sene theim gentill tame and meke
> That nowe are wyld and do not remembre
> That sometyme they put theimself in daunger
> To take bred at my hand; and nowe they raunge
> Besely seking with a continuell chaunge.[4]

This is neither the vulnerable voice of Geffrey nor the cold voice of Lydgate: this persona boldly drops without warning into extended metaphor. He knows the reader cares about his life and his feelings; he feels no need to assert higher or universal import to his experiences. They are here presented—emotions, experiences, memories—in a new dramatic language which needs no frame.

> Thancked be fortune, it hath ben othrewise
> Twenty tymes better; but ons in speciall,
> In thyn arraye after a pleasaunt gyse,
> When her lose gowne from her shoulders did fall,
> And she me caught in her armes long and small;
> Therewithall swetely did me kysse,
> And softely saide, dere hert, howe like you this?
>
> (lines 8–14)

The lyric continues, creating its persona as a character neither by description nor by dream report; what we learn of this man we surmise, from errant turns of phrase, from the erupting bitterness as the metaphor (among other things) is dropped, from the sudden, passionate encounter. The picture of the embittered lover that Wyatt creates here in seven lines would have taken Chaucer a poem the size of the *Book of the Duchess* to achieve—though only because this new lyricism would have seemed to Chaucer a brash and vulgar shorthand.

It was no dreme; I lay brode waking.
But all is torned thorough my gentilnes
Into a straunge fasshion of forsaking;
And I have leve to goo of her goodenes,
And she also to use new fangilnes.
But syns that I so kyndely ame served,
I would fain knowe what she hath deserved.

(lines 15-21)

Thus, what for Chaucer would have been a "straunge fasshion" and "new fangilnes" is a poetry written by and for people who are ready to express, accept, and sympathize with the deepest and most powerful emotions, writers and readers who do not need the device of the shared dream to knit together their individual sensibilities. A tide had turned, the oldest verities had been questioned and even forsaken, a new poetry had replaced the old.

NOTES

Introduction

1. Compare Tzvetan Todorov's sense of the requirements for responsible genre criticism:

> [A genre study] must constantly satisfy requirements of two orders: practical and theoretical, empirical and abstract. The genres we deduce from the theory must be verified by reference to the texts: if our deductions fail to correspond to any work, we are on a false trail. On the other hand, the genres which we encounter in literary history must be subject to the explanation of a coherent theory; otherwise we remain imprisoned by prejudices transmitted from century to century, and according to which (an imaginary example) there exists a genre such as comedy, which is in fact a pure illusion. The definition of genres will therefore be a continual oscillation between the description of phenomena and abstract theory.

Tzvetan Todorov, *The Fantastic: A Structural Approach to a Literary Genre*, tr. Richard Howard (Ithaca: Cornell University Press, 1975), 21.

2. "Convention as Structure: The Prologue to the *Canterbury Tales*," *MP* 49 (1952): 172–81; reprint in *Tradition and Poetic Structure: Essays in Literary History and Criticism* (Denver: Alan Swallow, 1960).

3. See Donald R. Howard, *The Idea of the Canterbury Tales* (Berkeley: University of California Press, 1978), 30–35. The earlier tradition, that sees the reference to "some comedye" as Chaucer's promise of a treatment of love's *saints* to match the *Troilus* (making the "comedye" a reference to the *Legend of Good Women*), is articulated in J. S. P. Tatlock's classic essay, "The Epilog of Chaucer's *Troilus*," *MP* 18 (1921): 625–59.

4. See F. X. Newman, "Somnium: Medieval Theories of Dreaming and the Form of Vision Poetry" (Ph. D. diss., Princeton, 1963), 253–331, for a complete discussion of typical or frequent motifs in dream-poetry, including the naive dreamer, the book as a soporific, the *locus amoenus*, the river, and many others. It is impossible to quarrel with Newman's collection of such motifs, but, as I argue above, their presence needs to be shown to be *necessary* for the operation of the poem, or at least integral to its technique. For another discussion of the motif of the dreamer reading, see Sheila Delaney, *Chaucer's House of Fame: The Poetics of Skeptical Fideism* (Chicago: University of Chicago Press, 1977), 40.

5. This distinction is itself a good index to the eclectic diversity of the form. The talking birds of the *Parlement of Foules* seem to be descendents of earlier talking animals in the French love visions of the thirteenth century (and possibly as well of talking birds in folk literature and allegories of the "Owl and Nightengale" variety). The eagle of the *Hous of Fame*, however, is a comic Chaucerian version of Dante's eagle (and therefore derived ultimately from the iconography of the Apocalypse), all of which makes it unlikely that even this frequent or common motif is prescribed. All dream visions contain odd, and, in fairness, preternatural things, but the fact that the sources of these additions are so various and diverse—allegory, folk literature, eschatology, etc.—suggests that their inclusion in the poems is a device of dream-verisimilitude or "dream mimesis" rather than a conventional signpost of some sort.

6. The list of such studies is daunting. Among earlier essays on the figure of the dreamer, see James R. Kreutzer, "The Dreamer in the *Book of the Duchess*," *PMLA* 66 (1951): 543–71; Donald C. Baker, "The Dreamer Again in the *Book of the Duchess*," *PMLA* 70 (1955): 279–82; Stephen Manning, "That Dreamer Once More," *PMLA* 71 (1956): 540–41; R. M. Lumiansky, "The Bereaved Narrator in Chaucer's *The Book of the Duchess*," *TSE* 9 (1959): 5–17; and so on. Similar bibliographies can be generated for *Pearl*, the *Hous of Fame*, and *Piers Plowman*. Perhaps the best general discussion can be found in A. C. Spearing's *Medieval Dream-Poetry* (Cambridge: Cambridge University Press, 1976), especially 4–5, 28–29, and 73ff. For additional bibliography and a reinterpretation of the problem of the *Book of the Duchess* narrator, see Barbara Nolan, "The Art of Expropriation: Chaucer's Narrator in the *Book of the Duchess*," in *New Perspectives in Chaucer Criticism*, ed. Donald Rose (Norman: Pilgrim, 1981), 203–22.

7. M. Tullius Ciceronis, *De Re Publica*, ed. K. Ziegler (Leipzig: Teubner, 1969), 126; tr. H. A. Rice in *The Norton Anthology of World Masterpieces*, ed. Maynard Mack *et al.*, 4th ed. (New York: W. W. Norton, 1979), I, 572–73.

8. See Newman, pp. 70–77, on Macrobius' acceptance of the *Somnium Scipionis* as a comprehensive philosophical vision, and Paule Demats, *Fabula: Trois Etudes de Mythographie antique et medievale* (Geneva: Droz, 1973), 19 ff. for discussion.

9. See Ziegler's introduction, pp. xxxvi–xxxix, for the manuscript history.

10. Ziegler, pp. 135–36; tr. Rice, pp. 578–79.

11. Cf. Newman, pp. 326–31, on the dazed, naive dreamer, and how this allows the dream vision to depict truths freed from the personal credibility of this dreamer.

12. Discussions of the notion alluded to here, that ancient and medieval people's minds work in ways qualitatively different from ours, range in expression from Carolly Erickson's measured meditation in *The Medieval Vision: Essays in History and Perception* (New York: Oxford University Press, 1976), through the careful collaborative research of Jacques LeGoff in *Time, Work, and Culture in the Middle Ages*, tr. Arthur Goldhammer (Chicago: University of Chicago Press, 1980), to the radical theories of Julian Jaynes in *The Origin of Consciousness in the Breakdown of the Bicameral Mind* (Boston: Houghton Mifflin, 1976).

13. Boethius, *The Theological Tractates and the Consolation of Philosphy*, ed. R. F. Stewart, E. K. Rand, and S. J. Tester, Loeb Classical Library, (Cambridge: Harvard University Press, 1918, rev. 1973), 130; *The Consolation of Philosophy*, tr. Richard Green, The Library of Liberal Arts (New York: Bobbs Merrill, 1962), 3.

14. Boethius, 132; Green, 3.

15. *Sweet's Anglo-Saxon Reader*, ed. Henry Sweet, rev. Dorothy Whitelock (Oxford: Oxford University Press, 1967), 153–54; translation mine.

16. Sweet, 157; translation mine.

17. Guillaume de Lorris and Jean de Meun, *Le Roman de la Rose*, ed. Felix Lecoy (Paris: Librarie Honore Champion, 1965), I, 1; tr. Geoffrey Chaucer in *The Complete Works of Geoffrey Chaucer*, ed. Fred Norris Robinson, 2nd ed. (Boston: Houghton Mifflin, 1961), 565.

18. On Guillaume's use of Macrobius as a *dis*authenticating device, see John V. Fleming, *The* Roman de la Rose: *A Study in Allegory and Iconography* (Princeton: Princeton University Press, 1969), 54; Charles Dahlberg, "Macrobius and the Unity of the *Roman de la Rose*," *Studies in Philology* 58 (1961): 573–82; and Marc-René Jung, *Etudes sur le poeme allegorique en France au moyen age* (Berne: Francke, 1971), 292–93.

19. Dante Alighieri, *The Divine Comedy*, ed. and trans. Charles S. Singleton, Bollingen Series 80 (Princeton: Princeton University Press, 1970), 2–3.

20. Compare Charles Singleton:

> The poet is deliberately leading the reader into double vision, to place him on what he had every right to assume would be the most familiar of scenes. There is this about that landscape at the beginning: we may not mark its whereabouts on any map. And, when we stand at the doorway of Hell and look back to where we were before, if we ask

ourselves where that was, we know that we may not exactly say. But that is not the important point. The point is that the scene was designed to locate us.

Dante Studies I: The Commedia: Elements of Structure (Cambridge: Harvard University Press, 1954), 7.

21. See Giuseppi Mazzotta, *Dante: Poet of the Desert: History and Allegory in the Divine Comedy* (Princeton: Princeton University Press, 1979), 254, on the disjunction between the poet and the wayfarer: "The poet knows more than the pilgrim does," a disjunction which, we will see, differs from the "pseudo-eyewitness" narrative mode of the dream vision. See also Kevin Brownlee, *Poetic Identity in Guillaume de Machaut* (Madison: University of Wisconsin Press, 1984), 12, on *dedoublement* in dream poetry, as distinct from the situation in *Inferno* I. For the *Divine Comedy* as a dream vision, see Newman, pp. 339–57.

Chapter One

1. On the notion of the dream vision as a pseudo-apocalypse, see Morton Bloomfield, *Piers Plowman as a Fourteenth Century Apocalypse* (New Brunswick: Rutgers University Press, 1961), 11; Bernard Huppé and D. W. Robertson, Jr., *Fruyt and Chaf: Studies in Chaucer's Allegories* (Princeton: Princeton University Press, 1963), 33, 42–43; B. G. Koonce, *Chaucer and the Tradition of Fame: Symbolism in the House of Fame* (Princeton: Princeton University Press, 1966), 51; and C. S. Lewis, *The Discarded Image: An Introduction to Medieval and Renaissance Literature* (Oxford: Oxford University Press, 1971), 63–64. Ultimately, the view can be traced to distinctions about dreams in Walter Clyde Curry's *Chaucer and the Mediaeval Sciences* (New York: Barnes and Noble, 1926, rev. 1960).

The competing view, that the dream vision is not intended to be seen as a fictive revelation and springs from the poets' desire to imitate the actual experience of dreaming in verse ("dream mimesis"), is equally well represented among critics. See, for example, Spearing, *Medieval Dream-Poetry*, 53–57; Charles Muscatine, *Chaucer and the French Tradition* (Berkeley: University of California Press, 1957), 102 and elsewhere; Constance Hieatt, *The Realism of the Dream Vision: The Poetic Exploitation of the Dream-Experience in Chaucer and His Contemporaries* (The Hague: Mouton, 1967), 20 and elsewhere; James Winny, *Chaucer's Dream Poems* (New York: Barnes and Noble, 1973), 28–35; John Lawlor, "The Earlier Poems," in *Chaucer and Chaucerians: Critical Studies in Middle English Literature*, ed. D. S. Brewer (University: University of Alabama Press, 1967), 42; and James I. Wimsatt, "Chaucer and French Poetry, " in *Writers and Their Background: Geoffrey Chaucer*, ed. Derek Brewer (Athens: Ohio University Press, 1975), 28–29.

2. Todorov, *The Fantastic*, 25.

3. Cf. Giuseppi Mazzotta:

The poem [the *Commedia*], it must be stressed, is neither the imitation of God's way of writing nor a prodigious crystal, an idolatrous self-referential construct; it occupies the ambiguous space between these two possibilities; and allegory, as I see it, dramatizes the choice with which the reader is confronted.

Dante: Poet of the Desert: History and Allegory in the Divine Comedy (Princeton: Princeton University Press, 1984), 237.

4. *The Epic of Gilgamesh*, tr. N. K. Sandars (Harmondsworth: Penguin, 1972), 66.

5. *Gilgamesh*, 66.

6. Aeschylus, *The Oresteia*, tr. Richmond Lattimore (Chicago: University of Chicago Press, 1953), 112, lines 423–39.

7. *The Oresteia*, p. 43, line 275.

8. *The History of Herodotus*, tr. George Rawlinson, ed. Manuel Komroff (New York: Tudor, 1941), 362.

9. *Herodotus*, 362.

10. *Herodotus*, 364.

11. Scriptural quotations are taken from the *Biblia Sacra juxta Vulgatam Clementinam*, ed. Alberto Colunga and Antonio Turrado (Madrid: Biblioteca de Autores Cristianos, 1977) and will be cited in text. Translations are mine.

12. A survey of Church Fathers on this subject can be found in Morton Kelsey, *God, Dreams, and Revelation: A Christian Interpretation of Dreams* (Minneapolis: Augsburg, 1968, rev. 1974), especially 130–44. Kelsey's treatment of medieval oneiromancy includes several useful quotations from Eastern thinkers such as Athanasius, Gregory of Nyassa, Basil the Great, St. John Chrysostom, and Synesius of Cyrene, as well as most of the Western Fathers mentioned in this present study.

Kelsey is aware that these thinkers did not have an important influence on *Western* Christian thinking on dreams, but this fact actually suits his purposes well. His thesis, a correct one at least historically, is that Christianity's original acceptance of oneiromancy survived in the Eastern Church but was consciously suppressed by Neo-Aristotelean thinkers in the European Middle Ages.

On the notion of psychic openness, sleep *in bono*, as it emerges in Western *mystical* thought, see note 19 below.

13. The designation is probably old enough to be contemporary with the Gospels. Macrobius quotes Cicero as using the term: "φαντασμα, quod Cicero, quotiens opus hic nomine fuit, visum vocavit" (" . . . *phantasma*, which Cicero, when the term was called for, called *visum*") (*Commentarii in Somnium Scipionis*, ed. Iacobus Willis [Leipzig: Teubner, 1963], 8, with my translation). For other Greek oneiromantic terms and their equivalents, see Kelsey, 80–86.

14. *Publii Vergili Maronis Opera*, ed. R. A. B. Mynors, Oxford Classical Texts (Oxford: Clarendon Press, 1969), 184, lines 265–76; *The Aeneid*, tr. Allen Mandelbaum (New York: Bantam, 1972), 90.

15. Mynors, 193, lines 554–70; tr. Mandelbaum, 100.

16. It is likely that this reading is light–years away from Vergil's intended meaning, but such is medieval studies. I suggest the reading in the spirit of Macrobius, taking cognizance of the specific language of the apparition and in an encyclopedic reading of *Aeneid* IV. If Mercury is a vision and "the image of Mercury . . . returned" a day-residue dream, their proximity in the text would have struck medieval commentators as an inescapable *integumentum*.

17. *PL* 32, cols. 691–92; St. Augustine, *Confessions*, tr. John K. Ryan (Garden City: Doubleday, 1960), 91 (Chapter 11). See F. X. Newman, "Somnium: Medieval Theories of Dreaming and the Form of Vision Poetry," (Ph. D. diss., Princeton, 1963), 109, for discussion.

18. *PL* 32, col. 692; tr. Ryan, 91.

19. The apocalypse—see Kelsey on "ἀποκαλυψις," 85—was an important literary genre in Semitic, Old Testament writing, but it is not clear what influence these works had on the Christian apocalyptic tradition, which begins, of course, with St. John and Revelation. Two very useful studies of the Biblical and medieval apocalypse are Bernard McGinn, "Early Apocalypticism: the ongoing debate" (pp. 2–39) and Marjorie Reeves, "The development of apocalyptic thought: medieval attitudes," (pp. 40–72), both in *The Apocalypse in English Renaissance Thought and Literature*, ed. C. A. Patrides and Joseph Wittreich (Ithaca: Cornell University Press, 1984). McGinn (p. 21) notes Revelation's departure from Semitic convention in explicitly identifying its author, who is usually anonymous or pseudonymous (in sharp distinction to the dream vision's carefully determined persona).

20. This is a very complicated notion, caught up in the infamous metaphorics of medieval mysticism. Spearing, in *The Gawain-Poet: A Critical Study* (Cambridge: Cambridge University Press, 1970), considers the issue briefly with reference to *Pearl*, 107–17, and concludes that the Aristotelean notion of sleep as the time when the senses and conscious mind are quiescent could be applied literally to dream-apocalypses. To this end, Spearing cites Richard of St. Victor on the "sleep of the senses and passions" (p. 115). The bulk of mystical writing, however, tends to treat sleep as a metaphor for the aspirant's *conscious* self-absention from quotidian sensory stimuli, passions, and concerns. *The Cloud of Unknowing*, for example, calls such an absention "a cloud of forgetting":

> Just as the *cloud of unknowing* lies above you, between you and your God, so must you fashion a *cloud of forgetting* beneath you, between you and every created thing.

(ed. William Johnston, S. J. [Garden City: Doubleday, 1973], 53, Book I, chapter 5).

A close reading of "mystic" writers from Dante to San Juan de la Cruz will, by and large, bear out a persistent *metaphorical* sense of sleep as the state of revelatory readiness (sleep *in bono*), typically alongside a sense of sleep as a state of unmitigated sin (sleep *in malo*). For the case that metaphoric uses of the dream in Neo-Platonic thought constituted "figurative extensions of prior dream theories," see Newman, 64 and 158–85 (on the dream as metaphor in Hugh of St. Victor). This solid evidence notwithstanding, the safest course (I believe) is to reject any prescriptive, literalist interpretation of sleep in such texts and to recall the ubiquitous cautions against vain dreaming and credulousness in the mainstream writers of the period.

21. *Apochrypha Anecdota*, ed. Montague Rhodes James, in *Texts and Studies*, ed. R. Armitage Robinson, vol. 2, no. 3 (1893), rpt. Nendelm: Kraus, 1967), 11; translation mine. This text, along with many other apochryphal visions, is translated in volume 10 of *The Ante-Nicene Fathers: Translations of the Writings of the Fathers down to AD 325*, ed. Alexander Roberts and James Donaldson (Grand Rapids: Eerdmanns, 1953).

22. Walahfrid Strabo, *Visio Wettini: Text, Translation and Commentary*, ed. and tr. David Traill, Lateinische Sprache und Literatur des Mittelalters (Frankfurt: Peter Lang, 1974), 193; 46.

23. *Visio Wettini*, 13: " . . . most visions are recorded by someone other than the visionary."

24. *Medieval Latin*, ed. K. P. Harrington (Berkeley, University of California Press, 1964), 384; translation mine.

25. On "obsolescence" in medieval literature—especially in the *Canterbury Tales*—see Donald R. Howard, *The Idea of the Canterbury Tales* (Berkeley, University of California Press, 1976), esp. 90–105.

Chapter Two

1. *The Medieval Vision: Essays in History and Perception* (New York: Oxford University Press, 1976), especially 1–28. Erickson's second chapter, "Visionary Imagination" (pp. 29–47), contains a brief survey of medieval oneiromancy which focuses on her major theme of perceptual openness in the Middle Ages. More standard surveys of medieval dream lore can be found in Walter Clyde Curry, *Chaucer and the Mediaeval Sciences*, rev. ed (New York: Barnes and Noble, 1960); George G. Fox, *The Medieval Sciences in the Works of John Gower* (New York: Haskell House, 1966); and Morton T. Kelsey, *God, Dreams, and Revelation: A Christian Interpretation of Dreams* (Minneapolis: Augsburg, 1974). See also Jacques LeGoff, *Time, Work, and Culture in the Middle Ages*, tr. Arthur Goldhammer (Chicago: University of Chicago Press, 1980), 203–204 and F. X. Newman, "Somnium: Medieval Theories of Dreaming and the Form of Vision Poetry,"

(Ph.D. diss., Princeton, 1963), especially 42–53 for discussion of physiological causes.

2. C. G. Jung, *Psychology and Religion: West and East,* in *Collected Works,* 11 (New York: Random House, 1968), 19ff.

3. Dream science outside the West is much older. A. Leo Oppenheim has edited an extremely ancient Assyrian dream manual in "The Interpretation of Dreams in the Ancient Near East, with a Translation of an Assyrian Dream Book," in *Transactions of the American Philosophical Society* 46, no. 3 (1956); 179–373. By way of summary in the Introduction, Oppenheim reports that, even in this work,

> . . . dream experiences were recorded on three clearly differentiated planes: dreams as revelations of the deity which may or may not require interpretation; dreams which reflect, symptomatically, the state of mind, the spiritual or bodily health of the dreamer, which are mentioned but never recorded; and thirdly, mantic dreams in which forthcoming events are prognosticated. (p. 184)

On conjectural sources for some of Plato's ideas on dreams, see Carl Alfred Meier, "The Dream in Ancient Greece and Its Uses in Temple Cures (Incubation)," in *The Dream in Human Societies,* ed. Gustave E. von Grunebaum and Ernest Caillois (Berkeley: University of California Press, 1966), especially 304; and E. R. Dodds, *The Greeks and the Irrational* (Berkeley: University of California Press, 1961), especially 102–34.

4. Cf. Newman, pp. 38–42, on dreams as revelations.

5. *The Timaeus,* tr. Benjamin Jowett (New York: Bobbs Merrill, 1949), 55.

6. *The Republic of Plato,* tr. Francis MacDonald Cornford (New York: Oxford University Press, 1939), 296 (9, 570).

7. Ibid., 297.

8. Ibid., 297.

9. *On the Soul, Parva Naturalia, On Breath,* ed. and tr. E. S. Scott, Loeb Classical Library (Cambridge: Harvard University Press, 1935), 394.

10. Ibid., 365.

11. Ibid., 377. For additional discussion, see Meier, "The Dream in Ancient Greece . . . ," Dodds, and Kelsey, especially 49–78; Kelsey's unsympathetic view of Aristotle is due, of course, to his bias in favor of the dream as a revelation.

12. Titi Lucretii Cari, *De Rerum Naturae Libri Sex,* ed. Cyril Bailey (Oxford: Clarendon Press, 1947), I, 410; I, 409–11.

13. Ibid., I, 410–12; I, 411–13.

14. Ibid., I, 412; I, 413.

15. Ibid., I, 362–64; I, 363–65.

16. *De Senectute, De Amicitia, De Divinatione*, ed. and tr. William Armistead Falconer, Loeb Classical Library (Cambridge: Harvard University Press, 1923, rtp. 1964), 139; 140; "Cicero's arguments against dream divination are many and intelligent, and probably represent the attitude of pious and humane Roman rationalism," Newman, 56.

17. On the interpretation of dreams in this work, see Artemidorus of Daldis, *The Interpretation of Dreams*, tr. Robert J. White (Park Ridge: Noyes Press, 1975), esp. pages 14–16. On Artemidorus' central position in Arab oneiromancy, see Artemidorus d'Ephese, *Le Livre des Songes, traduit du Grec en Arab par Harnayn B. Ishaq*, ed. Toufic Fahd (Damas: Institut Francais de Damas, 1964), xiii. Claes Blum (in *Studies in the Dream Book of Artemidorus* [Uppsala: Almquist and Wiksells, 1936]) shows graphically Macrobius' debt to Artemidorus (pp. 53–56) and their common sources in Posidonius and others (p. 56ff). Newman, p. 29f, sees the preface as "defensive" and "complicated," rather than responsible and careful.

18. Ambrosii Theodosii Macrobii, *Commentarii in Somnium Scipionis*, ed. Iacobus Willis (Leipzig: Teubner, 1963), 8; tr. William Harris Stahl (New York: Columbia University Press, 1951), 87–88.

19. Macrobii, 9; Stahl, 88.

20. Macrobii, 10; Stahl, 89.

21. Macrobii, 10; Stahl, 84–85.

22. *PL* 40, col. 798; translation mine.

23. *PL* 32, col 687; St. Augustine, *Confessions*, tr. John K. Ryan (Garden City: Doubleday Image, 1960), 83.

24. *PL* 40, cols. 591ff.

25. *PL* 34, col. 455; translation mine.

26. *PL* 34, col. 469; translation mine.

27. *PL* 75, col. 827; tr. Kelsey, 158–59.

28. *PL* 75, col. 827; tr. Kelsey, 158–59 (except Scriptural quotation, mine).

29. *Commentarium in Ecclesiasticum, PL* 109, col. 1005; translation mine.

30. *Liber de Modo Bene Vivendi, PL* 184, col. 1301; translation mine. A quaint but powerful version of this notion, that belief in dreams is an occasion of sin, can be found in the writings of Richard Rolle:

> The fyrste comandement es, "Thy Lorde God þou sall loue and til him anely þou sall serue." In this comandement es forboden all mawmatryse, all wychecrafte and charemynge, the wylke may do na remedy till any seknes of mane, woman, or beste, for þay erre þe snarrys of þe develle by þe whilke he afforces hym to dyssayve mane-

213

kynde. Alswa in þis comandement es forboden to gyffe trouthe till sorcereye or till dyvynynges by sternys, or by dremys, or by any swylke thynges.

("A Notabill Tretys off the Ten Comandementys," in *English Prose Treatises of Richard Rolle de Hampole*, ed. George G. Perry, EETS OS 20 [London, 1866], 9).

31. *The World Order*, ed. and tr. M. J. Charlesworth, vol. 15 of *Summa Theologicae, Latin Text and English translation*, gen. ed. Thomas Gilby, O. P. (London and New York: Blackfriars, Eyre and Spottiswoode, and McGraw Hill, 1970), 26–27.

32. *Superstition and Irreverence*, ed. and tr. Thomas Franklin O'Meara and Michael John Duffy, vol. 40 of *Summa Theologicae* . . . , 58–59.

33. *Ioannis Saresberiensis Episcopi Carnotensis Polycratici*, ed. Clemens C. J. Webb (Oxford: Clarendon Press, 1901), 2, 87: *Frivolities of Courtiers and Footprints of Philosophers, Being the Second and Third Books and Selections from the Seventh and Eighth Books of the Polycraticus*, tr. John Dickinson (New York: Columbia University Press, 1927), 75.

34. See Newman, 135–41, who finds John of Salisbury's suppression of the relevant dream confusing and contradictory; see also LeGoff, 204, who asserts that "with John of Salisbury, the dream took its place in a veritable semiology of knowledge."

35. *Polycratici* 2, 97; tr. Dickinson, 84.

36. *Giovanni Boccaccio de Casibus Illustrorum Virorum*, Facs. Paris Ed. (1520), ed. Louis Brewer Hall (Gainesville: Scholars Facsimiles and Reprints, 1962), 66; *The Fates of Illustrious Men*, tr. and ed. Louis Brewer Hall (New York: Frederick Ungar, 1965), 64.

37. Ibid., 66; 65.

38. *On the Properites of Things: John of Trevisa's Translation of Bartholomeus Angelicus' De Proprietatibus Rerum*, ed. M. C. Seymour (Oxford: Clarendon Press, 1975), 336.

39. Ibid., 336.

40. *PL* 101, col. 1403; translation mine.

41. Macrobii, 11; tr. Stahl, 90.

42. *Marcus Tullius Cicero De Republica*, ed. K. Ziegler (Leipzig: Teubner, 1969), 127; "The Dream of Scipio," tr. H. H. Rice, in *The Norton Anthology of World Masterpieces*, ed. Maynard Mack et al. (New York: W. W. Norton, 1979), 1, 572.

43. *Piers Plowman: The Prologue and Passus I–VII of the B Text as Found in*

Bodleian MS. Laud 581, ed. J. A. W. Bennett (Oxford: Clarendon Press, 1972), 1, lines 1–10.

44. *Pearl,* ed. E. V. Gordon (Oxford: Oxford University Press, 1953, rpt. 1972), 2–3 lines 49–56.

45. Macrobii, 9; tr. Stahl, 88.

Chapter Three

1. On language as the "celebration of truth" in Augustine, see Marcia Colish, *The Mirror of Language: A Study in the Medieval Theory of Knowledge* (Lincoln: University of Nebraska Press, 1968), especially 40ff; see also John A. Alford, "The Grammatical Metaphor: A Survey of Its Use in the Middle Ages," *Speculum* 57 (1982): 737 on language as "the reflection of God in human institutions."

2. *PL* 32, col. 670; St. Augustine. *Confessions,* tr. John K. Ryan (Garden City: Doubleday Image, 1960), 55–56.

3. *PL* 32, cols. 670–71; tr. Ryan, 56–57.

4. See Colish, esp. 20, and Alford, esp. 737.

5. *PL* 34, col. 47; St. Augustine, *On Christian Doctrine,* tr. D. W. Robertson, Jr. Library of Liberal Arts (New York: Bobbs Merrill, 1958), 51.

6. *PL* 32, col. 720; tr. Ryan, 136.

7. *PL* 32, col. 762; tr. Ryan, 202.

8. *PL* 32, col. 762; tr. Ryan, 202.

9. *PL* 32, col. 762; tr. Ryan, 202.

10. See Colish, especially 17.

11. *PL* 32, col. 686; tr. Ryan, 82; see Alford, 741, for thoughts on the medieval response to the "humble style" of Scripture.

12. See Jesse Gellrich, *The Idea of the Book in the Middle Ages* (Ithaca: Cornell University Press, 1984), esp. 113–22, on the breakdown of the tripartite sign in Augustine.

13. Ambrosii Theodosii Macrobii, *Commentarii in Somnium Scipionis,* ed. Iacobus Willis (Leipzig: Teubner, 1963), 3; tr. William Harris Stahl (New York: Columbia University Press, 1951), 83.

14. The best discussion of the *narratio fabulosa* in Macrobius is Paule Demats, *Fabula: Trois Etudes de Mythographie antique et medievale* (Geneve: Droz, 1973), 19ff. On the later history of the *narratio fabulosa,* see Winthrop Wetherbee, *Platonism and Poetry in the Twelfth Century: The Literary Influence of the School of Chartres* (Princeton: Princeton University Press, 1972) and Lisa J. Kiser, *Telling*

Classical Tales: Chaucer and the Legend of Good Women (Ithaca: Cornell University Press, 1983), 39–42.

15. Macrobii, 5; tr. Stahl, 83.

16. Macrobii, 6; tr. Stahl, 84.

17. Macrobii, 6; tr. Stahl, 85.

18. Macrobii, 7; tr. Stahl, 86–87.

19. Peter Dronke, *Fabula: Explorations into the Uses of Myth in Medieval Platonism*, Mittellateinische Studien und Texte, 9 (Leiden: E. J. Brill, 1974), 74–75; p. 48.

20. Dronke, 75; p. 49.

21. Cf. Demats, 21: "Mas le divin est aussi le sacré, et comme tel il s'offre aussi bien a la méditation de l'elite pensante qui en pénetre la vérité profonde, qu'a la vénération du vulgaire qui s'arrête aux images. La fable est, comme le mystere, une pédagogie divine, assez souple pour conduire les initiés, suivant leurs aptitudes, a la contemplation des essences ou a l'adoration des symboles." See also Wetherbee, *Platonism and Poetry* . . . , especially 36–48 on the concept of the *integumentum* in Guilaume de Conche and Abelard.

22. *PL* 34, cols. 38–39; tr. Robertson, 37.

23. These notions are strikingly parallel to modern ones on, for example, the arbitrary motivation of the sign. For example, see Umberto Eco, *Semiotics and the Philosophy of Language* (Bloomington: Indiana University Press, 1984), 16 and elsewhere.

24. *PL* 34, col. 21; tr. Robertson, 11.

25. Guillaume de Lorris et Jean de Meun, *Le Roman de la Rose*, ed. Felix Lecoy (Paris: Librarie Honore Champion, 1965), 1, 1; tr. Geoffrey Chaucer, in *The Complete Works of Geoffrey Chaucer*, ed. Fred Norris Robertson, 2nd ed. (Boston: Houghton Mifflin, 1961), 565.

26. Lecoy, 1-2; Chaucer, 565.

27. Lecoy, 2; Chaucer, 565.

28. Lecoy, 2; Chaucer, 565.

29. William Ockham, *Ockham: Philosophical Writings*, ed. and tr. Philotheus Boehner, O. F. .M. (London: Nelson, 1957), 41a; 41b.

30. The best discussions of the *via moderna* and Chaucer are Sheila Delany, *Chaucer's House of Fame: The Poetics of Skeptical Fideism* (Chicago: University of Chicago Press, 1977), 7–21; and Larry Sklute, *Virtue of Necessity: Inconclusiveness and Narrative Form in Chaucer's Poetry* (Columbus: Ohio State University Press, 1984), 13–19.

31. Boehner, 42a; p. 42b.

32. Boehner, 44a; p. 44b.

33. Russell Peck, "Chaucer and the Nominalist Questions," *Speculum* 53 (1978): 757. See also J. Stephen Russell, "Skelton's *Bouge of Court*: A Nominalist Allegory," *Renaissance Papers 1980* (1980): 1–9, for a dicussion of nominalism in a dream vision.

Chapter Four

1. Among much that has been written on the dreamer figure in the dream vision, Spearing's comment puts the problem of the ambivalence of the dreamer best:

> . . . the dream-framework inevitably brings the poet into his poem, not merely as the reteller of a story which has its origin elsewhere, but as the person who experiences the whole substance of the poem.

(*Medieval Dream-Poetry* [Cambridge: Cambridge University Press, 1976], 5).

Spearing goes on to note that this appearance has ambiguous effects, allowing the poet both to call attention to himself and to disappear from his text. This perception of unmitigated ambiguity is a function of Spearing's large claim that the form itself is ambiguous, either "the product of divine inspiration or . . . the expression of a merely human mood or fantasy" (p. 5).

2. Guillaume de Lorris et Jean de Meun, *Le Roman de la Rose*, ed. Felix Lecoy (Paris: Librarie Honore Champion, 1965), 1, 4; tr. Geoffrey Chaucer in *The Complete Works of Geoffrey Chaucer*, ed. Fred Norris Robinson, 2nd ed. (Boston: Houghton Mifflin, 1961), 566.

3. Viktor Shklovsky, "*Tristram Shandy Sterna: Stilistichesky kommentary,*" in *Sterni i teoriya romana* (Petrograd, 1921); tr. as "Stern's *Tristram Shandy*: Stylistic Commentary" by Lee T. Lemon and Marion J. Reis, eds., *Russian Formalist Criticism: Four Essays* (Lincoln: University of Nebraska Press, 1965), esp. 57:

> The idea of *plot* is too often confused with the description of events— what I propose provisionally to call the *story*. The story is, in fact, only material for plot formulation. The plot of *Eugene Onegin* is, therefore, not the romance of the hero with Tatyana, but the fashioning of the subject of this story as produced by the introduction of disrupting digressions.

Such a distinction works quite nicely for the dream vision, the plot of which, ultimately, is similarly the fashioning of a subject—the dreamer—a figure which will become both subject and object in the final analysis.

4. Lecoy, 1, 44–45; Chaucer, 579. See Kevin Brownlee, *Poetic Identity in Guillaume de Machaut* (Madison: University of Wisconsin Press, 1977), 12 on "dedoublement" in Guillaume de Lorris.

5. Lecoy, 1, 45; Chaucer, 579.

6. Lecoy, 1, 47; Chaucer, 579.

7. John Fleming makes this point—the irrelevance of the well's *sentence* as interpreted by Amant—quite forcefully: The glossator's perspective on the well "has much in common with that which sees *Othello* as a warning that ladies should look after their linen." *The Roman de la Rose: A Study in Allegory and Iconography* (Princeton: Princeton University Press, 1969), 96.

8. Lecoy, 1, 47; Chaucer, 579.

9. Compare Sheila Delay: The dream vision form " . . . involved the reader more intimately than straightforward narrative, for the reader becomes both the interpreter of the dream and the judge of its truth," *Chaucer's House of Fame: The Poetics of Skeptical Fideism* (Chicago: University of Chicago Press, 1977), 38. In fact, as I show below, the involvement of the reader is more intimate and complex than even this quotation suggests, since the status of the dream (and hence of the dreamer) are yet two more separate but interdependent interpretive problems for the reader.

10. William Langland, *Piers Plowman: The Prologue and Passus I-VII of the B Text as Found in Bodleian MS. Laud 581*, ed. J. A. W. Bennett (Oxford: Clarendon Press, 1972), 1, lines 11–20.

11. *Pearl*, ed. E. V. Gordon (Oxford: Oxford University Press, 1953, rpt. 1972), 9–10, lines 241–52.

12. *The Dream Thought of Piers Plowman* (New Haven: Yale University Press, 1974), 25.

13. Cf. Paul Piehler, *The Visionary Landscape: A Study in Medieval Allegory* (Montreal: McGill-Queens University Press, 1971), 19, 144–62 (the chapter on *Pearl*), for the dream allegory as a therapeutic experience.

14. Compare Kirk:

> In places this method succeeds in transmitting to the reader the vivid immediacy and almost intolerable pressure of actual dreams, in which we are taken possession of by something we can recognize as our own experience but stripped of the controls and modulations consciousness can always impose on empathy. In such states, complete empathy and total strangeness coexist. [*Dream Thought*, p. 181]

Chapter Five

1. I argue this in detail in "Lady Meed, Parsons, and the *Piers Plowman Visio*," *Mediaevalia* 5 (1982): 239–57.

2. This is a fairly radical departure from the critical tradition on the *Book of the*

Duchess. In his diplomatic survey of the critical literature on the poem in *Companion to Chaucer Studies* (ed. Beryl Rowland [New York: Oxford University Press, 1968]), D. W. Robertson can legitimately begin, "*The Book of the Duchess* is an elegy for Blanche, Duchess of Lancaster, who died of the plague on September 12, 1369" (p. 332). Although Robertson's survey shows that there has been considerable movement within this basically elegiac definition—notably his own and Bernard Huppé's *Fruyt and Chaf*—we are only now beginning to question this fundamental view of the poem. See, for example, Barbara Nolan, "The Art of Expropriation: Chaucer's Narrator in *The Book of the Duchess* in *New Perspectives in Chaucer Criticism*, ed. Donald Rose (Norman: Pilgrim Books, 1981), 203–22; R. A. Shoaf, " 'Mutatio Amoris': 'Penitentia' and the form of *The Book of the Duchess*," *Genre* 14 (1981): 163–89; "Stalking the Sorrowful H(e)art: Penitential Lore and the Hunt Scene in Chaucer's *The Book of the Duchess*," *JEGP* 79 (1980): 313–24.

3. Throughout this discussion and that of the *Hous of Fame*, I will consistently refer to the Chaucerian dreamer-narrator and dreamer-character as "Geffrey" when there is no reason to distinguish between character and narrator. I will use "Chaucer" consistently to refer to the poet.

4. Cf. Nolan, "The Art of Expropriation" and John Gardner, "Style as Meaning in the *Book of the Duchess*," *Language and Style* 2 (1969), for whom the *Book of the Duchess* is a dilation on "the uplifting force of love" (p. 145) developed through a critical dramatization of the artificial courtly language of French poetry.

5. "Routhe" or "reuthe" is, according to the *Oxford English Dictionary*, a word with a decidedly Anglo-Saxon flavor. The *OED*'s earliest entries for the word are in the twelfth century, but the root of "routhe," probably Old English "reccan" ("to care") is much older. There is, of course, no hard evidence that Chaucer deliberately chose "routhe" over the newer, French "pitee" to emphasize plainness or rusticity, but, given the overall French flavor of the *Book of the Duchess*, the word does jar.

6. Quoted in D. S. Brewer, ed., *Chaucer and Chaucerians: Critical Studies in Middle English Literature* (University: University of Alabama Press, 1967), 2; my thanks to Professor Rupert Pickens of the University of Kentucky for help with the translation. See also Nolan, "The Art of Expropriation," especially 209, and Phillip Boardman, "Courtly Language and the Strategy of Consolation in the *Book of the Duchess*," *ELH* 74 (1977): 567–79.

7. Brewer, 3.

8. Charles Muscatine (in *Chaucer and the French Tradition: A Study in Style and Meaning* [Berkeley: University of California Press, 1957]) sees this double thrust of the conventionality of the poem:

> The style of the *Book of the Duchess*, then, shows two concurrent movements in the light of the French tradition: one toward a func-

tional use of courtly convention, the other toward a realism that suggests comic disenchantment. (p. 107)

9. See Nolan, "The Art of Expropriation," 217, for Ceys and Alcion.

10. Mother Angela Carson, O. S. U., in "Easing the 'Hert' in *The Book of the Duchess*," *Chaucer Review* 1 (1966): 156–66 sees the story of Ceys and Alcion as told "matter-of-factly and at a quick tempo" with "the impression of indifference rather than compassion on the part of the narrator" (p. 157).

11. Compare Muscatine:

To "thilke Morpheus" he [Geffrey] makes a comically literal offer of a featherbed, then throws into the bargain an array of bedroom finery that would do credit to a mercer's apprentice; for sleep he will pay Juno too. Here are the makings of him who rimed the tale of Sir Thopas. (p. 104)

This may overstate it a bit—the bed comes from Machaut—but Muscatine is correct that Geffrey thoroughly botches the detail with tastelessness and a bourgeois nose for the price tag.

12. R. A. Shoaf in "Stalking the Sorrowful H(e)art," (p. 316), sees the whelp as an image of the penitent's conscience, which chases the fox (sins) into its den (the heart of the penitent). On this point he cites *Le Livre de Seyntz Medecines* of Henry de Gourmont, father of Blanche of Lancaster. If this association is intended, then the whelp is clearly more than a transitional device, though finally these penitential associations do not argue against this present reading. If the *Book of the Duchess* is about communication and communion, then the whelp, in bringing together Geffrey and the Black Knight, represents the wordless will to sympathy.

13. In conventional expectations, see Muscatine, especially 98–101; Alfred David (in *The Strumpet Muse: Art and Morals in Chaucer's Poetry* [Bloomington: Indiana University Press, 1976]): "[In the *Book of the Duchess*] . . . the audience is prepared to hear an allegory of love" (p. 18); and W. H. French (in "The Man in Black's Lyric," *JEGP*, 56 [1957]): "He [Geffrey] is a confirmed lover on the most approved courtly model . . . " (p. 236).

14. For another view, see John M. Steadman, "Chaucer's 'Whelp': A Symbol of Marital Fidelity," *Notes and Queries*, 1 (1956): 374–75.

15. For the various views on the reaction to the lament, see note 4 to the Introduction above; Robertson (*Companion to Chaucer Studies*), especially 333–34; A. C. Spearing, *Medieval Dream-Poetry* (Cambridge: Cambridge University Press, 1976), esp. 66–68; and Muscatine, who describes the narrator's " . . . kinship with the Man in Black—they are both disappointed lovers,—but his characterization is such that we cannot take his affairs so seriously" (p. 103).

16. French, p. 241:

Himself a person out of the pages of Ovid, Guillaume de Lorris, Machaut, Froissart and the rest, he supposed he saw before him another of the same breed.

17. Compare Nolan:

As the argument of the Duchess proceeds, we come to understand that this plea for common sense (lines 16–21) points to the poem's most serious themes. We will learn that the poetry of feeling and the platitudes of bookish, high-toned consolation cannot fully encompass or assuage personal grief. One is faced, finally, with the undecorated statement of fact, "She is ded." ["The Art of Expropriation," p. 213]

18. Compare Gardner:

Ironically, his [Geffrey's] art is as obscure as the Knight's allegory of Fortune. Though we understand his unhappiness in love, just as the narrator understands the Knight's grief when he first overhears him lamenting in the woods, Chaucer's narrator has failed to make the necessary open statement, relinquishing art for self-surrender. ["Style as Meaning," p. 170]

19. For useful summaries of the origins of the formal and doctrinal controversies concerning *Pearl*, see Rene Wellek, "The *Pearl*: An Interpretation of the Middle English Poem," *Studies in English by Members of the English Seminar of Charles University* (1933), rpt. in *Sir Gawain and Pearl: Critical Essays*, ed. Robert J. Blanch (Bloomington: Indiana University Press, 1971), 3–10, and A. C. Spearing, *The Gawain-Poet: A Critical Study* (Cambridge: Cambridge University Press, 1970), 129, note 1. In brief, the earliest students of the poem, notably ten Brink, Gollancz, and Osgood, saw it as an elegy satisfying the father's wish to know that his little daughter is in Heaven. Reacting to this view (which grew to encourage excessive biographical speculation), a group of critics including Carleton Brown ("The Author of *Pearl* Considered in Light of His Theological Opinions," *PMLA*, 19 [1904]) and Sister Mary Madeleva (*Pearl: A Study in Spiritual Dryness* [New York: Appelton, 1925]) began to treat the poem as allegorical, doctrinal, apocalyptic, or otherwise homiletic. Most contemporary analyses of *Pearl* must by rights be considered broadly "allegorical," though I single out the discussions of Spearing and Blenker below.

20. *The Gawain-Poet: A Critical Study*, 96–170.

21. *The Gawain-Poet: A Critical Study*, 128.

22. "The Theological Structure of *Pearl*," *Traditio* 24 (1968): 43–75; rpt. in *Pearl: Critical Essays*, ed. John Conley (South Bend: University of Notre Dame Press, 1970), 220–71.

23. On formal similarities between *Pearl* and the *Piers Plowman Visio*, see J. Stephen Russell, "Meaningless Dreams and Meaningful Poems: The Form of the Medieval Dream Vision," *Massachusetts Studies in English* 7 (1980): 20-32.

24. *Pearl*, ed. E. V. Gordon (Oxford: Oxford University Press, 1953, rpt. 1972), 16, lines 421–28. Hereafter cited in text by line numbers.

25. On the egotism and self-absorption of the *Pearl* narrator early in the poem, see Lynn Staley Johnson, *The Gawain Poet* (Madison: University of Wisconsin Press, 1984), 165ff.

26. See Johnson, *The Gawain Poet*, 188–89, on the special appropriateness of this tag line.

27. See Wellek, "The *Pearl* . . . ," and D. W. Robertson, Jr., "The 'Heresy' of *Pearl*: The Pearl as Symbol," *MLN* 65 (1950): 152-62, rpt. in Conley, 291-96, which illustrate the complexity of the poem's response to the Bradwardinians.

28. The point of the *Visio*, in fact, seems to be the irrational and gratuitous "mede" of salvation and the challenge this concept presents to the human mind; even in his attack on the strumpet Lady Meed in Passus Four, the strait-laced character Conscience seems compelled to admit that there is most certainly a sense of meed *in bono*: God's meed of salvation. See Russell, "Lady Meed, Pardons, and the *Piers Plowman Visio*."

29. *PL* 175, cols. 116–17; tr. Henry Osborn Taylor, *The Medieval Mind* (Cambridge: Harvard University Press, 1949), 2, 388–89, quoted in Blenker, 227-28.

30. I use the term "oracular" here in its technical sense in medieval oneiromancy. Spearing, in *The Gawain-Poet*, 145–52, discusses this context, noting the poignance of the inverted parent-child relationship.

31. *The Cloud of Unknowing and the Book of Privy Counselling*, ed. William Johnston, S. J. (Garden City: Doubleday Image, 1973), 60. For another suggestion on mystical connotations in *Pearl*, see Spearing, *The Gawain-Poet*, especially 107-17; Spearing cites Richard of St. Victor on sleep as a metaphor for the true contemplative's spiritual openness to divine visitation (p. 115). The conventional frame narrative of the apocalypse, however, regularly insists that the visionary is not asleep, not even in a "sleep of the senses and passions."

32. *The Cloud of Unknowing*, 52. Contemporary "Cloud mysticism," called "centering prayer," still emphasizes this emptying of the mind of even excellent thoughts and images. Basil Pennington, O. S. C. O., a teacher of centering prayer, tells the story of an old Trappist who sought him out troubled after reading injunctions against thoughts and images in prayer. "Does this mean," he asked, "that I should struggle against ecstatic visions of Jesus?" Father Basil answered yes.

The anecdote is relevant because, under the rubric of the dream vision that I am suggesting, both the dream and the poem are thrilling impediments to true spiritual communion. If I am correct about *Pearl*'s deconstruction of the discourse of eschatology, then the final lesson of the poem is to cast it away.

33. *Chaucer's House of Fame: The Poetics of Skeptical Fideism* (Chicago: University of Chicago Press, 1977). See also Piero Boitani, *Chaucer and the Imaginary World of Fame* (New York: Barnes and Noble, 1984) and Laurence K. Shook's "The House of Fame" in *Companion to Chaucer Studies*, ed. Beryl Rowland (New York: Oxford University Press, 1968), 241–54, which summarizes the relationships among Syferd, Patch, Ruggiers, and Koonce.

34. Delany, 3, 34–35.

35. Walter Clyde Curry, *Chaucer and the Mediaeval Sciences* (New York: Barnes and Noble, 1926, rev. 1960), 240; Clive Staples Lewis, *The Discarded Image: An Introduction to Medieval and Renaissance Literature* (Oxford: Oxford University Press, 1971), 63–64; and B. G. Koonce *Chaucer and the Tradition of Fame: Symbolism in the* House of Fame, (Princeton: Princeton University Press, 1966), 5, 46, 55.

36. The fullest account of the Proem to the *Hous of Fame* is in B. G. Koonce's *Chaucer and the Tradition of Fame* . . . , 45–56. Koonce explicates the Proem very carefully, providing patristic analogues for Chaucer's statements about the variety of causes for dreams, showing, not surprisingly, that there are solid Scriptural and scientific bases—*auctores*—for all of Chaucer's contradictory theories about dreams. This scholarship is undercut, it seems to me, by Koonce's implicit trust in Geffrey's identification of this particular dream as an *avisioun* and by just what this identification might mean.

Koonce is equally unclear on precisely what the status of a feigned or fictive *visio* or *somnium coeleste* or what have you might be; real *visiones* are prophetic, certainly, but feigned ones, Koonce says, require interpretation (pp. 5–6). This does not speak to the status of the *content* of the dream but addresses only its allegorical form. If, as Koonce claims, the *Hous of Fame* is a fictive *visio* or *somnium*, then its contents are somehow fictively prophetic, a category rather inscrutable in either medieval or modern terms. In any case, even stipulating that Geffrey identifies this dream as an *avisioun* tells us nothing really, for the statement is made rather backhandedly in a Proem that displays, at best, random oneiric knowledge—including six terms for Macrobius' *five* varieties—and prays twice that everything will turn out all right.

Delany's discussion of the Proem (pp. 36–44) is fittingly more diffuse and ambivalent than Koonce's: she claims (as Spearing does in *Medieval Dream-Poetry*, p. 75) that the Proem is an ironic deviation from traditional truth topoi, which complicates rather than settling questions of authenticity.

37. Compare Delany:

The *House of Fame* takes us to what, for the poet, is the heart of pluralism: the tradition itself. Not incoherency but incongruity is the characteristic of the *House of Fame*: indeed it is its subject, because incongruity is the essence of Fame. (p. 35)

38. See Larry Sklute, *Virtue of Necessity: Inconclusiveness and Narrative Form in Chaucer's Poetry* (Columbus: Ohio State University Press, 1984), 138, on "saugh I grave."

39. Compare Boitani, who nicely captures the peculiarly participatory nature of the Dido episode:

Thus Dido's words and the laments resound, not in space, but in the mind, in an absolute physical silence. They echo in thought, which can then digress and extend to famous cases of betrayed heroines: Chaucer drops the formula 'saugh I grave' precisely at the beginning of the Dido episode, picking it up again as soon as the latter is finished. In silence the *Aeneid* is recreated and lives on the walls, inscribed by the poet's pity, external and intimate at the same time.

Chaucer and the Imaginary World of Fame (New York: Barnes and Noble, 1984), 10.

As a maker himself, Geffrey is implicated or involved in the implicit attack on authority and tradition in the Dido episode. See also Jesse Gellrich, *The Idea of the Book in the Middle Ages* (Ithaca: Cornell University Press, 1984), especially 184, on deciding between Vergil's and Ovid's Dido.

40. Compare Delany: [In attempting to face the conflicting senses of the historical Dido,] " . . . Chaucer grants the validity of conflicting truths and confronts the problem with no way of deciding between them" (p. 57). I would agree that conflicting claims and their as yet unassailable authority are the themes of this poem, but I question Delany's sense that *deciding between them* is the ultimate issue or that the poem counsels acquiescence to double truth. If the *Hous of Fame* is Chaucer's "art poetical" as many have claimed, then it would be more consonant with that sense of the poem to hope that Geffrey and the reader might come to decide *beyond* rather than *between* conflicting authorial claims. I agree, in fact, with Donald Howard (in *The Idea of the Canterbury Tales* [Berkeley: University of California Press, 1978], 330–32) that the pluralism which emerges in the *Hous of Fame*, both here and especially at its conclusion, make it a fitting introduction or preamble to the *Canterbury Tales*, in which pluralism is an organizing principle as well as a theme.

41. *PL* 34, col. 38; St. Augustine, *On Christian Doctrine*, tr. D. W. Robertson, Jr., Library of Liberal Arts (New York: Bobbs Merrill, 1958), 36.

42. Compare Robert B. Burlin:

The dreamer-narrator listens in a literal-minded way; he sees and describes without comment, reads and transcribes without engaged response. He may occasionally be moved to pity and terror, but never for long or with sustained seriousness. He resides innocently upon the surface of his experiences, shaping and containing them by his presence, but rarely interpreting or generalizing the powerful sensations forced upon him. The dreamer's reactions are arrested at the first stage of perception, the Thomist *experimentum*; he stands before a brave new world not of his making, though nominally his by virtue of the dream fiction.

Chaucerian Fictions (Princeton: Princeton University Press, 1977), 27.

43. Compare Boitani:

Chaucer's Fame, suspended between heaven, earth and sea, between life and death, does not stand at the end of time, but in a prehistorical, eternal present. She creates history by determining who and what will survive in the memory of men, and with which connotations. Her 'dom,' her a-moral judgement, is not history, but historiography.

(*Chaucer and the Imaginary World of Fame*, p. 172)

44. Boitani (*Chaucer and the Imaginary World of Fame*) cites *Inferno IV*, line 113 as an analogue (p. 83).

45. Compare Boitani (*Chaucer and the Imaginary World of Fame*):

When the man of great authority appears in the poem's last line, we are back at square one. The *auctoritates* with whom Geffrey has identified himself and into whom he has refused to incarcerate himself— Virgil, Ovid, Dante—rise again. Chaucer, as the last line's derivation from *Inferno IV* testifies, is about to enter another Castle of Limbo. The *House of Fame*, like a short story by Borges, would repeat itself forever. (p. 208)

and Gellrich (*The Idea of the Book in the Middle Ages*):

The "man of gret auctorite" must be anonymous. To search for his name is to go in the wrong direction. Chaucer has led in the last line of the poem to the origin that myths always lead to: they are anonymous. (p. 198)

Epilogue

1. "Mum and the Sothesegger," in *English Verse: 1300-1500*, ed. John Burrow (London: Longmans, 1977), 258-59, (lines 854-68). Hereafter cited in text by line numbers.

2. *The Temple of Glass* in *John Lydgate: Poems*, ed. John Norton Smith, Claren-

don Medieval and Tudor Series (Oxford: Clarendon Press, 1966), 67, (lines 1-9). Hereafter cited in text by line numbers.

3. As evidence of this improbable thesis, consider that there are no witches or warlocks in Chaucer's poetry and at most one ghost—depending on how one interprets Dido in the *Hous of Fame*. Now consider Shakespeare. The reason for this is certainly not that the Middle Ages was a more *rational* period than the Renaissance: I suspect the reason devolves to Macrobius once more—only respectable, decent, and plausible fictions were available to poets and rhetors in the mainstream medieval tradition.

4. *The Anchor Anthology of Sixteenth Century Verse*, ed., Richard S. Sylvester (Garden City: Doubleday Anchor, 1974), 138-39, (lines 1-7).

BIBLIOGRAPHY

Primary Sources

Aeschylus. *The Oresteia.* Tr. Richmond Lattimore. Chicago: University of Chicago Press, 1953.

Alighieri, Dante. *The Divine Comedy.* Ed. and tr. Charles Singleton. Bollingen Series 80. Princeton: Princeton University Press, 1970.

[Alcuin.] "The Prayer of Alcuin." In J. P. Migne, *Patrologia Latine,* vol. 101, col. 1403.

Aristotle. *On the Soul, Parva Naturalia, On Breath.* Ed. and tr. E. S. Scott. Loeb Classical Library. Cambridge: Harvard University Press, 1935.

Artemidorus d'Ephese. *Le Livre des Songes, traduit du Grec en Arab par Harnayn B. Ishaq.* Ed. Toufic Fahd. Damascus: Institut Francais de Damas, 1964.

Artemidorus of Daldis. *The Interpretation of Dreams.* Tr. Robert J. White. Park Ridge: Noyes Press, 1975.

Augustinus, Aurelius, St. *Confessiones.* In J. P. Migne, ed. *Patrologia Latine,* vol. 32.

————. *Confessions.* Tr. John K. Ryan. Garden City: Doubleday, 1960.

————. *De Cura pro Mortibus.* In J. P. Migne, *Patrologia Latine,* vol. 40.

————. *De Genesi ad Litteram.* In J. P. Migne, *Patrologia Latine,* vol. 34.

————. *Liber de Spiritu et Anima.* In J. P. Migne, *Patrologia Latine,* vol. 40.

————. *De Doctrina Christiana.* In J. P. Migne, *Patrologia Latine,* vol. 34.

————. *On Christian Doctrine.* Tr. D. W. Robertson, Jr. Library of Liberal Arts. New York: Bobbs-Merrill, 1958.

Bartholomeus Anglicus. *On the Properties of Things: John of Trevisa's Translation of Bartholomeus Anglicus' De Proprietatibus Rerum.* Ed. M. C. Seymour. Oxford: Clarendon Press, 1975.

Bernard of Clairvaux, St. *Liber de Modo Bene Vivendi.* In J. P. Migne, *Patrologia Latine,* vol. 184.

Boccaccio, Giovanni. *De Casibus Illustrorum Virorum.* Facs. Paris Ed. (1520). Ed. Louis Brewer Hall. Gainesville: Scholars Facsimiles and Reprints, 1962.

————. *The Fates of Illustrious Men.* Tr. and ed. Louis Brewer Hall. New York: Frederick Ungar, 1965.

Boethius. *The Theological Tractates and the Consolation of Philosophy.* Ed. R. F. Stewart, E. K. Rand, and S. J. Tester. Loeb Classical Library. Cambridge: Harvard University Press, 1918, rev. 1973.

————. *The Consolation of Philosophy.* Tr. Richard Green. The Library of Liberal Arts. New York: Bobbs-Merrill, 1962.

Ciceronis, M. Tullius. *De Re Publica.* Ed. K. Ziegler. Leipzig: Teubner, 1969.

————. *De Senectute, De Amicitia, De Divinatione.* Ed. and tr. William Armitage Falconer. Loeb Classical Library. Cambridge: Harvard University Press, 1923, rpt. 1964.

————. "The Dream of Scipio." In *The Norton Anthology of World Masterpieces.* Tr. H. A. Rice, ed. Maynard Mack *et al.,* 4th ed. New York: W. W. Norton, 1979.

Colunga, Alberto, and Antonio Turrado, eds. *Biblia Sacra juxta Vulgatam Clemintinam.* Madrid: Biblioteca de Autores Cristianos, 1977.

Gordon, E. V., ed. *Pearl.* Oxford: Oxford University Press, 1953, rpt. 1972.

Gregory the Great, St. *Moralia in Job.* In J. P. Migne, *Patrologia Latine,* vol. 75.

Guillaume de Conche. *Commentary on the Commentarium in Somnium Scipionis,* in *Fabula: Explorations into the Uses of Myth in Medieval Platonism.* Ed. and tr. Peter Dronke. Mittelateinische Studien und Texte, 9. Leiden: E. J. Brill, 1974.

Guillaume de Lorris et Jean de Meun. *Le Roman de la Rose*. Ed. Felix Lecoy. Paris: Librarie Honore Champion, 1965.

————. Tr. Geoffrey Chaucer in *The Complete Works of Geoffrey Chaucer*. Ed. Fred Norris Robinson. 2nd ed. Boston: Houghton Mifflin, 1961.

Harrington, K. P., ed. "Apocalypsis Golias." In *Medieval Latin*. Berkeley: University of California Press, 1964.

Herodotus. *The History of Herodotus*. Tr. George Rawlinson, ed. Manuel Komroff. New York: Tudor, 1941.

Hugh of St. Victor. *Nineteen Homilies in Salomis Ecclesiasten*. In J. P. Migne, *Patrologia Latine*, vol. 175.

James, Montague Rhodes, ed. *Visio Sancti Pauli*, in *Texts and Studies*, ed. R. Armitrage Robinson, vol. 2, no. 3. 1893, rpt. Nendelm: Kraus, 1967.

[John of Salisbury] Johannes Saresburiensis. *Polycraticus*. Ed. Clemens C. I. Webb. 2 vols. Oxford: Clarendon Press, 1901.

————. *Frivolities of Courtiers and Footprints of Philosophers, Being the Second and Third Books and Selections from the Seventh and Eighth Books of the Polycraticus*. Tr. John Dickinson. New York: Columbia University Press, 1927.

Johnson, William, S. J., ed. *The Cloud of Unknowing and the Book of Privy Counselling*. Garden City: Doubleday, 1973.

Langland, William. *Piers Plowman: The Prologue and Passus I-VII of the B Text as Found in Bodleian MS. Laud 581*. Ed. J. A. W. Bennett. Oxford: Clarendon Press, 1972.

[Lucretius] Carus, Titus Lucretius. *De Rerum Naturae Libri Sex*. Ed. Cyril Bailey. 2 vols. Oxford: Clarendon Press, 1947.

Macrobius, Ambrosius Theodosius. *Commentarii in Somnium Scipionis*. Ed. Iacobus Willis. Leipzig: Teubner, 1963.

————. *Commentary on the Somnium Scipionis*. Tr. William Harris Stahl. New York: Columbia University Press, 1951.

Plato. *The Timaeus*. Tr. Benjamin Jowett. New York: Bobbs-Merrill, 1949.

————. *The Republic of Plato*. Tr. Francis MacDonald Cornford. New York: Oxford University Press, 1939.

Rhabanus Maurus. *Commentarium in Ecclesiasticum.* In J. P. Migne, *Patrologia Latine*, vol. 109.

Roberts, Alexander, and James Donaldson, eds. *Visio Sancti Pauli*, in *The Ante-Nicene Fathers: Translations of the Writings of the Fathers down to AD 325.* Grand Rapids: Eerdmans, 1953.

Rolle, Richard. "A Notabill Tretys off the Ten Comandementys."In *English Prose Treatises of Richard Rolle de Hampole.* Ed. George G. Perry. EETS OS 20. London, 1866.

Sandars, N. K., trans. *The Epic of Gilgamesh.* Harmondsworth: Penguin, 1972.

Strabo, Walahfrid. *Vision Wettini: Text, Translation and Commentary.* Ed. and tr. David Traill. Lateinische Sprache und Literatur des Mittelalters. Frankfurt: Peter Lang, 1974.

Sweet, Henry. *Sweet's Anglo-Saxon Reader.* Rev. Dorothy Whitelock. Oxford: Oxford University Press, 1967.

Thomas Aquinas, St. *Summa Theologicae, Latin Text and English Translation.* Ed. Thomas Gilby, O. P. London and New York: Blackfriars, Eyre and Spottiswoode, and McGraw Hill, various dates.

[Vergil] Publius Vergilius Maronis. *Opera.* Ed. R. A. B. Mynors. Oxford Classical Texts. Oxford: Clarendon Press, 1969.

———. *The Aeneid.* Tr. Allen Mandelbaum. New York: Bantam, 1972.

William of Ockham. *Ockham: Philosophical Writings.* Ed. and Tr. Philotheus Boehner, O. F. M. London: Nelson, 1957.

Secondary Sources

Alford, John A. "The Grammatical Metaphor: A Survey of Its Use in the Middle Ages." *Speculum* 57 (1982): 726–60.

Baker, Donald C. "The Dreamer Again in the *Book of the Duchess.*" *PMLA* 70 (1955): 279–82.

Blanch, Robert J., ed. *Sir Gawain and Pearl: Critical Essays.* Bloomington: Indiana University Press, 1971.

Blenker, Louis. "The Theological Structure of *Pearl.*" *Traditio* 24 (1968): 43–75. Rpt. in *Pearl: Critical Essays.* Ed. John Conley, 220–71. South Bend: University of Notre Dame Press, 1970.

Bloomfield, Morton. *Piers Plowman as a Fourteenth Century Apocalypse.* New Brunswick: Rutgers University Press, 1961.

Blum, Claes. *Studies in the Dream Book of Artemidorus.* Uppsala: Almquist and Wiksells, 1936.

Boardman, Phillip C. "Courtly Language and the Strategy of Consolation in the *Book of the Duchess." ELH* 74 (1977): 567–79.

Boitani, Piero. *Chaucer and the Imaginary World of Fame.* New York: Barnes and Noble, 1984.

Brewer, Derek S., ed. *Chaucer and Chaucerians: Critical Studies in Middle English Literature.* University: University of Alabama Press, 1967.

————, ed. *Writers and their Background: Geoffrey Chaucer.* Athens: Ohio University Press, 1975.

Brownlee, Kevin. *Poetic Identity in Guillaume de Machaut.* Madison: University of Wisconsin Press, 1984.

Burlin, Robert B. *Chaucerian Fictions.* Princeton: Princeton University Press, 1977.

Calin, William C. *A Poet at the Fountain: Essays on the Narrative Verse of Guillaume de Machaut.* Lexington: University of Kentucky Press, 1974.

Carson, Mother Angela, O. S. U. "Easing the 'Hert' in *The Book of the Duchess." Chaucer Review* 1 (1966): 156–66.

Colish, Marcia. *The Mirror of Language: A Study in the Medieval Theory of Knowledge.* Lincoln: University of Nebraska Press, 1968.

Conley, John, ed. *Pearl: Critical Essays.* South Bend: University of Notre Dame Press, 1970.

Cunningham, J. V. "Convention as Structure: The Prologue to the *Canterbury Tales." MP* 49 (1952): 172–81.

Curry, Walter Clyde. *Chaucer and the Medieval Sciences.* New York: Barnes and Noble, 1926, rev. 1960.

Dahlberg, Charles. "Macrobius and the Unity of the *Roman de la Rose." Studies in Philology* 58 (1961): 573–82.

David, Alfred. *The Strumpet Muse: Art and Morals in Chaucer's Poetry.* Bloomington: Indiana University Press, 1976.

Delany, Sheila. *Chaucer's House of Fame: The Poetics of Skeptical Fideism.* Chicago: University of Chicago Press, 1977.

Demats, Paule. *Fabula: Trois Etudes de Mythographie antique et medievale.* Geneva: Droz, 1973.

Dodds, E. R. *The Greeks and the Irrational.* Berkeley: University of California Press, 1961.

Dronke, Peter. *Fabula: Explorations into the Uses of Myth in Medieval Platonism.* Mittelatein ische Studien und Texte, 9. Leiden: E. J. Brill, 1974.

Eco, Umberto. *Semiotics and the Philosophy of Language.* Bloomington: Indiana University Press, 1984.

Erickson, Carolly. *The Medieval Vision: Essays in History and Perception.* New York: Oxford University Press, 1976.

Fleming, John R. *The Roman de la Rose: A Study in Allegory and Iconography.* Princeton: Princeton University Press, 1969.

Fox, George G. *The Medieval Sciences in the Works of John Gower.* New York: Haskell House, 1966.

French, W. H. "The Man in Black's Lyric." *JEGP* 56 (1957): 231–41.

Gardner, John. "Style as Meaning in the *Book of the Duchess*." *Language and Style* 2 (1969): 143–71.

Hieatt, Constance. *The Realism of the Dream Vision: The Poetic Exploitation of the Dream-Experience in Chaucer and His Contemporaries.* The Hague: Mouton, 1967.

Howard, Donald R. *The Idea of the Canterbury Tales.* Berkeley: University of California Press, 1978.

Huppé, Bernard, and D. W. Robertson, Jr. *Fruyt and Chaf: Studies in Chaucer's Allegories.* Princeton: Princeton University Press, 1963.

Jaynes, Julian. *The Origin of Consciousness in the Breakdown of the Bicameral Mind.* Boston: Houghton Mifflin, 1976.

Johnson, Lynn Staley. *The Gawain Poet.* Madison: University of Wisconsin Press, 1984.

Jung, C. G. *Psychology and Religion: East and West.* In *Collected Works*, vol 11. New York: Random House, 1968.

Jung, Marc-René. *Etudes sur le poeme allegorique en France au moyen age.* Berne: Franke, 1971.

Kelly, Douglas. *Medieval Imagination: Rhetoric and the Poetry of Courtly Love.* Madison: University of Wisconsin Press, 1978.

Kelsey, Morton. *God, Dreams, and Revelation: A Christian Interpretation of Dreams.* Minneapolis: Augsburg, 1968, rev. 1974.

Kirk, Elizabeth D. *The Dream Thought of Piers Plowman.* New Haven: Yale University Press, 1974.

Kiser, Lisa J. *Telling Classical Tales: Chaucer and the* Legend of Good Women. Ithaca: Cornell University Press, 1983.

Koonce, B. G. *Chaucer and the Tradition of Fame: Symbolism in the House of Fame.* Princeton: Princeton University Press, 1966.

Kreutzer, James R. "The Dreamer in the *Book of the Duchess.*" *PMLA* 66 (1951): 543-71.

Lawlor, John. "The Earlier Poems." In *Chaucer and Chaucerians: Critical Studies in Middle English Literature.* Ed. D. S. Brewer, 39-64. University: University of Alabama Press, 1967.

LeGoff, Jacques. *Time, Work, and Culture in the Middle Ages.* Tr. Arthur Goldhammer. Chicago: University of Chicago Press, 1980.

Lewis, Clive Staples. *The Discarded Image: An Introduction to Medieval and Renaissance Literature.* Oxford: Oxford University Press, 1971.

Luniansky, Robert M. "The Bereaved Narrator in Chaucer's *The Book of the Duchess.*" *TSE* 9 (1959): 5-17.

Madeleva, Sister Mary. *Pearl: A Study in Spiritual Dryness.* New York: Appelton, 1925.

Manning, Stephen. "That Dreamer Once More." *PMLA* 71 (1956): 540-41.

Mazzotta, Giuseppi. *Dante, Poet of the Desert: History and Allegory in the Divine Comedy.* Princeton: Princeton University Press, 1979.

McGinn, Bernard. "Early Apocalypticism: the ongoing debate." In *The Apocalypse in English Renaissance Thought and Literature.* Ed. C. A. Patrides and Joseph Wittreich. Ithaca: Cornell University Press, 1984.

Meier, Alfred. "The Dream in Ancient Greece and Its Uses in Temple Cures (Incubation)." In *The Dream in Human Societies.* Ed. Gustave E. von Grunebaum and Ernest Caillois. Berkeley: University of California Press, 1966.

Muscatine, Charles. *Chaucer and the French Tradition*. Berkeley: University of California Press, 1957.

Newman, F[rancis] X[avier]. "Somnium: Medieval Theories of Dreaming and the Form of Vision Poetry." Ph. D. diss. Princeton, 1963.

Nolan, Barbara. "The Art of Expropriation: Chaucer's Narrator in *The Book of the Duchess*." In *New Perspectives in Chaucer Criticism*. Ed. Donald Rose, 203-22. Norman: Pilgrim, 1981.

Oppenheim, A. Leo. "The Interpretation of Dreams in Ancient Near East, with a Translation of an Assyrian Dream Book." In *Transactions of the American Philosophical Society* n. s., vol. 46 (1956), 179-373. No. 3. Philadelphia: IPS, 1956.

Patrides, C. A., and Joseph Wittreich, eds. *The Apocalypse in English Renaissance Thought and Literature*. Ithaca: Cornell University Press, 1984.

Peck, Russell. "Chaucer and the Nominalist Questions." *Speculum* 53 (1978): 745-60.

Piehler, Paul. *The Visionary Landscape: A Study in Medieval Allegory*. Montreal: McGill-Queens University Press, 1971.

Robertson, D. W., Jr. "*The Book of the Duchess*." In *Companion to Chaucer Studies*. Ed. Beryl Rowland, 332-40. New York: Oxford University Press, 1968.

―――. "The 'Heresy' of *Pearl*: The Pearl as Symbol." *MLN* 65 (1950): 152-62, rpt. in part in *Pearl: Critical Essays*. Ed. John Conley, 18-26. South Bend: University of Notre Dame Press, 1970.

Rose, Donald, ed. *New Perspectives in Chaucer Criticism*. Norman: Pilgrim, 1981.

Rowland, Beryl, ed. *Companion to Chaucer Studies*. New York: Oxford University Press, 1968.

Russell, J. Stephen. "Lady Meed, Pardons, and the *Piers Plowman Visio*." *Mediaevalia* 5 (1982): 239-57.

―――. "Meaningless Dreams and Meaningful Poems: The Form of the Medieval Dream Vision." *Massachusetts Studies in English* 7 (1980): 20-32.

―――. "Skelton's *Bouge of Court*: A Nominalist Allegory." *Renaissance Papers* (1980): 1-9.

Shklovsky, Viktor. "Stern's *Tristram Shandy*: Stylistic Commentary." In *Russian Formalist Criticism: Four Essays*. Ed. Lee T. Lemon and Marion J. Reis. Lincoln: University of Nebraska Press, 1965.

Shoaf, Richard Allen. " 'Mutatio Amoris': 'Penitentia' and the Form of *The Book of the Duchess*." *Genre* 14 (1981): 163–89.

———. "Stalking the Sorrowful H(e)art: Penitential Lore and the Hunt Scene in Chaucer's *The Book of the Duchess*." *JEGP* 78 (1979): 313–24.

Shook, Laurence K. "*The Hous of Fame*." In *Companion to Chaucer Studies*. Ed. Beryl Rowland, 341–54. New York: Oxford University Press, 1968.

Singleton, Charles S. *Dante Studies I: Commedia: Elements of Structure*. Cambridge: Harvard University Press, 1954.

Sklute, Larry. *Virtue of Necessity: Inconclusiveness and Narrative Form in Chaucer's Poetry*. Columbus: Ohio State University Press, 1984.

Spearing, A. C. *Medieval Dream-Poetry*. Cambridge: Cambridge University Press, 1978.

———. *The Gawain-Poet: A Critical Study*. Cambridge: Cambridge University Press, 1970.

Steadman, John. "Chaucer's Whelp: A Symbol of Marital Fidelity." *Notes and Queries* 1 (1956): 374–75.

Tatlock, J. S. P. "The Epilog of Chaucer's *Troilus*." *MP* 18 (1921): 625–59.

Taylor, Henry Osborn. *The Medieval Mind*. 2 vols. Cambridge: Harvard University Press, 1949.

Todorov, Tzvetan. *The Fantastic: A Structural Approach to a Literary Genre*. Ithaca: Cornell University Press, 1975.

von Grunebaum, Gustave E., and Ernest Caillois, eds. *The Dream In Human Societies*. Berkeley: University of California Press, 1966.

Wellek, Rene. "The *Pearl*: An Interpretation of the Middle English Poem." *Studies in English by Members of the English Seminar of Charles University*. 1933. Rpt. in *Sir Gawain and Pearl: Critical Essays*. Ed. Robert J. Blanch. Bloomington: Indiana University Press, 1971.

Wetherbee, Winthrop. *Platonism and Poetry in the Twelfth Century: The Literary Influence of the School of Chartres*. Princeton: Princeton University Press, 1972.

Wimsatt, James I. "Chaucer and French Poetry." In *Writers and their Background: Geoffrey Chaucer*. Ed. Derek Brewer, 109–36. Athens: Ohio University Press, 1975.

Winny, James. *Chaucer's Dream Poems*. New York: Barnes and Noble, 1973.

INDEX